THE BROIDERED GARMENT

HILDA MARTINSEN NEIHARDT

The Broidered Garment

The Love Story of Mona Martinsen and John G. Neihardt

University of Nebraska Press
Lincoln and London

⊗

Library of Congress
Cataloging-in-Publication Data
Petri, Hilda Neihardt.
The broidered garment : the love story of Mona Martinsen
and John G. Neihardt / Hilda Martinsen Neihardt.
p. cm.
Includes bibliographical references.
ISBN-13: 978-0-8032-3351-5 (cloth : alk. paper)
ISBN-10: 0-8032-3351-5 (cloth : alk. paper)
1. Neihardt, John Gneisenau, 1881–1973—Marriage.
2. Authors, American—20th century—Biography.
3. Martinsen, Mona, 1884–1958—Marriage.
I. Title.
PS3527.e35z84 2006
811′.52–dc22
2005030894

Contents

Illustrations

Foreword

When I was first thinking about writing this book, I had a dream in which I was talking to my father, John Neihardt. I told him that I wanted to write the story of his and my mother's lives, but I did not know how to begin.

In the dream, which was unusually clear, my father appeared middle-aged, and his manner was quite serious. This is what he told me: "Read Proverbs 30, verses 18 and 19." That was all he said, and my dream was over. It had been so clear that I felt it was truly a visit.

When I awakened the next morning, I remembered the dream and went immediately to find the Bible given to me by my grandmother, Alice Neihardt. Though not particularly familiar with the book, I turned its pages quickly to the verses my father had indicated. I read the passage eagerly: "There be three things which are too wonderful for me, yea, four things I know not: the way of an eagle in the air, the way of a serpent upon a rock, the way of a ship in the midst of the sea, and the way of a man with a maid."

I was amazed as I read that very beautiful passage, for the "four things I know not" would all figure in the story I wished to write. Three of those "things" are fairly obvious in the story, and I shall let any persons who may read this book recognize them. The fourth—the serpent upon a rock—is the subject of a sequence in Neihardt's story of the great explorer, Jed Smith, which is an attempt to understand a most misunderstood creature:

> There was a whirring sound
> That made the land be still—and there he wound,

A deadly puddle stewing in the sun,
Head up to end what hunger had begun,
And weariness and thirst.

. . . .

Like a flower he grew,
Slow waving in a breeze that never blew
This side of heaven. Then he crawled away,
Still beautiful with what he couldn't say,
And scared because it never could be said.

Thus the entire biblical quotation my father suggested fits happily into the story I seek to tell. It has been an inspiration to me.

Let us, then, get about the story itself, with two brief comments. First, during the times told about here, proper and polite demeanor would never have permitted that John and Mona Neihardt be called by their first names. Mona would never have allowed that, but for us now, the use of their first names and those of others who figure in our tale is convenient. The usage here is most surely not intended to be impolite.

Second, with the introduction of sympathetic imagination to provide needed bridges and to "flesh out" known events, and with sufficient research as indicated in the bibliography to make the settings authentic, the following story is how life happened for John and Mona. Their letters, together with a couple of biographies, newspaper and magazine reports of the time, John's memoirs, and our own memories and memories of what they told us, provide the life sources for this work. It would be difficult, if not impossible, to tell their story in its entirety. No attempt is made here to portray in its totality the warp and woof of the fabric of their lives, but its main threads have been carefully presented. The unusual happenings, which some might term paranormal, are related simply and without ornamentation.

This book is dedicated, with love, to John and Mona and to anyone who may care as much about life as they did.

Acknowledgments

The following institutions were most helpful in my research for this book: the Wayne County Historical Museum in Richmond, Indiana; the Richmond Public Library, Richmond, Indiana; the Douglas County Historical Society, Omaha, Nebraska; the Cambridge City Public Library, Census Records, Cambridge City, Indiana; the United States Patent Office, University of Arizona, Tempe, Arizona.

I am grateful for the interest and assistance of my children. My daughter Gail Toedebusch of Richmond, Indiana, spent considerable time and effort in helping me find Ada Ernst. The writing of this book benefited greatly from her encouragement as well as the encouragement and technical assistance of my son, Robin Neihardt of Phoenix, and my daughter, Coralie Hughes of Coatesville, Indiana.

My sister Alice Neihardt Thompson, in addition to urging that this book be written, related to me the facts of the Olga Currier story, which she had learned from that lady when they met in New York around 1943.

Nancy Gillis, Executive Director, and Mary Lou Schweers, both of the John G. Neihardt State Historic Site in Bancroft, Nebraska, have been most helpful.

My sincere thanks to all.

A Note on the Text

Early in life John Neihardt changed the spelling of his last name from "Neihart" to "Neihardt." The original spelling is used in this text for the period of time in Neihardt's life before he made the change.

THE BROIDERED GARMENT

1

An International Financier Family

1

Ada Ernst

THE UNITED STATES OF AMERICA was still a very young country when it was shaken by a conflict that threatened to wreck its very foundation. Strife arose between the northern states, where slavery was neither practiced nor accepted, and the South, where the large plantations were owned by slaveholders. Much of the southern economy was based on labor performed by persons who had been sold in Africa to traders and brought to the new world, where they were sold again as slaves. There were other disagreements between the northern states and the southern, but the most urgent one was whether slavery should continue to exist, or whether the slaves should be set free.

Civil war appeared imminent when, on December 12, 1860, the state of South Carolina declared its intention to secede from the Union. Five other southern states followed in January of 1861, and the new state of Texas announced on February 1, 1861, that it would join the six and abandon the Union.

These events caused nationwide unrest, touching even Indiana, a state not directly involved with the conflict. Like many Northerners, Indianans had felt the stress of industrialization and social change. The people of that state, both young and old, realized that their Union was threatened, and many volunteered for the militia.

But men were not the only volunteers, for women in both the North and the South took on new roles. Homemakers organized more than ten thousand soldiers' aid societies, rolled bandages, and raised large sums of money to aid wounded troops. Many women served as nurses in front-line hospitals.

In the North people were uncertain about the real cause of the war. Some men risked their lives on battlefields because they wanted to preserve the Union or give freedom to the slaves, while sons of the wealthy were permitted by law to avoid military service with the payment of money or by hiring a substitute.

The governments of both the Confederacy and the United States expressed a similar uncertainty about the purpose of the war. Abraham Lincoln, who was elected in 1861, carefully avoided reference to slavery as the crux of the matter during the first part of his presidency, and Jefferson Davis, president of the southern states, told his people they were fighting for constitutional liberty.

It was at this unsettled and emotion-fraught time that Ada Ernst was born in the small but charming town of Cambridge City, Indiana. Her mother, Addi Ernst, had been only seventeen years old when she met Trenton Thorpe. Trenton was four years older than Addi and came from a fairly well situated family in Richmond, a small city just a few miles away. Addi fell head over heels for this well-educated "older" man, and Trenton found the eager young girl most attractive.

Addi was not like any girl Trenton had met before. A pretty, blue-eyed blonde, all five feet seven inches of her were vibrant and full of life. The war fever did not entirely prevent normal social events, and when Addi and Trenton attended an affair, the two young people made a handsome pair—he, well dressed and dignified in the way he carried himself, and she, pretty and bright and always smiling. Addi loved life, and Trenton was captivated by her. It was not long before he took Addi to Richmond to meet his mother, Mary Thorpe, who was the proprietor of a fancy dry goods store in that city.

Mary Thorpe had lived for a number of years with her husband in Richmond, and when she was widowed and realized that she would need to fend for herself, she had decided to start a business. Since she was unusually skilled in all forms of needlework, even during a time when most women sewed only out of necessity, Mary decided that a middle-aged woman like herself would be most likely to succeed with a store that catered to dressmaking. She explained her choice to a friend: "There is always a need for clothes, and people like them to be pretty,

I just really like sewing and dressmaking, and I am sure I can make a success of the business."

Mary lost no time in her search for a suitable location for her shop, and when she found one, she set about making arrangements for the space and seeking out sources for the wares she would offer. The Richmond newspaper carried the following notice of her venture: "Mrs. Thorpe has opened a Fancy Dry Goods Store on the east side of Fifth Street, four doors north of Main, where she has on hand a well-assorted lot of dress trimmings, embroidery, etc."

Mary's fancy dry goods store, with its predominantly local patronage, did not suffer from the war in the South as much as larger businesses did, and her little shop continued to yield enough income for the comfortable life she had always enjoyed in a town that, even at that early time, was a center for artistic events.

When Trenton brought Addi to meet his mother, Mary was immediately drawn to the girl, even though she was a bit disturbed by her independent and even headstrong conduct. "At least she *does* something," Mary told a friend, "she is not like so many girls who think only of fancy clothes and who just sit around, waiting for a man's attentions. She works and is busy. I like that."

Thinking that Addi might wish to help in the war efforts, Mary invited her to join in the volunteer work she and a number of her friends were doing. The ladies were making bandages, and each evening after Mary closed her shop, a group of them came to Mary's store. A large table used during the day to display bolts of cloth was cleared, and the women gathered around it, chatting and enjoying the news of the day—and perhaps even a bit of gossip—as they rolled the bandages. Mary had been able to get the soft, white cloth they needed at a good price, and the women cut it into strips, then put the long strips into rolls that would be easy for the nurses to use.

Trenton's young friend was as eager in bandage-rolling as she was in other pursuits. "Whatever she does," Mary told her son, "she does with her whole heart, and I certainly approve of that. But, Trenton, I am a bit worried about you and her. She is—Addi is—so different." The girl was not at all like her son. Trenton had always been a quiet boy, and as a young man he was serious-minded. She understood why her son was so attracted to Addi and was not at all surprised by it, for she also admired what she called Addi's "spunk."

"What is it that worries you about Addi, Mother?" Their relationship was simple to Trenton; he saw in Addi an especially attractive young woman who was, as he told his mother, "lots of fun."

"What worries me, Trenton, is that I can't help wondering if such a lively girl could ever settle down with a man. Every time I see her, she is talking about some big adventure she wants to take or some uncivilized place she wants to see. Trenton, I can't help wondering if she should ever get married. . . ."

"Mother, Addi and I are just having a good time. I like her lots, and I think she likes me, but we are not talking about getting married—not in these times. Not with this damnable war going on."

For the moment, Trenton's assertion settled the matter for Mary. She knew all too well that Trenton had not yet found his real niche in life and that he was no better prepared for marriage than was Addi. Although Trenton helped out in the store from time to time, Mary realized that he had no plans to take over her business.

Mary was only too aware of the difficulties that faced everyone— and especially young people—because of the war. "In such uncertain times," Mary thought, "how could a young couple plan to marry?" Even though it seemed she should have been relieved by what her son had told her, Mary was troubled. Addi attended the bandage-making sessions regularly for some time, then she appeared at the work sessions at Mary's store less and less frequently, and finally she did not come at all. Mary had noticed that Addi was troubled by something, but she always had plausible excuses to give when Mary or someone else inquired about her problems.

At the time, Mary was not overly concerned herself with Addi's absences, but she did wonder and worry why it was that her son rarely came to see her. Then one day Trenton came to the store mid-afternoon, and Mary was shocked at his appearance. Normally fastidious in his dress, Trenton's suit was rumpled, and his handsome, usually bright and open face was dark and nearly expressionless. He hugged his mother and attempted to smile at her, but his greeting did nothing to soothe her concern, nor was she happy to hear what he had to say.

"Mother, I came to tell you that I am leaving Richmond. I cannot really explain why. It is just that I feel there is no future for me here, and everything is so mixed up. Mother, everything is just so mixed up now. I told some friends of mine that I would leave tomorrow with them. They are going to sign up with the militia. I haven't decided that I want to enlist, but I just have to get away from here. Mother, I hate to leave you now. I certainly would not go if I didn't feel sure that you will be all right without me. Besides, I haven't done much for you these last months, have I?"

Mary noticed that her son was fighting back tears as he spoke. Trenton's announcement, so obviously upsetting to him, left her almost speechless. She was a woman who had weathered many of life's storms, and the fact that her grown son was leaving should not have upset her as much as this news had. It was because he seemed so upset himself, and so sad, that she was disturbed.

"Trenton, *why*? Why are you leaving in this way? I can see that you are sad and very upset about something, and it seems to me that you don't really want to go. Why, please tell me, why are you leaving us now?"

It was not easy for Trenton. "Mother, I can't stay here and be the only fellow my age who is doing nothing about the war. Sometimes I think I really should join the militia. What do you think? At least, Mother, I ought to be doing something, not just hanging around here as I have been doing. I just have to leave, and you must know that I love you very much. I do love you, dear Mother!" With that brief statement, and with a hint of tears in his eyes, Trenton embraced his mother, gently released himself from her arms, then turned, walked quickly to the buggy left standing at the edge of the street, and drove away. Mary would not hear from her son for a long time.

A week or so after Trenton's announcement, Addi Ernst appeared at Mary's door. Happy to see her, Mary eagerly invited her in. The vivacious smile with which Addi normally greeted Mary was gone, and a worried expression now clouded her pretty face. Mary noticed more than the lack of a smile; Addi's whole appearance was different. She looked at Addi a moment or two, then quickly realized what had happened. "Why, you dear girl," she blurted out, "are you—are you *in trouble*?"

In spite of the shock she felt, Mary knew that this was no time for anything but kindness, and with more than usual gentleness she ushered the young woman to a comfortable spot in her living room. "Tell me all about it," she urged.

Addi was now quite shaken, and it was not easy for her to talk. "Mrs. Thorpe, you have been so good to me, and I love you. I really do. What's the matter is that Trenton has left. He didn't say why—he just left. He did tell me that he might join the militia, and he said he would try to send money to help me, but he just couldn't stay. Why, *why* couldn't he stay with us? Mrs. Thorpe, I just can't understand. Didn't he want our baby? Why would he leave?"

Addi's questions, so like her own, were puzzles that the soon-to-be grandmother could neither understand nor answer. All she could do was put her arms around the weeping young woman and pat her gently on the back. "Now, Addi, don't you worry. Just don't you fret. I will help you. You can stay right here with me, and together you and I will take care of the baby. I will arrange everything so that we can be comfortable in this house. This old house will be glad to have young people in it again."

Addi did little but sob and cling to this gentle woman who now seemed a tower of strength. "I am so sorry, Mrs. Thorpe. You have been very good to Trenton and to me. I am so sorry to do this to you. I really am very sorry."

Mary surprised even herself, for she was not tempted to blame Addi for what she had done. She felt only tenderness toward this young woman, and she also had a sense of responsibility for what she perceived as her son's lack of proper manliness. A warm surge of feeling she had never experienced before came over Mary, and she knew that she would welcome the chance to take care of this grandchild.

Mary felt a sense of renewed strength, almost of happiness, rise up within her. It had always been like that when she was faced with a problem; instead of being crushed by things that most people would label "bad," she was energized and excited by facing difficulty. Being a practical woman, she began to plan for her grandchild.

On February 27, 1862, a strong, eager, blue-eyed, blond girl was born, and Addi named the child after herself: Ada Ernst. "My name is really 'Ada,' " the young mother explained. " 'Addi' is just a kind of a nickname, but I have always used it." When Addi brought the baby girl to her grandmother's home, Mary Thorpe took little Ada in her arms, and she almost begged Addi to let her make a home for both of them.

"I have planned how we can arrange the house so you and Ada will have your own little apartment. Then, when you need to work or go someplace, I will take care of Ada. I really think that would be best, don't you? Addi, you and your baby will be welcome here. Little Ada is a part of me, and I love you both."

"No, Mrs. Thorpe, I can take care of my baby myself. I love her so much, and I want to be a good mother for her. But, who knows? If it turns out that I really can't give her as good a home as you can, I will remember what you said. But I do thank you very, very much!"

"At least stay here tonight, Addi!"

Addi and little Ada did spend the night with Grandma Mary, but just after they had finished breakfast in the morning they left for the modest rooms where Addi lived. Mary did her best to smile and wave as Addi left, carrying her baby so casually in her arms, but when they were gone, a lonely grandmother went into her house and made no effort to control her weeping.

People in Indiana did the best they could to keep their lives on an even keel; nevertheless, the war between the states continued to be the focal point for them and for most citizens in the North, even though the fighting for the most part took place on southern ground. For people at home, as well as for most soldiers, the overall policymaking by political and military leaders was far from their minds. Their thoughts were with the men fighting away from home—the men who had been conscripted or who had volunteered and who were enduring great hardship and risking death.

The citizens of Richmond were not immune to the privations caused by the "conflict between brothers," and they continued to join the fighting forces. News from the battle lines was not good, but most residents followed it eagerly. The months passed. Away from his family, Trenton had been caught up in the war, and Mary heard all too seldom from him. Strangely, Addi heard nothing.

Little Ada was now living in Richmond with her grandmother. Addi and Mary had talked it over many times. "I never had a real home like this," Addi admitted, "and I want my little girl to have it better than I did. What with your good education and all, and this nice house you have, I know that Ada will be more likely to have a really good life than she would if I kept her with me. But, Grandma Mary, I still can come to see you both, can't I?"

"You will be most welcome to come at any time. You should know that! And Ada and I will plan for some good times we can have together— just the three of us. And you must know, Addi, that I would never do anything to come between a little girl and her mother. *Never!*"

Addi had found it very difficult to work at the jobs she was able to get and give proper care to Ada. Most women who might have served as babysitters for Ada were employed in war work, and Addi worked long hours herself. So it happened that Mary once more found herself caring for a little one, and she delighted in being a grandmother. Addi did not move in with Mary, but she came by her home almost daily to help in any way she could.

Together, Mary and Addi watched as the tide of battle began to turn in favor of the Union. In July of 1863 two battles—Vicksburg and Gettysburg—brought defeat to the Confederacy and diminished its hope for independence. The southern troops fought with courage and dedication, but the results of both battles were disastrous.

Richmond was safely removed from most wartime problems, but Mary heard about food riots occurring in the spring of 1863 in many southern cities. In rural areas of the South, there was opposition to wartime measures, and farmers refused to accept certificates of credit, in lieu of cash, for their products, as the law required. Men of draft age were hiding out in the forests.

It was much the same in the North. There was opposition to the war and resentment of the draft, and the Union army faced desertion rates as high as those of the Confederate army. Volunteer workers increased their efforts, and little Ada, seemingly oblivious to grown-up problems at her advanced age of two, often played in the store while her mother and grandmother rolled bandages.

The war became increasingly one-sided, for the Union was much richer than the South in many ways. President Lincoln was more successful than Jefferson Davis in communicating with the people. He wrote letters to newspapers and to soldiers' families, and in this way he was able to make the people feel that their grief was also his. In spite of those good efforts, however, nothing could quell the popular protest against the war.

Mary and her friends now talked mostly about the war at their work sessions. After all, it was the most important happening of the time. What they did not learn from newspaper reports they picked up from letters received from hometown men engaged in the fighting. What Trenton had called "this damnable war" was taking a long time—a long, weary time for all concerned. Victory for either side was slow to come.

Citizens in Richmond, Indiana, were encouraged as Grant advanced his troops against Lee, but the Union troops suffered tremendous losses despite their superior numbers. Relatives learned that many Union soldiers placed pieces of paper bearing their names on their backs, certain that they would be mowed down by Lee's forces.

The end finally came in the spring of 1865, when General Lee—his army hemmed in by federal troops, short of rations, and numbering fewer than thirty thousand men—surrendered to Grant at Appomattox Courthouse. The war was over, but any relief for people on both sides blended uncomfortably with the uncertainty that faced the nation. The massive damage done by the war would mean years of struggle and rebuilding.

During the war Mary had had little news from Trenton, but she did know that he was in New Orleans. In September 1867, the news came to her that he had died on the third of the month. He had not been killed in battle but had died of yellow fever. Mary was deeply saddened, and for weeks she found it difficult to keep up with all that she had to do.

So it happened that Ada lost her father, whom she never saw or knew, when she was only five and was just beginning her formal schooling. For Mary, the loss of her son was not less tragic because he had been away from home so long, but her pain was undoubtedly softened because she had his child with her. She dearly loved her granddaughter, and Ada—so full of life and so intensely involved in all that went on around her—brought happiness into an old woman's heart. Mary had done her best during those five years to make Ada feel that she did have a father, but his absence made her feel helpless. For his child, it was almost as if Trenton had never existed.

For Addi the news of Trenton's death was disturbing, but she did not seem overly distressed. Her heart went out to the bereaved mother, whom she truly loved, but what she said about Trenton seemed almost to reveal a lack of feeling. "I am sorry for you, Mary, and for my little girl who never had a father. I've been sorry about Trenton for five years now, and that's long enough. I just can't feel sad about him anymore."

The reluctant tears dampening Addi's eyes as she spoke seemed to contradict her words, and she clutched Mary's outstretched hands in hers. "I sometimes think," she added, "that Ada would be just as well off without either her mother or father. We haven't been much good, have we? Perhaps I should just give up too and let you take care of her alone."

"And that I am very happy to do. Just don't you worry any, not any at all, Addi!"

Mary's devotion to her granddaughter did not change, and now that Ada was beginning her schooling, there was much more that a grandmother could do for her. Ada was one of the best-dressed girls in her class when she was enrolled in school. Grandmother Thorpe, entrepreneur-seamstress, took great pleasure in dressing her pretty granddaughter in the favored fashion of the time. "She is such a dear; she looks just like a doll," Mary's friends often remarked.

Such compliments pleased Mary, but she did much more than dress Ada "like a little doll." She encouraged her granddaughter to express herself. When Ada was just a little girl, Mary had noticed her marked talent for acting, and this ability came out in her daily life as well as in school. Wisely, though, Mary helped Ada to do well in all her studies.

Mary knew the importance of a good education. Her mother had attended a girls' college in the East and had been a teacher before her marriage and had seen to it that Mary was well educated. Mary, in her turn, was determined to provide a good education for her granddaughter and to give her every advantage possible. Never forgetting her own particular talents, Mary taught Ada to sew and to knit while she was still very young, and Ada seemed interested in working with brightly colored yarns.

In spite of what she had confessed about her ability as a mother, Addi did not abandon her daughter; she came every week or so to Mary's home to see Ada. Still, Mary Thorpe had not misjudged Addi in her belief that the young mother would be unlikely to "settle down" and pursue a life that would fit society's notions of what she should do or be. It became more and more evident that Addi could never measure up to such expectations; she wanted something, Mary knew, but *what*?

The Civil War was no longer the center of interest, and the big news of the time for many men and women was the exciting opportunity for a good life that might be found in the only partially explored areas of the western United States. In Richmond, as in other parts of the country, eager young people met and talked excitedly about the possibilities. Among those adventurous souls was Addi.

She was particularly interested in the Southwest and had learned about that territory from a young man she knew who had only recently returned from New Mexico. What tales he did tell her! "Addi, in the Southwest, everything is big and open and new, and a person can feel free down there. Down there, you have the feeling that you could just do anything. It is mostly huge ranches, with cattle and horses—lots of horses!" The last part of his remarks had particularly caught Addi's attention, for she loved horses. As often as she was able, she had taken her daughter riding, and Ada already sat a horse very well.

On many of her visits to Mary's house, Addi spoke of her growing fascination with the New Mexico ranch country. Although Mary was also a woman of some energy and ambition, she did not share Addi's enthusiasm about the unsettled areas of the West. To her, the danger they presented outweighed the opportunity they promised. Addi, however, could think of little else.

"Just imagine, Grandma Mary, the things a person could do in that country! Everybody says the sky is the limit down there! I just know I could find something to do if I went west. I wouldn't be so held in as I am here. You know, I don't really like the kind of life we have here in Indiana. I want to do something different—something really big!"

"Yes, I know that, Addi. But, don't you see? You would be much better off here, and it's best for Ada too." Mary understood how Addi felt, but it troubled her—not for Addi but for her granddaughter.

When Ada was nearly eight years old, Addi came to tell her about an exciting idea. "How would you like to go with me away down to Santa Fe in New Mexico? It is beautiful down there! You would love it!"

Addi could see that Mary was shocked at what she had heard. "Addi! What on earth are you saying?"

Addi was not to be stopped. "Down there it is all new country and a new life. There are huge ranches, and people there can have a real chance at life. I would have a real chance to do something. Ada, you and I could take trips on horseback together. It would be a real adventure! What do you say, Ada?"

The child's bright blue eyes became even bluer and widened with expectation. "Yes, Mothie! Yes! Yes! When, Mothie, when?" The conversation Mary had overheard left her shocked and, for a time, speechless.

Addi saw how disturbed Mary was, and she quickly added, "I just meant we could go there for a trip, not to stay!"

The trip did not happen at once, and it was discussed, objected to, and promoted many times during the winter and into the spring of 1870. Mary, with a grandmother's caution and perhaps with more than a little common sense, was not in favor of a journey that seemed to her dangerous and even ridiculous.

Mary's opinion was shared by her friends. "Why, Mary," a close friend cautioned, "they would have to travel through dangerous country, where there are hostile Indians and Mexican bandits, and they would have to go by stagecoach. Or by wagon. And they would not be safe! New Mexico is not even a state, is it?" All of Mary's friends agreed that such a trip would be unthinkable.

Addi was not entirely uncaring about the grandmother's concern and tried to reassure her. "I have a friend who works where I do. He just came back from a trip down there, and he knows of a good place we could stay. It's a rooming house with a friendly Mexican family. He says the Mexican people are very friendly and kind."

"Really," she said to Mary, whose face was drawn with worry, "it would be quite safe. I have checked it all out—how we would travel and where we might stay. Grandma Mary, I'm not talking about a real move, just a trip. Please let her go with me. I will bring her back safe and sound . . ."

After weeks of consideration and much discussion and explanation, it was settled. Strange, even outrageous, as such an adventure seemed to the grandmother, she finally agreed. It was evident that Addi had carefully planned the proposed venture to the unsettled desert area of New Mexico and that her heart was set on including her daughter in those plans. Mary Thorpe was not the sort of woman who would wish to deprive a child of what might be an enlightening experience, and eventually she relented, although reluctantly.

They would go! The three chose the clothes that would be needed for such a trip, and Addi spent considerable time deciding on and arranging the route they would travel. In 1870 the railroads had not progressed far beyond Kansas City, Missouri.

Addi had learned that travel by train ended near Junction City, Kansas, and from there travelers went by way of a stagecoach that came up from Santa Fe to meet the train. The railroad would not be able to take passengers all the way to Santa Fe for another ten years, not until 1880, when the tunnel at Raton was completed.

The fare on the train would be about one hundred and fifty dollars, a very large sum at that time, and after that the stagecoach would cost about the same. Addi had been working and saving most of her earnings for several years, and she believed she could meet the expenses and take care of Ada and herself. Wanting to assure the safety of both mother and daughter, grandmother Mary offered to help.

The Columbus, Chicago, and Central Indiana Railway had three daily departures for Indianapolis, and Addi chose the early morning time. Arriving in Indianapolis, they boarded the next train for St. Louis. It was a smoky, dusty trip by train from Richmond to Indianapolis, then to St. Louis and on to Kansas City. The cars offered only straight-backed seats that were not very comfortable, but for young and eager people like Addi and Ada, it did not matter.

At St. Louis they found a little shop where they purchased some food for the next part of their journey. After a few hours of waiting they were directed to the train that would take them to Kansas City. The train was not crowded, so mother and daughter were allowed to curl up on two of the hard bench seats.

When they stopped along the way at a small town, they joined other passengers who left the train to find food. It was not long, however, before they heard the conductor call "B-o-o-o-a-r-d!" With the other passengers, mother and daughter scurried to the waiting train, where the conductor helped them get aboard. As the train began to move the conductor picked up the stepstool and climbed aboard himself.

When they arrived in Kansas City Addi learned that the train for Junction City, Kansas, would not leave for some five hours. After wandering around the station area for what seemed much longer than that, they found and boarded the train for Junction City. That train seemed in no hurry to leave, but it finally did depart, and after another dusty and smoky ride, they reached Junction City, Kansas. They were on the last leg of their journey!

In Junction City Addi inquired about the stage for Santa Fe, which, she was told, came only twice a week and would arrive in two days. Tired and feeling in need of a bath and a change of clothes, Addi found a small hotel nearby, where they enjoyed a good meal and slept in a real bed. After a couple of relaxing days, mother and daughter would be well rested and ready for the trip by stage to Santa Fe.

Travel by rail in 1870 was not overly comfortable, especially if one could not afford a pullman berth, but our adventurers found that stage travel was something quite different. The stagecoaches had been rather romantically described in the *Independence Missouri Commonwealth* in this fashion: "The stages are gotten up in elegant style, and are each arranged to convey eight passengers. The bodies are beautifully painted and made water-tight, with a view to using them as boats in ferrying streams. The team consists of six mules to each coach. The mail is guarded by eight men, armed as follows: Each man has at his side, fastened in the stage, one of Colt's revolving rifles, in a holster below one of Colt's revolvers, and in his belt a small Colt's revolver, besides a hunting knife."

Whether this is an accurate description of the particular coach in which Addi and Ada were to ride, we do not know, but it is likely that the use of the stagecoach on rocky and dusty roads had taken its effect on the vehicle and its passengers.

When a stagecoach arrived at its destination, the passengers were covered with dust and their clothes were rumpled. Surely it was not the glamorous arrival portrayed in motion pictures or in romantic Western novels, which often portray a West that never was, where every stagecoach was driven uphill and down at a breakneck gallop.

However the actual facts may differ from more romantic descriptions, the stagecoaches did make pretty good time. We are told that one hundred and fifty miles a day—equal to about six and a quarter miles per hour—was considered excellent.

Of course, this time included stops for meals and for changing teams at relay stations, which were set up at reasonably frequent intervals along the route. It was necessary to change horses often, for no animal—horse or mule—could travel for more than a few hours at stagecoach speeds.

The coach from Santa Fe arrived late one afternoon in Junction City, and Addi and Ada were told that it would leave for the return trip at six the next morning. They arrived about half an hour before the coach was to leave, and found two other passengers waiting at the staging spot. They were a Mexican couple who introduced themselves as Rafael and Maria Martinez. Addi thought them of somewhat advanced middle age, and to Ada they seemed almost as old as Grandmother, but they were very friendly.

Rafael Martinez had graying hair worn rather long and was dressed in clothes suiting his occupation, which he said was that of a merchant. "Maria and I went to Kansas City," he told them, "partly for a little vacation, which we both needed. But we mostly went to see about new-style clothing. Santa Fe is a big town now—a thousand people!—and our customers want to keep up with the new styles. Senora Ernst, you must come to see our store while you are in Santa Fe!"

Maria Martinez was equally well dressed and was a handsome woman, although no longer as slim and pretty as she once had been. Both were very friendly, and Addi looked forward to a pleasant trip in their company.

Although there were only four passengers for the trip to the Southwest, there was a goodly amount of mail. Several large pouches and four or five boxes were put on top of the coach and made secure with leather thongs. The passengers' valises were also thrown up on top of the coach, where they were kept from falling off by a low railing. Both luggage and mail pouches would be exposed to dust and weather on the trip.

When it was time for departure, the four passengers gathered at the door of the stagecoach, and as they entered, they noted that the driver had a second man sitting beside him. Inside, they took seats facing each other, the Martinez couple looking forward and Addi and Ada looking toward the back.

Rafael volunteered information concerning the second man on the seat up front. "He is," Rafael said, "riding shotgun to protect the mail—and us too. At many spots along our way there might be robbers or bandits. He is no doubt a professional gunman, so we can feel pretty safe." It was all very exciting—and a bit scary—to Ada. The presence of the armed man made Addi feel more secure.

The journey from Kansas to Santa Fe took about two weeks, with frequent stops for changing the horses or for food and rest at a way station. It was a grueling trip, and the dust thrown up by the hurrying teams filled the coach in spite of the drawn side curtains. The four passengers were soon covered with dust, and at times it became difficult even to breathe.

Sitting with their backs to the front of the coach, Addi and Ada were able to view through the dusty side curtains something of the countryside as it swept past them. Now and then they slept, with Ada's head against her mother's shoulder, and with Addi's head bouncing precariously atop her daughter's.

The stagecoach arrived at Santa Fe on a warm—perhaps we should say hot—day in mid-July. It was welcomed by a small group of people, two of whom came in a buggy for Senor and Senora Martinez. There was no one for Addi and Ada, but a rather rough-looking, poorly clad Mexican came up to Addi and asked if he could take them someplace. Addi said they had been told there was a rooming house nearby.

The Mexican nodded, then led them to a small buckboard to which two rather sad-looking horses were hitched. With unexpected deference the man helped them to climb into the seat of the buckboard, put their bags into the rear of the vehicle, and then drove them to an adobe house a few blocks away. On the front of the building was a small wooden sign that read, "Rosita's—Room and Board." Addi paid for the ride, and they went inside.

Rosita Cortez was a plump, cheerful woman of perhaps fifty years or more. In her facial appearance she favored her Indian ancestry more than the Spanish, but she wore her black hair pulled back and fastened with a silver comb, a piece that obviously was a source of pride and status to her. The house was small and quite plain, but Rosita kept it clean enough, and Addi could see that the sandy, rocky front yard was swept regularly.

Addi and her pretty blond daughter were a new experience for Rosita. She had never before had white women as her guests, but when they arrived, covered with dust, it is likely that only the shape of their faces and their blue eyes revealed that they were white.

Although she had a marked Spanish accent, Rosita spoke English quite well. She made it evident that she was pleased to have the "fine ladies" stay at her place, and she used all her Latina charm to make them feel comfortable. After showing them to a small room that boasted only a bed, two chairs, and a washstand, Rosita brought warm water to fill the blue pottery bowl on the washstand.

It was a welcome relief for both mother and daughter to wash away the dust of the road and to remove their dusty travel clothes and put on clean dresses. Refreshed, they went to the kitchen, where Rosita was busying herself with preparations for the evening meal. When Addi showed an interest in her cooking, Rosita was flattered. "Just let me know what you like, and I will make it for you," she told them, then added, "and tell me if I can do anything for you—anything!"

There were only two people for supper that evening, and Rosita, in a gesture of friendliness, sat with them. Addi—always willing to try something new—enjoyed the hot Mexican food that Rosita served, even though she was unaccustomed to it. Ada had a child's natural distrust of eating anything different, but she watched as her mother and Rosita ate and rather gingerly sampled some herself. She did not wish to hurt Rosita's feelings.

Addi wanted to learn something about the community and the surrounding countryside, and Rosita was eager to answer her questions. About herself, she volunteered, "My husband, Manuel, was killed last year, and I have had to make my own way since then. We had this house then. Manuel trained horses, and he was riding a big black stallion that a man wanted him to break.

"That horse was crazy, and all of a sudden he just stood up on his back legs—just right straight up!—and then he fell over backwards, right on top of Manuel. It was all so fast that he could not roll away. I could not believe it happened, because Manuel was so quick that he had never got caught by a horse before. But this time he did . . ." Rosita's dark eyes conveyed a sorrow that she was not able to fully express in her words.

That evening they were treated to a bath in their room, using the metal tub and the warm water Rosita brought for them. Both were tired from their long journey, and they wished only to go to bed. They lay down together on the corn-husk mattress, near an open window that let in the much cooler, light desert air, and, even though they were excited to be safely in New Mexico, sleep came easily to them both.

To people accustomed to the continual warmth of summer in the East, the air still seemed cool when they awoke the next morning and dressed. Being unusually hungry, they hurried to the kitchen for breakfast. Rosita had noticed Ada's reluctance at dinner the evening before, and she thought it best not to put any of the good hot sauce on the eggs she served her. Rosita had scrambled the eggs, and she showed Ada how to roll them up in the tortilla. "See, Addita, you made a burrito."

Ada caught on at once, picking up the warm tortilla and biting off one end. "I like it, Rosita! It tastes just like Grandma's cornbread!"

After breakfast, Ada, now quite at home with her hostess, asked, "Senora Cortez, can I go outside? I want to see the chickens." "Si, Addita, you go out. The hens are friendly, but watch out for the rooster. He's a mean fellow!" Meanwhile, Addi remained at the table, enjoying yet another cup of the strong coffee that Rosita had brewed. Addi's thoughts turned to what they might do on that day.

"Rosita," she asked, "is there someone who might be a guide for us? I'd like to find some horses and go for a ride out in the desert." Rosita suggested that the livery stable would be the most likely place, and she told Addi how to get there. Addi found her daughter in the backyard, where she was watching the hens as they scratched here and there, pecking eagerly when they came across a seed or a hapless bug.

Ada had not seen many chickens before, and she found them quite fascinating. "They are so funny! Hello, chickie! Mothie, see how they look at me sideways when I talk to them." Addi agreed about the hens, then told her daughter where she wanted to go.

Together they walked down the road to the saloon, then turned left as they had been directed and walked about a quarter of a mile farther to a building marked "Livery." No one greeted them at the door, but when they went back into the stable area, they saw a stocky young Mexican man pitchforking manure into a wheelbarrow. It was quite obvious that English was not his usual language when he asked them what they wanted.

Addi explained that they desired to rent horses, provided there was someone who could be their guide to ride out into the surrounding countryside. Addi had to repeat her wish in the simplest way she could manage before he seemed to understand. The young Mexican was not used to women customers, and certainly white women were a new experience to him. That a young "gringo" lady and her little daughter should seek to go riding in the desert was to that young man almost incomprehensible, but he thought they seemed friendly, and the mother was quite pretty. He wanted to be helpful.

"We have horses but no one to take you out," he said. Then he thought better of it: " . . . but I would go with you. I know this desert. I work for *dos* years on a big ranch. If you like, Señora, I will ride with you."

This was all that Addi wanted. She introduced herself, and the young man responded, "I am José Castillo, and I am happy to take you, Senora and Senorita, riding on horses." They discussed the matter, and settled on a ride for the next day.

It was early morning and not yet light when José rode up to the rooming house on a fairly decent-looking palomino gelding, leading two rough, haltered and saddled horses. They obviously were of mustang origin, but they appeared to be tractable enough.

Rosita saw the entourage from her kitchen window, hurried to the doorway, and called to Addi, "José is here! He has two horses for you!" Hurriedly, they put on the riding outfits they had brought and went to the kitchen, where a cheery fire in the cookstove felt good to Addi. Even in July, early mornings are often cool in the desert.

Rosita went to the kitchen door, opened it, and called out to José, who was tying the three horses to the hitching rail in front of the house: "José, ven para comer con nosotros" Addi knew just a little Spanish, and she gathered that her landlady had invited José to have breakfast with them. She understood his reply: "Si, Senora, gracias!" José wasted no time in coming into the kitchen.

He was a stocky young man, not much taller than Addi, and she was struck again by how Indian he looked, except for the black moustache he was cultivating. Wanting to make a favorable appearance for the two ladies, José had dressed as well as he could, with clean brown pants of some rough-weaved fabric and a long-sleeved shirt of a similar material.

As he entered the kitchen he quickly removed his grimy leather ten-gallon hat, which he now held in his hand. "Buenas días, Señora! Nice day for a ride. Not too hot—not yet. Just right." Then, glancing briefly at Ada, who seemed to be staring at him, he took the place at the breakfast table that Rosita had indicated.

Breakfast was a hearty one: bacon, eggs, more tortillas, strong coffee for Addi and José and fresh milk for Ada. Afterward, anticipating what they would need on their desert ride, Rosita poured water into two jugs, one of which José would tie to Addi's saddle, and she also put some tortillas and a few hard-boiled eggs into a cloth sack that would fit into one of the worn leather saddle bags.

When Addi and Ada went outside to where the horses were standing, they saw that the saddles were not like those they were accustomed to using, having a high horn in front, a deep cantle, and leather-covered stirrups. Both saddles were badly worn and surely did not look comfortable, but mother and daughter were so eager for a ride that comfort mattered little to either of them. They were excited and could not wait to be off on their adventure.

José followed the girls out and quickly bridled the two horses. Then, noticing that they wore nothing on their heads, he asked abruptly, "No hats?" "We don't have any," Ada announced. "Can't go out in the desert without hat. Sun's too hot. Rosita has hats."

Rosita heard what he said and, quickly agreeing, went back into the house. She soon appeared carrying two big hats, one of which she explained had been her husband's and the other was hers. Addi chose the larger hat and put the smaller one on Ada. Although she had a bit of trouble keeping the hat from coming down over her eyes, Ada was quite delighted. "Now I look like a cowboy!" she said.

If either Rosita or José had felt some concern over the riding ability of the ladies, they were reassured when they saw how quickly the mother and her sturdy, well-grown daughter mounted. Their full-cut clothing permitted them to get on the horses easily and to ride astride as the saddles required. Addi had seen to that, for she had guessed that side-saddles might not be available in ranch country.

Addi was about the same height as José, so the stirrups on her saddle were the right length, but for eight-year-old Ada it was different. José was not able to make the stirrups on her saddle the right length, so she pushed her feet in between the leathers of the skirts, leaving the stirrups empty. This arrangement twisted her legs near the ankles, but many a child has ridden in such an uncomfortable manner, and Ada did not complain.

It was not yet warm when they started out. The sun was just coming up over the rugged hills, and the landscape—so new to the girls—spread strangely about them as they rode. In 1870 the whole area was sparsely settled, and the desert tended to be unforgiving, even to its natural inhabitants, as indeed it remains to this day.

As the three rode Ada and Addi marveled at the rough terrain and the beautiful views in all directions. On the ground beneath the horses there was only widely spaced bunch grass, with sage and prickly pears the predominant vegetation. Scattered about were an occasional piñon tree and numerous small, round, bushlike junipers.

As the day progressed, the uninterrupted sunshine in the light desert air made the temperature rise quickly, and it became uncomfortably hot for both horses and riders. The girls removed the jackets they had donned in the morning and tied them to their saddles. Only now and then a piñon or juniper gave slight shelter from the sun, and the advancing summer allowed the heat to rise so much that it seemed almost dangerous.

It must be said that the "ride out" that the Ernsts had chosen to take on that day would not have overly challenged a hardy local rancher. However, for the young woman from Indiana and her little daughter, entirely unaccustomed to such intense heat, the adventure almost got the best of them. Addi began to consider an early return to the town.

Searching for some relief from the heat, they stopped where low ground in a wash made it possible for a sizeable juniper on the bank to cast shade high enough to accommodate horses and riders. Mother and daughter dismounted and decided to rest awhile in that welcome patch of relief. Since neither of them had experienced desert heat before, it had become to them quite unbearable.

It was past midday, and the ever so slight but very pleasant coolness of the shade allowed them to notice that they were hungry, so Addi removed the cloth sack of food from her saddlebag. She and Ada were rather eagerly eating the tortillas and hard-cooked eggs that Rosita had given them when, quite suddenly, José, who had remained on his horse, shouted "Banditos! Banditos!"

Without any other explanation José spurred his horse, took off at a fast gallop down a rocky wash, and disappeared from view. At first they hoped he was just investigating the situation, perhaps looking for water for the horses, but when he did not return, the truth was evident. The guide they trusted had left them, and they were alone in the desert!

Mounting their horses the young woman and the girl set out in the direction José had gone, but no one was to be seen—not even the"banditos." The desert began to look strange to them. Try as she might in all that unfamiliar sameness, Addi could not decide which direction they should go. Bravely, she tried to hide the fear that she now felt.

Addi remembered the jug tied to her saddle and reached for it, only to find that they had already drunk most of the water. The jug was nearly empty, and they had eaten all the food Rosita had given them. How could they survive out in that wilderness alone? Addi sought to reassure her daughter: "We still have some water. Here, take a small drink. It will help us go on." Both drank, but the small amount remaining in the jug only whetted their thirst.

"Has José really left us, Mothie? Oh . . ." Addi saw that tears began to fill the girl's eyes. "Mothie, can we find the way back?"

Addi assessed their situation. The larger jug of water had been tied on José's saddle. Without that, and with their own jug now empty, they were left with nothing to drink. Added to this misfortune was the realization that they could easily get lost in desert terrain, which has a certain sameness and which, particularly for strangers, had no readily distinguishable landmarks.

They were, she feared, already quite lost. Urging their now unwilling mustangs, they wandered for what seemed an interminable length of time, getting nowhere, seeming to ride in circles and returning over and over to places they knew they had been a short while before.

They looked for water in every crevace or depression but found none. Without water, and with the July heat becoming ever more oppressive, their tongues were now swollen in their mouths, and their lips were painfully dry and cracked.

Addi tried to appear confident in front of her daughter. She realized that they and the horses were really in danger, for the tired animals had plodded along much of the day without anything to drink. The sun was low in the western sky, and dusk would soon begin to fall.

Mother and daughter were exhausted by the unaccustomed heat and were in pain, and in their weariness they leaned forward and clung to the horns of their saddles for support. They spoke little, but Addi heard her brave little daughter whimpering as they rode.

As they came up over a small rise, Ada saw a dim figure on horseback, which caused her to cry out through her badly swollen lips, "Mothie, José is coming back. I see him!" She pointed toward a small hillock, where a lone horseman could be seen, riding towards them and waving his arms. It was José! He had come back for them! The weary mustangs neighed softly when they saw their approaching relative, and two exhausted riders sat up a bit straighter in their saddles.

When he reached Addi and the little girl, José was very quiet and seemed ashamed of what he had done, but the two were so glad to see him and were both so weary and almost ill that they did not complain or scold him, as Addi certainly otherwise would have done.

José did tell them that he had been frightened when he saw a group of horsemen who he thought were bandits and that on his dash away from the girls he had stopped at a ranch along the way. The rancher, a tough, grizzled old-timer, had stopped at the livery stable a few times when he was in town, and he was quite disturbed when José told him what had happened. "I was ashamed, too, when I got to thinking about you ladies out here alone," José said, "and I decided that I could not leave you alone and without anyone to help you. That is why I came back, even if I was worried about the banditos I thought I saw back there. Really, Senora, those fellows are plenty mean!"

When José told the rancher that he would try to find the girls, the man offered to give him some food and water to take along. José had taken as much as he could pack on his horse.

José told Addi, "We camp tonight. Too late now to ride. We go back in the morning." Painfully tired and sick from their lack of water and the extreme heat, mother and daughter quickly agreed.

The ladies drank sparingly but repeatedly from the jug José had brought, then nibbled lightly on the bread and cold meat. José gave the horses a small amount of the precious water, removed their saddles, and tied them to juniper trees where they could find some bunch grass and could also forage on the sagebrush.

Pulling a blanket from behind his saddle, José reminded Ada and her mother that they also had blankets tied behind their saddles. The sun had gone down, leaving behind a sunset that they barely noticed. It was almost dark, but enough light remained so they could look around for a safe place to sleep. They chose a spot that was fairly smooth, and when they had made sure that no snakes or scorpions were present, Addi spread her blanket on the dry, sandy ground, then she and Ada lay down, used their saddles as pillows, and covered themselves with the other blanket. José did the same, considerately choosing a spot somewhat removed from where the "senora and senorita" would sleep.

Weary from their long ride, the two girls had now calmed down from their earlier fear, and all three found that sleep came easily. So tired were they that neither mother nor daughter noticed the sky full of stars in the clear air above them. They did not see the tightly woven blanket of smaller stars that made a backdrop for the strangely large and brilliant ones outlining the constellations.

Toward morning they awoke, no longer feeling ill but chilled almost to the bone by the desert night. Reaching in the dark for their saddle blankets, they pulled them up over the other covering. Cuddling closely together, Addi and Ada were soon almost warm.

Before they went back to sleep, they did notice the myriad of stars and the brilliant constellations high above them. Without speaking, each felt as she gazed into the sky that she would never forget the overwhelming beauty of that desert night. The fear that they had experienced, together with gratitude for their escape from near-tragedy, served to emphasize their awareness of the beauty above them. All of this would remain long in their memories.

When the sun was barely visible over the eastern horizon and began to warm the air, the three arose and ate the rest of the bread and cold meat. Ada and Addi folded their blankets and helped José tie them and the other equipment to saddles. Wasting little time, José bridled and saddled the horses and gave them a little more—just a taste—of the water he had brought.

Eager to be on their way, the three mounted their refreshed horses and rode quickly in the relative cool of the morning. José was obviously at home in the desert, and he proceeded confidently and with no hesitation, seeming to have a natural, built-in compass somewhere in his being.

In a couple of hours they could see the first houses of the town, and mother and daughter knew that they were safe. The horses whinnied, happy that they were nearing their home, and the three riders rejoiced in their own way. Right about then, that little boarding house would have looked mighty inviting to the ladies from Indiana, and when they reached it, they were more than happy.

Rosita had been worried when they did not return the night before, and when she saw the three riders coming toward her house, she called out to them, "You are safe! I was worried! Come in and tell me all about your trip!" Ada excitedly tried to tell her how they had been lost in the desert, how José came back, and about sleeping on the ground. "It was scary, Rosita, but it was lots of fun too!"

Rosita did not invite José in as she had done before, and after he left for his home, she prepared an early lunch that mother and daughter ate with hungry enthusiasm. They chatted with Rosita a bit afterward, then spent the early part of the afternoon relaxing, doing nothing much at all.

After a time, they decided to walk about the town, and Addi needed directions from Rosita. "Do you know where the Martinez store is?"

"The store of Senor Martinez is near the blacksmith shop. The same side of the street. They have a big sign. You will see it."

Addi explained: "I thought we might stop in and see Mr. and Mrs. Martinez. They asked us to come by while we were in Santa Fe. We had a good time with them on the stagecoach, especially when we stopped, because everything seemed so different to us, and they showed us around and made us feel safe."

In 1870 Santa Fe was just a small town. About a thousand people lived there, and only a few were white men. There were no white women, and as they walked along the street, the two blondes from Indiana were a novelty, and they caused more than a little interest on the part of the few men who were standing about or lounging in front of the saloon. Addi and her daughter tried not to notice how the men stared at them or at least not to show that they did.

They stopped briefly at the blacksmith shop, where the rhythmic clang of the smith's hammer on the anvil enlivened that quiet part of town. The smith was a big, hearty Mexican, and he did not hide his surprise to see the two white ladies. He probably did not speak much, if any, English, for he made no effort to talk to them.

The smith did not put down the horseshoe that he was shaping on the anvil. He did, however, nod his head once or twice, sending a wide smile in their direction, a happy smile that ended in deep crinkles at the edges of his eyes.

Mother and daughter resumed their walk down the street from the blacksmith shop. "There it is," Addi said, pointing to a low stucco building only a few yards ahead. "Let's go in and see Señor and Señora Martinez."

The sign on the Martinez building was more professional than Rosita's simple little announcement. In fact, it bragged a bit: "R. Martinez Clothing and Outfitting. Finest yard goods. Hats and Gloves. Everything in Wearing Apparel."

The store had few windows, and since there were no lights, it was hard to see when they first entered out of the bright sunlight. As soon as their eyes adjusted, they saw that in the back of the store Senora Cortez was helping a woman with some dress goods, spreading the brightly colored cloth out on a long table not unlike the one that Grandmother had in her shop in Richmond.

As soon as she was finished with her customer, Señora Martinez greeted Addi and Ada: "I am so glad to see you. I thought that you were not coming to see us. Do come in. Rafael has gone out, but he will be back soon. Tell me, what have you been doing in Santa Fe? Did you find a good place to stay?"

Words and questions just tumbled out of that friendly lady's mouth, and finally Addi was able to answer the senora. "We are staying at Rosita's, and she is very good to us. We had a chance to ride out with José from the livery stable—out into the desert. That was something!"

Ada was walking about the store, looking at all the items displayed but particularly at the cowboy hats. "Go ahead, put one on," the Senora urged. Ada chose one that seemed about her size—a hat of some rough cloth, not leather. It was solid gray in color, but its red band had caught Ada's eye.

She put the hat on, then looked at herself in a small mirror that hung nearby. "Oh, Mothie, I love this! May I have it? It would be such fun to wear it in Richmond. No one has a hat like this!" Addi inquired of its cost, which was not excessive, and agreed that she would buy it for Ada.

"We must also find something to take to Grandmother. Why don't you look around for a gift you think she would want?" After Ada had suggested a number of things she liked, they agreed on a bright scarf.

"I am sure Grandmother would love one of those pretty baskets you showed me," Addi counseled her daughter, "but it would be hard to take back with us; there would not be room in our bags for it." They left the store in a happy mood, and Ada was wearing her "cowboy" hat.

A bit farther down the street they passed a small, iron-barred, one-windowed jail that was quite empty, and as they continued walking they passed by the saloon. Loud sounds came from the open doorway— husky men's voices but also the tinkling, tinny sound of a piano accompanying a sultry-voiced woman singing a sad song of her man's unfaithfulness.

"Every little town has its saloon," Addi said, "even big towns like Richmond. Towns like Indianapolis and Richmond, they have more than one, and some men go there to drink and spend money that is needed for their families. I have seen that happen, back home. 'Dens of iniquity,' they call them." Ada's experience in life did not allow her to fully understand what her mother had said, but she did feel sorry for the neglected families.

The two Adas continued to walk around the town for a while, then returned to Rosita's. At supper they ate only lightly, then went early to bed, finding that the day and a half spent riding in the desert and their walk around the town had left them quite weary. In fact, they were so tired that the rude mattress on their bed seemed almost comfortable.

Morning soon came, and after another hearty breakfast, Addi decided to venture out into the desert on foot. Rosita cautioned her, "Don't go too far. Remember what happened yesterday!" Addi had not forgotten that frightening experience, and she did not wander far, keeping the edge of town always in sight.

Ada was interested in Rosita's cooking, done partly on a wood stove in the kitchen but mostly—because of the heat—on a fire outside. She asked if she might stay to watch. Her Mexican landlady assured Addi, "Ada is no trouble. I like to have her, and I'll teach her how I cook. She can make tortillas."

They spent several happy days with Rosita, and twice more they rented horses and took rides in the desert surrounding the town. Addi loved the desert, with its long views and the mountains in the distance. Not wishing a repetition of their earlier experience, they both were very careful to keep the town in their sight or at least not to ride very far past where they could see Santa Fe. Addi had a sense of freedom from restraint in that wild land, and it was a feeling that her spirit needed. Ada was a younger version of her adventurous mother, and she too delighted in the many newnesses around them.

It was a happy time, and both of them felt surprisingly at home in the desert town, but Addi knew that they must soon return home. On the next stagecoach day, they set out for Junction City, Kansas. Again they rode twelve or fourteen dusty, hot days, stopping at the regular stage stops to change horses and to eat or sleep at the roadside inns, until they reached Kansas. From there they traveled by train to Kansas City, St. Louis, Indianapolis, and finally to Richmond. They arrived safely but were weary and rumpled and covered with dust and grime, and it was a happy and relieved grandmother who welcomed them home.

So it happened that a journey that might have ended in tragedy became a warm and happy memory. Addi had kept her word to Mary; she had brought her grandchild home safe, and Ada was happy to be home with Grandmother once more. Addi, however, had changed. She had tasted the exhilarating freedom that the New Mexico Territory awakened in her, and she could not forget.

A few weeks after their return, secure in the suitability of her daughter's home with Grandmother Thorpe, Addi reached a decision about her own future. It was a warm Saturday afternoon when Addi stopped by for her regular visit with Mary and Ada. She had just returned from a horseback ride and was dressed in the tan cotton riding habit she had worn in New Mexico. Addi bounded up the steps to the front porch, and her daughter met her at the door. She seemed unusually excited, a broad smile brightened her face, and she hugged Ada soundly when she came to the door. Inside, the parlor was bright and friendly. Addi looked around the room. "Where is your grandmother?"

Just as Addi was asking about her, Mary came in from the kitchen. "Well, Addi, we wondered when you would come by. I am so glad to see you. Will you have a cup of tea? Ada and I just finished making some oatmeal cookies."

"Yes, thanks. Tea and cookies sound just fine! Can I help you?" She followed Mary into the kitchen. "Grandma Mary, your kitchen is such a happy place. I do like to think of Ada being here with you. It makes me happy just to think about it. You are so good to her—to both of us."

Out in the kitchen, Mary put water on to boil, and soon the kettle began to whistle. She poured boiling water on the loose tea that she had spooned into the teapot, and while they waited for the tea to brew, she put a plate of cookies on the kitchen table, along with cream and sugar. Ada had taken cups and plates from the cupboard and a spoon for each from the silverware drawer.

"Now we can have a good visit," Mary suggested, "let's have our tea and cookies and a nice, long chat!" She looked at Addi, and it struck her that something might be amiss, for a very serious look had come across the young mother's face. "Addi, is something wrong?"

"Nothing is wrong, Grandma Mary, but I do have something I want to talk to you and Ada about. It is something that I have thought about a lot lately. I hardly know how to begin," she faltered. Ada stopped chewing on her cookie but said nothing. Mary, seeing the troubled look on her granddaughter's face, spoke quickly: "Addi, what is it? Tell us, please!"

"Well, Grandma Mary, as I said, it seems to me that Ada is happy with you, and I know that you are giving her the kind of life she deserves. You are giving her all the things I could never manage to do. Education, a really nice home, and a place where she can invite her friends to come. Grandma Mary, I want all that for Ada; I really do!"

"But what do you want for yourself, Addi? What do you plan for yourself?" Mary had a notion she knew what was coming.

"I am sure you have noticed how much I talk about New Mexico. Grandma Mary, I just loved it down there—the desert and the little towns and the big open spaces where there are no people. I love to see the deer, the big jackrabbits, and the coyotes. I love the pine trees and the junipers and even the prickly pear cactus.

"I just love it all, dear Grandma Mary, and I want to go back. I want to go to a place where everything is new and big and . . ." For a moment Addi was silent, then she added, with more than a touch of emotion, "someplace where there is *hope* and where I can amount to something! Please tell me you understand!"

Addi turned to her daughter, who was staring hard at her mother as she talked. "Ada, my wonderful Ada, I do love you. I love you so very much! But I want the best possible life for you, and I know that I can't give it to you, at least I can't now.

"Grandmother can, and she loves you too! I will come back to see you, and perhaps you and Grandma can come to see me when I find a place there. What do you think of that?"

For once, Ada did not immediately find words to speak. She just reached for her mother and wept. Addi tried to comfort her daughter: "I won't be gone forever, Ada. But I just have to leave here and go someplace where I can feel alive and at home. Can you understand that?"

After a few minutes Ada looked at her mother and said softly, "Mama,

I guess I understand. I guess I do." Then she got up from her chair and went over and buried her head in her grandmother's arms.

Mary pushed her chair away from the table to make a lap for the grieving young person. "Yes, Addi, I understand. You must go where you will be happy, and I am so very happy to have Ada stay right here with me. This is her home." Ada was getting too big to sit on her grandmother's lap, but Mary held her tightly. "Yes, dear Ada, this is your home."

Addi left by train on the next Wednesday. It was after three weeks that they received her letter from Santa Fe, saying that she had arrived safely and was looking for a way to make her living. "It is great here," she said, "but I miss you dear people. I will write often." Addi's letter seemed happy enough, but Mary felt an underlying tension in it that was worrisome.

As the weeks passed, Addi's letters came less frequently, and when one did arrive late in summer, it had unpleasant news. "Things have not worked out well here in Santa Fe, and we are leaving soon to go to California, where we hope to find work and perhaps a good place to live." Addi made no effort to explain the "we," and the final sentence in her letter, which she doubly underlined, had an air of finality to it.

"My darling Ada, you must never forget that your mother loves you very, very much. Take good care of Grandmother, and please be good to yourself. Do the best you can in school and be happy. Do this for your mother, who will always love you."

The letter was written in ink and with great care. The last two or three lines seemed a bit smudged, as if they might be tearstained. Ada did not know it then, but she would never again hear from her mother.

2

Mary Thorpe, Grandmother

THE INDIANA SUMMER HAD BEEN a hot one, but Ada and her grandmother lived pleasantly in the comfortable, high-ceilinged home on Fifth Street, and when fall came, Ada returned to school. Caught up in the many activities offered and with the need to apply herself to her studies, Ada's sadness after that last letter from her mother gradually lessened, and Grandmother Thorpe's loving care helped Ada to feel completely at home. Life was good with her grandmother and her young friends.

The years passed, and Ada, occupied with her schoolwork and the many artistic advantages the Richmond community offered, grew to healthy and well-rounded young womanhood. The lively child became a tall, vivacious young woman, still retaining the wavy blond hair and bright blue eyes of her childhood. And her eagerness—her eagerness for living—was undimmed.

Richmond, then a city of some eleven thousand, had already become an artistic center. An article that appeared regularly in a local newspaper kept citizens informed of "Art in Richmond." Two railroads served the town, and as a result a variety of traveling artists—singers, actors, lecturers—stopped and performed there. Mary Thorpe was interested in the artistic events the city offered, and she took Ada often to Phillips Hall and to the Morrison Opera Hall.

Both loved fine music and plays, and they also enjoyed the numerous lectures that were a feature of the times. In the 1870s speeches by well-known people were a common form of entertainment, and the newspapers of the day featured poems and stories on their front pages, along with a faithful reporting of the most homely details of local news.

Ada enjoyed all these attractions, but her first love was acting. She sat entranced when she and her grandmother attended a performance by one of the better actors of the time. Because it was served by two railroads Richmond was fortunate to have many of the best-known actors of the time appearing there, among them Agnes Ethel, John Drew, Fanny Davenport, George Holland, Charles and Rose Coghlan, Otis Skinner, Maurice Barrymore, and John Gilbert.

A picture of Ada taken by "the best photographer in the U.S." (name and address unknown) at about the time she would be entering her teenage years, shows a young lady with her hair pulled back flat against her head. There is a serious expression on her face as she stands with her hands on the arm of a heavily ornate chair, her feet properly placed in a ladylike position.

In the picture a tall stove is partially shown in the background, and the dress she wears is bouffant, with something of a bustle and with rows of lace coming within a few inches of her high-top shoes. Grandmother made sure that our Ada was quite the young lady of fashion!

As she developed, Ada's inclination toward all things theatrical increased so much that it soon dominated her thoughts and aspirations. Teachers chose her for parts in many of the school plays, and Richmond playgoers agreed that Ada never failed to give an outstanding performance.

After Ada had been applauded for her portrayal of Juliet in a school performance, Grandmother Thorpe made a decision. Although Ada was just sixteen years old, Mary Thorpe decided that she should be sent to Europe for formal study in the theatre. Sending a young student abroad was not uncommon at that time; in fact it was very popular to send young people to Europe to study, if, of course, the family could afford it. Mary Thorpe was able to arrange such an opportunity for Ada.

After much inquiry, Mary chose Dresden, a city whose reputation as a center for the arts had spread widely in the United States. More particularly, she made arrangements for her granddaughter to study at the Dresden School of the Theatre.

One of the taller and more fully developed of the girls in her class at school, Ada felt quite grown up and full of confidence. In fact, that young lady was ready to take on the world! When Mary discussed with her the plans she had, Ada was more than happy. The prospect of going all the way to Dresden to study was exciting to her.

"Dear Grandmother," Ada exclaimed, "I am so very, very happy!" It was difficult for Ada to control her emotions, and surely this was no time to do so. "I am happy, happy, happy, and I promise you that I will make you proud of me!"

Grandmother was more serious and did not wish to lose this opportunity to emphasize all that she believed was important. "You must not forget, Ada, what I have taught you. You must continue to apply yourself to your studies, and—especially—you must be a good girl. Promise me that you will always remember, Ada, that you are a young lady, and you must behave like one!"

"I will, dear, dear Grandmother! Oh! This is just what I have dreamed about. Is it all really coming true?" Ada was not one to hide her feelings, and in her enthusiasm she kissed her grandmother soundly on the cheek. In her turn Mary, managed a smile but with a noticeable tenseness in her expression and held her eager granddaughter close to her breast.

The decision to send her granddaughter far—so very far—away had not been easy for Mary. "But," she had often reminded herself, "Ada is unusually talented. She is a born actress; she must have more education in what she loves, and she does love acting and the theatre. My Ada has always been a good girl; surely I have had no trouble with her. I must have faith that she will continue to be protected and always behave as she should, even if she is with strangers and far from home. I must have faith."

Mary Thorpe had put a tidy sum away for her retirement, and she used what was necessary to make Ada's dream—and her own grandmotherly wish—come true. In the early spring of 1879 she and her granddaughter took the train to New York. Arriving in the late afternoon, they found a small hotel and spent the night. Mid-morning of the next day Mary asked the bell captain to get a cab for them.

The doorman signaled to the line of small cabs that were waiting outside, and the one nearest the door drove up. It was a small, two-wheeled cab pulled by just one horse, and there was barely enough room in the vehicle for Ada's considerable luggage. After he had stowed the bags and helped the ladies to a seat in the cab, the driver took his seat high at the rear, leaving the forward view open for his passengers.

The trip from the hotel to the dock took more than an hour, and as they drove, Mary was nearly as excited as her granddaughter by the sights of New York. The driver took them to the dock from which Ada's ship—the *Bavaria* of the Hapag Line—would be leaving for Europe. After he had escorted the two ladies and obligingly carried Ada's luggage to the dock, Mary thanked and paid the driver.

As they walked to the dock both Ada and her grandmother were awed by the sight of the long, sleek vessel that lay at anchor. Hand in hand the two ladies—one youthfully exuberant and the other unsure of whether she was happy or sad—crossed the gangplank and climbed the stairway leading to the *Bavaria*'s deck.

Mary noticed a tall, rather dignified, unusually well dressed young man standing at the rail. He wore a top hat, beneath which one could see that his dark hair was cut in the prevailing longer fashion, ending on either cheek in long sideburns.

She particularly noticed his eyes. Mary had always believed that eyes reveal one's personality, and she thought that this young man's eyes were unusual. Framed by dark lashes, they were large, wider than most, and of a soft bluish-gray, and to Mary they seemed both kind and firm. Then she noticed his mouth, which had such a kindly air about it that it seemed its owner was about to smile.

The young man had been conversing with a passenger beside him, but now he stood quietly at the rail, looking at the throng of people on the docks below. Something in his overall mien gave Mary Thorpe a most remarkable idea and the courage to follow it through. She stopped directly in front of the young gentleman and spoke to him.

"Sir, forgive me for being so forward. As you can see, I have my granddaughter with me. We have arranged for her to go to Dresden for studies in the theatre, and she is traveling alone, since I cannot go with her. We live in Richmond, Indiana, where I have a business, and my granddaughter has never been away from home before.

"What I am asking you, sir, is this: Would you be so kind as to watch over Ada on the voyage? I should be so grateful, so very . . ."

Before Mary could finish what she meant to say, the young man smiled, removed his top hat, bowed slightly, and spoke. His cultured, warm voice held a charming accent that Mary could not identify.

"Madame, I shall be very happy to watch over this lovely young lady and make sure that she arrives in Europe safely. When we land in Hamburg I will see to it that the rest of her journey is in order. Madame, let me introduce myself. I am Rudolf Vincent Martinsen from Amsterdam, where I am employed by Boissevain and Company. We are a banking firm much interested in the development of your great country." Young Martinsen's manner, though it was obvious to Mary that he came from a world unlike that of her own American Midwest, was warm and gracious, and he put her so at ease that she almost gushingly responded:

"Sir, how can I thank you for your kindness? I cannot say how relieved I am. Now I am sure that Ada will be safe on the voyage. Oh! I almost forgot. I am Mary Thorpe, and this is Ada Ernst, my granddaughter. We are from Richmond, Indiana, as I said, where I own a small business establishment." The introductions were properly acknowledged by Martinsen's dignified bow and by something of a curtsy from the ladies.

Mary and Ada had arrived not much in advance of the *Bavaria*'s time for departure, and it was not long before they heard the loud clanging of a bell warning that all guests should leave the ship, for she would soon put out to sea. Mary Thorpe was unusually emotional as she again thanked Mr. Martinsen, then bade her granddaughter a fond farewell, wished her success in her studies, renewed her caution about proper behavior, and urged Ada to write often.

Eager to begin the new adventure, Ada embraced her grandmother and promised everything. "Yes, Grandmother, I will, I will! Grandmother, you will be happy that you have given me this chance! I will write you often. Oh, I shall miss you so very much, dear Grandmother!"

Overflowing with emotion, Ada brushed tears from her eyes as she watched her grandmother make her way carefully down the stairway and across the gangplank to the dock below. Mary Thorpe was a pretty woman, a few inches shorter than her granddaughter and perhaps a little stout, as one might expect of a woman her age. Her graying hair was done up in a neat bun, and she was tastefully dressed in a dark blue wool suit with a floor-length, straight skirt, under which one could barely get a peek at her black high-top shoes.

Grandmother carried herself with confidence as she walked, and Ada felt a warm surge of pride and love for this remarkable woman who was so good to her. Ada watched as her grandmother adjusted the small hat that completed her ensemble and which had been pushed askew by the enthusiastic good-bye hug Ada had given her when they parted. Noting the tears in her eyes Rudolf Martinsen took Ada's hand in his and pulled her a bit closer to his side. A series of loud blasts from the ship's horn warned that the vessel would soon be moved from the docks. Small vessels towed her away from the pier and out into the bay. Once out in the harbor, a breeze freshened, the steam engines were started, the sails hoisted, and the Bavaria began to glide out to sea. The shouting of the crew, so loud at first, soon became faint as Mary watched from the docks.

Mary Thorpe was happy to see that young Martinsen was standing beside her granddaughter as they waved to her from the rail. She could make out the excitement and happiness on Ada's face, which soothed her grandmotherly concerns. "Rudolf Vincent Martinsen . . . from Amsterdam." Mary thought about their chance meeting with the altogether engaging young man, and she wondered about the unaccustomed temerity she had shown in speaking so openly to a stranger, and especially to a man.

She felt only gratitude as she recalled his promise and his friendly assurances. "What a fine young man," she mused, "How old might he be? Twenty-five or so? I do like him. I trust him. Yes, for some reason I trust Mr. Martinsen. Ada will be safe; he will see to that. My Ada will be safe, and she will find her dream."

3

Rudolf Vincent Martinsen

MUCH HAS BEEN WRITTEN about the romantic attributes of an ocean voyage, and some travelers have ventured so far as to claim that during every crossing of an ocean, love—passionate love—flowers. Without commenting on that extravagant assertion, we can surely say that the voyage just begun—Ada's first—was full of excitement for her. The *Bavaria* was large, and although it was a steamer, it still gained part of its power from sails and was built much like the latest models of a sailing vessel.

Ada had a second-class cabin, but it was, she thought, most wonderful. The second cabin, as those rooms were called, was amidships. The first-class cabins formed a long row on each side of the ship, and each had a porthole. From the cabins, one stepped directly into the long, narrow salon that lay between them and served as both a dining and a sitting salon. Lighting came from above via sky lights.

Rudolf Martinsen was entirely faithful to his promise to Mary Thorpe; in fact, he thought it a most pleasant diversion to help his vivacious young charge become acquainted with the ship and its offerings. During the first few days he escorted her at mealtimes to the dining salon, then as the days passed the two entered into some of the social activities provided on the vessel. Increasingly, however, they preferred just to enjoy each other's company.

They spent long hours walking about the *Bavaria* or perhaps just sitting in steamer chairs and looking out over the broad ocean. During such times, Rudolf told Ada something of his life and the work he was doing, and Ada sat entranced, for she was being introduced to an exciting world that she had hardly known existed at all.

In response to Rudolf's interest, Ada told him about her mother, her life with Grandmother in Richmond, her experiences in school, her trip to New Mexico, and—most of all—her hopes for an acting career.

In the evenings after dinner the salon of the *Bavaria* was arranged for dancing, and Rudolf found that he had a most eager and agile dancing partner who quickly learned any steps that were new to her. It was all so wonderfully *shiny* to Ada, and so exciting.

A chance observer might well have thought it surprising how well the two got along together—he, a man from the Old World and an internationally successful financier; she, a young, inexperienced girl from the American Midwest. Ada was seventeen, and Rudolf was twenty-seven, but the difference in their ages seemed of no importance to either of them.

Rudolf was charmed as he had never been before by the enthusiastic and dramatic Ada, and she—well, Ada had in her young life never seen or met anyone even remotely like this tall, good-looking man of the world. Rudolf was so attentive, so gallant, so knowledgeable; in no way was he like the schoolboys she had known in Richmond. Indeed, it was a first for both of them; Rudolf had never met a girl like Ada either.

The voyage across the Atlantic took approximately two weeks, but before that time had passed, Rudolf realized that his feelings for Ada had become much stronger than he would have anticipated when he was first asked to watch over her. He wondered, "Have I fallen in love with this young girl?"

In fact, Rudolf had fallen in love, for when he thought about Ada, his pulse quickened and a new thrill passed through his very being. Rudolf found himself thinking of little else but this young lady, and he knew that he must do something before it would be too late.

On the evening before the *Bavaria* was scheduled to arrive in Hamburg, the two stood together by the rail, bewitched by the beauty of what lay before them. All around them there was moonlight—soft light that played in a wondrous way on the ocean as it rose and fell, wave upon wave. And there was music coming from the grand salon, romantic dancing music that accentuated the gentle movement of the boat and wove itself into the moonlight and the moist evening air, and into the hearts of the two who listened.

As was the style of the time, both Ada and Rudolf were in evening dress, and Ada could not help feeling that all eyes were upon them as they entered the salon for dinner that evening. Her dress was of a light blue silk, and Grandmother Thorpe had made certain that it fit her lovely young figure well. Ada had "done up" her hair into a small bun, and the soft color of the dress urged her eyes to outdo themselves in their blueness.

Now, together with Ada on the deck in the moonlight, Rudolf was overcome. Although he had been thinking intently about her during the past few days and had gone over in his mind what he wanted to say to her, when he did speak, his words came tumbling formlessly out.

"Oh, Ada, I love you, and I want you with me always. Dear Ada, will you marry me? Oh, I will be so good to you! I will take care of you always. I promise you, Ada, you will never want for anything!"

His arms were around her, and Ada was lost in the magic of the moment and the strong warmth of his love. "Oh, yes, Rudolf! I will, I will marry you!" She told him then that she wanted to be his wife, although—as she in later years told a granddaughter—"at the time, all I really wanted was to cuddle."

Ada was so young, so inexperienced.

When they reached Hamburg, Rudolf did not start Ada on her way to Dresden to attend the School of the Theatre there. Instead, he took her directly to his mother's home in north Germany. Satisfied that she would be quite all right in his mother's care, he boarded the next available ship for America. From New York he proceeded immediately to Richmond, where he would see Grandmother Thorpe.

As he had told Ada and Grandmother Thorpe when they first met aboard the Bavaria, Rudolf was employed by the eminent Amsterdam banking firm of Boissevain et Cie. His main efforts at that time were to work with other Dutch interests in financing certain business ventures in the youthful and thriving United States of America. Martinsen's financial interest in "the new world" was coupled with a particularly firm belief in its future, and when he met Ada and her grandmother aboard the Bavaria, he was returning from business in New York.

Rudolf Martinsen was born in Reval, Russia, on August 10, 1851. Although they had lived for many years in Russia, the Martinsen family was not native to that country, having moved there from Schleswig-Holstein in north Germany. It is probable that they were among the many Germans invited by Katherine of Russia to come to her country, with the hope that they would bring with them the arts and the culture that her own nation lacked.

His grandfathers, both on his father's and his mother's sides, were bankers. Rudolf's paternal grandfather's interests were in Reval, and those of his maternal grandfather were in Riga. His maternal grandfather was mayor of Riga, at a time when the office was an entirely honorary position and was not achieved through politics.

The Martinsens in Reval lived in a comfortable, refined manner as prosperous bankers, and Rudolf attended the Russian schools. He showed early on a marked ability in music, particularly the piano, and he developed a singing voice that grew into a warm, melodious baritone. Wishing to provide the best possible education for their son, his parents sent him to school in Vevey, Switzerland, then widely respected as an educational center.

Young Martinsen continued to do well in his studies, and he obtained a position as a clerk in a Swiss banking house when he was only sixteen. Rudolf showed such remarkable aptitude and trustworthiness that he was quickly promoted to the position of cashier, which gave him the authority to sign for the firm.

In 1871, when he was only twenty, Rudolf went to Amsterdam, where he had relatives, and became a member of another well-known banking institution, H. W. Bildenstein and Co. In 1873 he became a stock exchange member of that firm, and in 1876 he was made a member of the banking association of Adolph Boissevain et Cie.

When he reached Richmond it was mid-afternoon, and Rudolf at once hired a horse-drawn cab to take him to a hotel, and then to Mary's shop. Although Mary immediately recognized Rudolf, she at first was caught up in an understandable grandmotherly fear that he might have bad news about Ada. Her greeting expressed that concern.

"Mr. Martinsen, how good to see you!" Then she frowned slightly. "Is there something wrong? Is Ada all right?"

"No, Madame Thorpe, there is nothing wrong, and Ada is quite safe. But I must talk to you. May I come in?"

"Oh, certainly. Please forgive me; I was just very surprised to see you. Please, sir, do come in." Mary showed Rudolf to a comfortable armchair near a window at the back of her shop, then seated herself in a rocking chair nearby. "Now, sir, we can talk."

"Madame, let me first say that I find your granddaughter a truly charming and unusual young lady. For me, it was pleasing to see that she enjoyed herself and felt at ease on our voyage. As I promised you, it was my firm intention to see that she was safely on her way to Dresden after we arrived in Hamburg. But, Madame, I did not do that. Instead, I took her to my mother's home in Germany, where she is happily installed and quite safe. My mother and all my relatives there loved Ada at once. . . ."

Noting a worried, questioning look in Mary's eyes, Rudolf determined that he must quickly explain his intentions. "I must tell you, Madame Thorpe, in those few days on the ship I have come to care for your granddaughter. In fact, I love her dearly, and I have come here from Germany with but one thought in mind.

"I ask you for Ada's hand in marriage, and I assure you that I am in a position to give her a fine home and the truly good things in life. Ada loves you very much, and she would want your blessing on her marriage. If you do agree that she may become my wife, Ada will want for nothing; I promise you that."

Mary stopped rocking, and, in her great surprise, she said nothing. Instead, she tried to control the emotion she felt. Rudolf pressed on: "May I have your answer, Madame?"

This was a turn of events for which Mary Thorpe was not prepared. If Ada married so young—so very young—what was to become of her dream of being an actress? "And yet," Mary thought, "the life of an actress is not a certain thing, by any means. Perhaps her life would be better with this young man . . ."

Mary turned her attention to Rudolf as he waited for her response, and again she felt a reassuring, warm certainty when she looked into his eyes. She wondered at her own confidence in this man she had known such a short time, but something about the warmth of his personality and the steadiness with which he looked directly into her eyes made

Mary feel that she could trust him. She did not speak at once, and Rudolf waited until she rather haltingly broke the silence.

"Mr. Martinsen, you will understand that what you have said comes as such a surprise to me that I am at a loss for words. How about Ada? There has not been time for her to write me about this. How does Ada feel about giving up her plans for the theatre? Marriage—so soon—how does she feel about it?"

"Madame Thorpe, I could not ask for her hand in marriage if I did not believe that she loves me too. That would indeed be a foolish thing to do. If you saw us together, I am sure you would realize she does love me. On our last evening on the ship before landing in Hamburg, I asked Ada to marry me. She agreed—oh, she agreed, I can assure you of that. Ada is young, I know, but many women do marry at seventeen, and I am ready and eager to take on the responsibility of caring for her as my wife. Ada will be safe with me, and to make her happy will be my joy. Do you not believe me?"

"I do believe you, Mr. Martinsen, and I could hardly wish for a finer husband for my Ada." For a moment Mary hesitated, still somewhat unsure; then a feeling of confidence overcame her hesitation, and she gave Rudolf her answer. "Yes, I do give my consent. You and Ada may be married. But tell me, when do you wish to marry?"

"Right away! At once! Just as soon as we may make plans. I think we should be married in Amsterdam, but I know that Ada could not think of a wedding unless her dear grandmother is with her." Mary started to interrupt, but Rudolf continued. "Oh, yes, Madame Thorpe, you must be with us, and I shall arrange it. Now you will have to make plans to be away from your business for a few weeks. Madame, you have made us very happy!"

Mary smiled, with only the bright hint of a tear, and opened her arms to this young Russian who would marry her Ada. Rudolf reached out for her, and, tenderly hugging, they became relatives.

"And now," Rudolf asked, "may I have the pleasure of dining with you? Which is your favorite restaurant in Richmond?"

4

Marriage

IT WAS SO LIKE RUDOLF MARTINSEN. He booked rail and ocean passage for Ada's grandmother to travel to Amsterdam for the wedding, and Mary was overcome with surprised happiness when she saw with her own eyes the comfort and the luxury that had come into her granddaughter's life. It was so much more than she, Mary, could give her and far more than Ada's young parents could have offered. For a moment she thought of her son's early death, and for another fleeting moment she wondered, "Where are you, Addi? What has happened to you?" It was months, even years, since Mary had heard from Ada's mother.

Rudolf and Ada were married in Amsterdam on July 22, 1879, and the *Richmond Telegraph* carried this bit of news: "Miss Ada Ernst, granddaughter of Mrs. Thorpe, with whom she lived from her childhood, was married at Amsterdam, Holland, on the 22nd. Her husband is a young banker of that city named Rudolph Vincent Martinsen, who, while returning from a visit to their branch office in New York, met her aboard ship. They are off on a six months bridal tour and expect to eat their Christmas dinner in this city at the residence of Mart. Nixon with whom Mrs. Thorpe resides."

Thus it happened that Ada Ernst was not destined to fulfill her youthful desire to attend a school of the theatre, nor would she become a professional actress. Nevertheless, it would be often noted in later years by those who knew her best that Ada Ernst Martinsen *acted* the rest of her life. Had Fate permitted her to release her emotions through acting, could her later, highly emotional mindset have been avoided?

The long honeymoon tour was a delight to Ada, for it was devoted to seeing strange new places and enjoying a wide variety of entertainment, and it provided only the slightest hint of the responsibilities of married life. Moreover, the experience revealed to her the joys of world travel, which no doubt resulted in her later pronounced habit of not staying overly long in one place.

Rudolf took his bride first to Paris, both because he knew she would love it and also because he had not seen enough of "Gay Paree" himself. To use a common phrase, they "did the town" together—and to be together was what they both wanted. How can one describe the delights they experienced in that city that specializes in delight? Suffice it to say that it was Rudolf, not Ada, who decided they should leave Paris, but Rudolf knew how well his romantic young wife would love Italy.

In Italy they spent a week or more in Rome, another week in Florence, and many days in the quaint small towns between. In both cities they reveled in the art and the music that was everywhere to be enjoyed. It seemed to Ada that everyone in Italy was a singer, for she heard so many good voices there, even in the streets. To hear an operatic aria or a passionate love song coming from the untrained voice of an ordinary Italian was not at all unusual, but it seemed so to Ada.

When they left Italy, they traveled to Vienna, a city about which one dreams. In that beautiful, unspoiled metropolis they attended the opera and enjoyed many a carriage ride through the fabled Vienna Woods. In the magnificent palace built for his horses by the emperor of Austria, they attended a dressage performance by the Spanish Riding School. The horses were of a type Ada had never seen before—big, white Lippizaner stallions. She imagined that they were dashing descendants of the chargers used by medieval knights.

A horse lover from her girlhood, Ada marveled at how the riders sat their mounts—so upright and tightly glued to the saddles. Never had she seen horses put through such intricate movements. It was all new to her—new and thrilling.

Seeing how fascinated Ada was, not only with the horses but also with the palace itself, Rudolf arranged for them to attend another type of performance there—a musical evening. It was a grand party, just about the grandest that Ada could even imagine, and they dressed for it in their finest evening attire. Entertainment was provided by a large orchestra and singers from the Vienna Opera. Surely it was an evening to be remembered! Rudolf told Ada that when the great Beethoven was still living, he had conducted an orchestra of several hundred musicians in that very room!

How Ada did love Vienna! To her, it completely lived up to its reputation as "the city of dreams."

They remained in Vienna more than the week they had planned, then went on to Russia. Rudolf took her to the place where he was born and where he had grown to young manhood—the beautiful, medieval city of Reval. He was proud to introduce his bride to his relatives, who seemed as happy to greet her as they were to see Rudolf again.

The home that Rudolf had been born in—the Martinsen home—was overwhelming to Ada, who had only known the simple houses she had seen in Indiana. Built of carefully hewn stone, it seemed to young Ada more like a castle than a house. The interior revealed an even more impressive appearance. Everywhere, everything was polished; everything gleamed softly. Ada felt that she was dreaming.

There was much to see in Reval, and it was like no other city Ada had ever seen. It was walled and its streets were of cobblestones. She had only read stories about cities like Reval.

Ada gazed at the onion-topped structures of the government buildings and the churches, and she felt that she was in a world different from any she had known. In fact, she *was* in a new and different world, and because it was the homeland of the husband she adored with all her romantic heart, she absorbed the atmosphere eagerly.

The buildings, the streets, and the people impressed her, as did the fine carriages that were everywhere to be seen. The carriages were not at all like the plain cabs and wagons that plied the streets of Richmond. To Ada everything in Russia seemed like something out of a storybook. She was fascinated by it all.

Rudolf wanted to show his bride everything in the city he knew and loved so well, but, always the caring husband, he could see that his usually active wife had spells when she did not feel well. He greatly curtailed certain activities and satisfied his desire to entertain her with many carriage rides through the cobbled streets. He showed her the fine homes that climbed up Toompoea Hill, and they stopped at points where she could get a view of the Baltic Sea.

Weeks passed, and the time came for the newlyweds to return as planned to Richmond for Christmas. During their stay with the Martinsens, Ada had become very fond of her in-laws, and it was a bit sad to say good-bye to them and begin the long journey to Indiana.

Together they took the train across Europe to Hamburg, boarded the ship that would take them to the United States, and then traveled by rail to Richmond. Ada had brief spells during the long journey when she did not feel well.

Their return to Richmond was a happy one, and Grandmother Mary and her daughter and son-in-law, the Martin Nixons, spared nothing to make it a truly festive celebration. Ada and Rudolf had brought with them from their travels many beautiful and novel gifts for Mary and the family, and there were appreciative "oohs" and "aahs" as packages were unwrapped.

Perhaps for Mary, however, the most exciting gift of all was when Ada whispered in her ear that she might be expecting a child. Ada—who was herself little more than a child to Mary—was to be a mother!

Later, alone in her room, Mary's thoughts went back to the time of Ada's birth, and she felt a warm thrill of gratitude that this new experience would be a happy one. How fortunate that this child-to-be would come into a home that offered love and all the comforts of life! She could not avoid contrasting Rudolf's evident fatherly enthusiasm with the seemingly uncaring attitude of her own son, Ada's father.

"How much Trenton missed!" she said out loud. "And how happy have been my own love-filled years with Ada!" Mary looked back over the years of planning and giving—yes, even of sacrifice—occasioned by her care of Ada from childhood. As she lost herself in that remembering, an old familiar saying came to mind that had to do with casting one's bread upon the waters . . .

"Oh, I have been richly rewarded for it all. I have been blessed, truly blessed!" Mary breathed.

Rudolf and Ada did not stay long in Richmond, leaving after the New Year for New York, where he promptly checked in at his company's branch office. They remained in New York, and during their stay there, the happy couple enjoyed some of New York's famed entertainment. Before they left to return to Amsterdam, Rudolf took Ada to Tiffany's. In that beautiful jewelry store, they were promptly greeted by a formally dressed clerk. "What may I do for you, sir?" he asked, to which Rudolf responded, "I want to buy my wife a ring."

They were shown to an alcove containing a number of comfortable chairs. The clerk was solicitous: "And what kind of a ring are you looking for, sir?" Rudolf replied that he wished to buy a diamond ring, and asked that they be shown "a few of your best diamonds." The clerk needed more information: "And what size stone do you desire?" Ada would never forget Rudolf's response: "I want a diamond, young man, the size that a *lady* can wear."

A tray of diamonds in various settings was brought, and together they looked carefully at each. One, bearing a modest-sized but particularly brilliant diamond, intricately set in yellow gold, caught Ada's eye, and she would have no other. She picked up the ring, placed it on a long, slim finger, and held up her hand to view the effect. The ring dangled a bit loosely, but how it did sparkle and gleam!

The attendant smiled. "Your wife has an unerring sense of value, sir! May I put the ring in a case for you?"

Rudolf was pleased that a choice was so quickly made. "No," he said, "Mrs. Martinsen will wear it as soon as you have made it the proper size. But, do give us a suitable box for its safekeeping." Rudolf asked that the ring be sized at once, for they would be leaving the next day for Holland.

The voyage back across the Atlantic was not as enjoyable as the first one had been, for Ada had unpleasant spells of morning sickness, and the passage seemed long. Eager to be home, the crossing was tiresome for both of them. Rudolf was impatient, not only to be back at work but also to arrange for their new home.

After arriving in Amsterdam, they lived for a few months in his bachelor apartment, but, although it was well arranged for one person, it never was intended to be a family home. In the days ahead they looked for something more suitable, and they found what they wanted in another apartment. It was larger, and it was set in a parklike neighborhood that would be more enjoyable for Ada when she was at home while Rudolf worked.

"And when our baby comes, I can take him airing in the park." Ada was already enjoying the new home. "Yes, my dear, you can do that, and I shall go with you whenever I am here." Both of them were happily anticipating parenthood.

They would need new furniture for their home, and together they chose from the handsome, hand-carved mahogany pieces that were made in Holland.

Table linens were ordered with the initial M woven into them, and the accompanying napkins were large enough to fit a modern card table. Ada was surrounded by luxury she had never known before, but such was the adaptable nature of her personality that she soon grew quite accustomed to it.

Rudolf experienced a feeling of satisfaction as he saw his young wife so comfortably in charge of their home. Stylishly dressed in the manner of the times, Ada carried herself with a dignity most remarkable for one so young, and she thoroughly charmed their guests.

Ada from Richmond, U.S.A., was quite the model of a European banker's wife, and no one would have suspected that having servants and managing a fine home were new to her. It occurred to Rudolf that an acting ability can be useful both on stage and in daily life. He liked watching this delightful young woman who so graced his home. Rudolf was happy.

Though European by birth, upbringing, and education, Rudolf's fascination with the New World, his informed and unswerving belief in the future of the United States, and no doubt also his marriage to a girl from Indiana, made him decide to become a naturalized American citizen.

He arranged for that step soon after his marriage to Ada, and he determined that, as children were born to them, they also would be American citizens. And so it happened that when the time neared for their first child to be born, he took Ada to New York, and there on August 20, 1880, a boy was born. They named him after his father: Rudolf Vincent Martinsen.

5

A Tragic Loss

WHEN LITTLE RUDI WAS ONLY a month old, Ada asked if she might take him to Richmond. "Oh, Rudolf," she said, "Grandmother must see our baby. While we are in New York, can't we go to Richmond?" Her husband responded that he was too involved with business at the time, but he made arrangements for Ada and little Rudi to go.

It was a heartwarming reunion for Ada and for Grandmother Thorpe, who proudly showed her great grandson to family members and to the friends who "could hardly wait" to see Ada's baby. Mary had prepared a special place for Rudi, and when bedtime came, she sat holding him in her rocking chair and sang sweetly as she had done years before with Ada. Her soft, grandmotherly voice calmed the little fellow, and—feeling safe in grandmotherly arms which held him just right—he soon was sleeping soundly.

In spite of Mary's warm welcome and her enthusiasm about her great grandson, Ada was a bit worried about her grandmother. She could not quite put her finger on what it was, but Grandmother did not seem like her old self. Ada did not think that the change she noticed in Grandmother was entirely caused by aging. But when Ada spoke to Mary about her concern, she promptly tried to put Ada at ease.

"Now, don't you fret any about me, Ada. I am just fine. A bit tired, perhaps, because there has been so much to do of late. That's all it is, Ada; I am just a bit tired. A few days' rest, and I'll be good as new again!"

Ada returned to her husband in New York, and soon the three Martinsens traveled to their beloved home in Germany. Concerned when her grandmother's letters became infrequent, Ada wrote to her aunt, Mary

Nixon, who informed her that Grandmother had been diagnosed with cancer of the stomach and that her condition was not at all good.

Rudolf and Ada had just arrived in New York for a short business trip when they heard the bad news. As soon as possible, Ada traveled to visit Mary Thorpe, who was living in her daughter's home, where she could receive the care she needed. Grandmother was frail and ill, but she nevertheless was delighted to have Ada with her.

As for Ada, she was desperately aware that she was about to lose the person who had been her whole family and the source of her early inspiration. She remained in Richmond for as long as she could, but when Rudolf informed her they must leave at once for Europe, she joined him in New York. Ada did not know it then, of course, but she would never again see the grandmother she loved.

A cable arrived in late October of 1881, telling of the death of Mary Thorpe. Ada could not be present at her funeral, for the ships of 1881 could not make the journey in time. Mary Nixon sent Ada copies of notices that appeared in the Richmond paper.

The first, dated October 27, 1881, read as follows: "Mrs. Mary M. Thorpe, who had been a resident of this city for about twenty years, died at the residence of her son-in-law, M. N. Nixon, at 12:30 Monday morning, after a protracted and painful illness in the sixty-fifth year of her age."

The second article carried this announcement: "The funeral of Mrs. Mary M. Thorpe will take place tomorrow at 2 o'clock P.M. from the residence of her son-in-law, Martin M. Nixon, 203 North Ninth Street. Friends of the family are invited without further notice."

Rudolf was away from home when the news came of Mary's death, but when he returned, Ada told him, the always-ready tears dampening her cheeks. "Darling Rudolf, Grandmother was so good to me, and she was the only real family I ever had. Oh, I shall miss her; I shall always miss Grandmother!"

"Yes, dear," Rudolf comforted his wife, "and I too shall miss her. Your grandmother was a truly remarkable lady. You know, I feel that I am greatly in her debt, for it was she who brought you to me. I do thank her for that, dear Ada. Yes, we shall both remember your grandmother."

6

Vrohmberg

FOR THE TIME THAT HIS family would spend in New York, Rudolf had acquired a home on Fifty-fourth Street just off Fifth Avenue. In Europe they had purchased another home—a large, imposing house on a hill above the village of Gernsbach near Baden-Baden in the Black Forest of southern Germany. The castle-like home was set in substantial grounds, and a driveway marked "Martinsenstrasse" led through stone gateposts from the main road—Hildastrasse—to the entry, with its many concrete steps leading up to the house. It was a happy home.

In the spring of 1882, they traveled to New York, where on April 3, a second boy was born. They named him Ottocar Hielbig. Two years later, on May 26, 1884, a little girl was born. She was named after her mother, Ada Ella. Little Ada, as she came to be called, was also born in New York, and before her birth, the family made another voyage to the United States. Then, as soon as travel was feasible, they returned to their home in Gernsbach. They had named the home they so loved "Vrohmberg," using the initials of the first names of family members.

Little Rudolf—Rudi as they affectionately called him—seemed healthy enough, though not particularly strong, and he was a good-looking lad. When he was only a few years old, he evidenced an unusual thoughtfulness and something of his mother's emotional makeup. But those who were close to him could not escape a growing premonition, a feeling that hovered strangely about the son named after his father, that Rudi did not have a happy future.

Ottocar was different; from the first he was strong and cheerful. A husky, outgoing little fellow, he favored his mother in appearance, but he had a steady, firm manner that reminded Ada of her husband.

Little Ada was her father's own daughter, and the love that developed naturally between them was to have a powerful influence on her life. Rudolf adored that bright, eager little feminine creature with the mass of blond hair and the gray Russian eyes so like his own. He called her "Baby," and that nickname, along with her own creation—Adalibooli— remained with her for many years.

The three children played happily on the spacious grounds of Vrohmberg. Hammocks situated between the large trees provided solace for some and entertainment for others in the family. One day three year-old Baby was lying in a hammock, and her playful brothers began pushing her in it, causing it to swing dangerously high. Baby was squealing with delight, but her mother was afraid she would fall and hurried out from the house.

Mother Ada cautioned the little girl to hold on tightly, and the child's reply was so comically endearing that she made a note of it in her album:

> "Be careful, Ada! Hold on tightly!"
>
> "Mamaliboo, I won't fall. I'm holding on to myself! I got hold of my leg!"
>
> The little fat limb in question was clutched spasmodically by a dear little dimpled brown hand.

Little Ada had made up affectionate nicknames for members of the family. She was "Adaliboo" or "Adalibooli," Papi was "Papalibooli," and mother was "Mamaliboo." How she came upon those names is not known, except that Adaliboo was a most unusual child.

She did not at all like being called "Little Ada." She was growing and maturing and becoming better acquainted with her own independent personality. Since she was a lone girl with two brothers, Ada played with them when she was at home. They did very well together, for Ada was a strong girl and was determined to "keep up" with her older brothers.

One particular day, while she was busily playing outside with Rudi and Ottocar, she heard her mother calling excitedly from the house, "Little Ada, be careful! Don't play so roughly with Ottocar. You might get hurt!"

Adalibooli waved at her mother in acknowledgment, but the play continued, with the little girl happily tussling with her brother. Again a call from the house, this time from her governess: "Kleine Ada, komm' herein! Kleine Ada, mach' schnell!"

Quite upset, Adalibooli ran to where her mother and the governess stood just outside the door of the house. Before either could say a word, the young girl voiced her complaint: "Ich bin nicht Kleine Ada. Ich bin—I am—moi!" Seeing a concerned look on her mother's face, she corrected the language but not the meaning, of what she had said: "I am not 'Little Ada'; I am me; I am myself!"

It had not occurred to Ada that her daughter would be so disturbed by what was merely a customary way of distinguishing between a parent and child having the same name. Realizing how upset she was, Ada put her arms around her daughter. "Of course you are your own self, daughtie dear! We all know that. I will remember not to call you 'Little Ada' again. What shall we call you instead?"

"Just call me Adalibooli, Mother!"

"I will, dear; I will!" Most of the time after their exchange, Ada did remember her promise to her daughter.

Life in the Black Forest countryside was beautiful when the Martinsens were there, as indeed it remains to this day. The rolling, hilly land was covered with pine trees, and the unusually dark foliage of the pines gave the forest area its name.

The air was clear, and the climate was pleasant. Few or no insects interfered with the life of the fortunate inhabitants of the Schwarzwald, and no screens were needed on their houses. Only a short distance from the well-known town of Baden-Baden, the whole area, including Gernsbach, was a popular destination because of its famed health spas, but it had not become unpleasantly crowded. It was a splendid place to live, as Adalibooli long remembered, even years after she had changed her name to Mona.

Because of his increasing business involvements, Rudolf found it necessary to be frequently away from home, either elsewhere in Europe or in the United States. Ada was so caught up in the social life she loved, and what was expected or even demanded of her as Mme. Rudolf Martinsen, that she turned over the greater part of the care of her offspring to a series of governesses.

This circumstance, which to Ada seemed only an enjoyable and practical necessity, proved troublesome for her children. It seemed to the children that as soon as they became so comfortable with a certain governess that a bond of love was apparent, Ada became jealous and the unfortunate woman was dismissed. Happy, fun-loving Bertha was replaced with Marta, an older, more severe woman, and when she relaxed a bit and lost some of her severity, making the children seem happy in her company, she too was replaced. And so it continued.

This succession of caretakers was disconcerting to Rudi and Ottocar, but it affected the naturally loving Adalibooli so much that she gradually became disappointed in her mother. She was hurt each time a governess she liked was taken from her. Instead of the stylish, vibrant, part-time maternal parent she had, her daughter would have preferred a mother who could spend more time with her.

On more than one occasion, Adalibooli made her feelings known: "When I am big, I will take care of my babies myself!"

It was different when her father was home; then Baby was truly happy, and all was right with her world. She loved to sit close to him when he was at the piano, and the music his fingers drew from the keyboard of his grand piano satisfied a need she felt within her. At times he improvised, and if he happened to be sad or troubled over some problem, Baby could feel that emotion in his music and was sad with him.

After dinner, when the family left the dining room and Papilibooli repaired to the library to relax or read a bit, Baby would run to him, and his warm, fatherly smile let her know she might climb up in his lap. In his quiet and familiar way he held his daughter close, sang Russian folksongs in a melodious and cultured baritone, and told her little tales he remembered from his own childhood.

Adalibooli felt completely safe and secure with her father. She felt in him the calm dignity of a mature person, and this gave to her the sense of stability and security that a child needs. His warmth and the kindness of his strength enveloped her.

Often, on one of these perfect evenings, the mother's or the governess's bedtime call came to Adalibooli as an unwelcome interruption, for it ended that little girl's happiest of times, when she sat curled up on her father's lap.

7

Big Business

As a Dutch-related magazine of the day noted, Rudolf Martinsen had become well known in financial circles in Europe and in the United States. Through his representation of Dutch and English financial interests in the United States, he became convinced that a great future was in store for that young nation, and he wanted to be a part of its future. Already a naturalized U.S. citizen, he decided to move his business headquarters to the United States. He retired in 1881 from the Boissevain firm in Amsterdam and opened a private office in Exchange Place in New York. Later, in 1885, he moved his offices to their permanent location at 44 and 46 Broad Street.

It was the "gilded age" in the new country, a decidedly rough-and-tumble, ruthless time in the business world and in politics. Martinsen was a contemporary of such financial giants as Gould and Morgan, but he did not always approve of business tactics in the United States.

Rudolf was involved in a variety of business endeavors, including railroads, gold, silver, and coal. In 1883 he represented a group of Dutch financiers in a syndicate that had amassed some thirty million dollars to build the Canadian Pacific Railway. When the road was completed, the syndicate was liquidated, and Rudolf Martinsen became a member of the Board of Directors of the Canadian Pacific Railway.

Much more was happening in the United States than business and politics. It was also the time of the Great Migration, and news that free land was available in the West lured many to leave their homes in the East and travel by covered wagons to take advantage of the wondrous opportunities awaiting them. In one year some ten thousand wagons left from Missouri occupied by many thousands of men and women who sought their fortunes in the fabled West.

In the American Southwest large areas of land had been won for the new country after the war with Mexico. When on August 15, 1848, the United States of America acquired by invasion and conquest the land known as New Mexico, it also inherited troublesome land grant problems. For more than three centuries the area had been under Spanish rule, during which time a multitude of rules and regulations regarding the granting or transfer of land in the colonies had been in effect.

Mexico had acquired this same territory after achieving independence from Spain in 1821. Mexico's land grant policy was not consistent when it acquired the area known as New Mexico, however, and previous rules regarding the transfer of land were amended and repealed. Those desiring to acquire land under their names learned that the many legal problems would make the transfer difficult.

The 1848 treaty between Mexico and the United States that had ended the Spanish-American War did attempt to handle the matter of land ownership fairly and to assure the rights of persons living on the lands. Congress had also made a similar effort, but the problems involving titles to land remained unsolved.

In 1870 Congress, which had previously confirmed a number of Spanish or Mexican land grants, suddenly changed its policy and refused to do anything with regard to New Mexican land matters. It was in this very year that eight-year-old Ada and her mother were adventuring in the Santa Fe area. The Maxwell Land Grant in New Mexico, named for that colorful pioneer Lucien B. Maxwell, was among those that had been confirmed by Congress.

Without attempting to tell the entire history of New Mexico we can get some idea of the nature and value of that land from a petition filed in 1841 to the governor of Santa Fe. That document claimed that the New Mexico Land Grant included within its borders "an abundance of water, forests, wood, and useful timber. . . . [Its] soil, containing within its bosom rich and precious metals."

The Maxwell Land Grant had caught the attention of many adventurous promoters, including our own Rudolf Martinsen. He was attracted by the obvious challenge to his business ingenuity provided by the confused state of land titles that hampered normal progress in the area.

Rudolf's judgment told him that there might be real opportunity in New Mexico, and his financial interest in the project no doubt gained personal overtones because he remembered Ada's adventure as an eight year old in the desert near Santa Fe. He had thought her story surprising and almost unbelievable, and through the strange quality of that event, he had come to understand his young wife's nature.

Now there was another Ada at home in Vrohmberg—Adalibooli. Would she have the same adventurous spirit that her mother had shown? As he thought about these two people so central in his life, Rudolf experienced a warm glow somewhere inside him. Was it love or pride or admiration? Or was it all three of those sentiments?

Lucien B. Maxwell and his partner, Beaubien, sold their interests in the vast lands of the Maxwell Land Grant to the Maxwell Land Grant and Railway Company, a corporation that had been organized to acquire the lands. The bonds that were issued to finance the company were defaulted upon, and they were promptly bought up by a group of foreign speculators. Those financiers organized the Maxwell Land Grant Company, described as "a corporation created and organized under a charter from the King of the Netherlands, pursuant to the laws of the Kingdom of Netherlands, doing business within the Territory of New Mexico."

Rudolf formed a syndicate of investors in Amsterdam to gather funds needed to conduct the reorganization of the Maxwell Land Grant Company, and he was made president of its American board of trustees. It is not surprising that considerable legal action was necessary regarding the granting of titles and that numerous lawsuits were filed contesting the rights of the Maxwell Land Grant Company.

On May 12, 1887, the Supreme Court of the United States decided in favor of the Maxwell Land Grant Company. This victory was welcomed by the Company, but it was devastating to the many persons—Mexican, Indian, and American—who had believed they honestly owned the land on which they lived. Good business dictated that the Company file ejectment suits against such persons in possession of land.

It was not a happy situation, and we can only imagine the distress that Rudolf must have felt, distress that led him to sit at his piano and improvise the sad melodies that his little daughter heard with so much sympathy. Business and legal necessity led to that unhappy state of affairs.

It was, however, all necessity. Frank W. Springer, the attorney who had successfully handled the litigation for the company through the lower courts and to the Supreme Court, clarified the situation in an address in which he noted the need for certainty of ownership of land:

> The question is not whether we are in favor of grants or not. . . . It is not a question of sentiment we have to deal with. . . . But upon the broader question, which goes to the very life of the commonwealth, whether the grant titles shall be speedily settled, there can be no two opinions. . . . It is not the grant claimant alone that is affected by the uncertainty which prevails. If he cannot tell what land will ultimately be confirmed to him, the settler, seeking to acquire land upon the public domain, is no better off. He does not know at what moment a tract of land, now supposed to belong to the United States, may be claimed under some hitherto unknown grant.

So it was that another problem was settled, if not solved.

Important though it was, the New Mexico title situation was not the only matter with which Rudolf was involved, not the only serious problem that set him to further improvisations on his Steinway. The Missouri, Kansas, and Texas Railroad, of which he was president, was being attacked with a view to forcing it into bankruptcy. An article in the *New York Times* of September 26, 1888, under dateline of "St. Louis, September 24," carried these headlines:

DISPOSING OF THE WRECK

DISPUTING OVER ONE OF JAY GOULD'S VICTIMS

A Crowd of Lawyers After the Remains of the Missouri,
Kansas and Texas Railway

The article related that the Southern Hotel was crowded with lawyers, agents, capitalists, syndicate representatives, and candidates for the receivership and that a "Philadelphia lawyer" might find lucrative employment by contacting any of the business men gathered there. First and foremost of interest in the matter, the journalist wrote, were Simon Sterne of New York, R. V. Martinsen, the new president of the Missouri, Kansas, and Texas Railway, and others. Judge Brewer was to hear the arguments.

The *Times* quoted Martinsen in its record of the hearing:

> "I represent a large amount of Dutch stock and Dutch bonds, and as far as they are represented by me, their interests are identical."
>
> "What is the position of the stockholders in this matter?"
>
> "Simply this. We do not believe that the Road has been rightly managed by the Missouri Pacific, or has received what is justly its own. At the same time, we believe that the Road is not in such condition that the appointment of a Receiver is necessary. By the terms of the lease (to Missouri Pacific) it becomes void if there is a default in interest. There was such default June 1, consequently the Road reverts to us 6 months later, on December 1.
>
> "We expect to show the Court that we are abundantly able to take charge of the Road and manage it in such a way that there will not only be no deficit, but even a surplus. We maintain that if the Missouri Pacific had not taken money and business which properly belonged to our Road, there would have been no occasion for a default.
>
> "Why, two days before we took charge of the Road, after the election, the Missouri Pacific took some $3,000,000 of assets from the treasury of the Missouri, Kansas and Texas Railway, claiming that amount as due it from the International and Great Southern (Railway), which was leased to us, and that consequently we were liable for the debt. The securities thus taken consisted of International and Great Northern stock, Galveston, Houston and Henderson bonds, and other collateral which at the present market value amounted to $3,000,000."

The article continued, "President Martinsen says that the Missouri Pacific borrowed the money with which it paid its last two dividends. Simon Sterne represents the Missouri, Kansas and Texas Board of Directors and is opposed to the appointment of a Receiver."

Although the *Times* article quoted above did not report how the court hearing ended, other news of the time indicated that Martinsen was successful in reorganizing the Missouri, Kansas, and Texas Railway. Those persons who had tried to scuttle the railroad did not succeed in doing so. Rudolf Martinsen, its president, had won.

8

Family Life

THE MARTINSEN FAMILY CONTINUED to live well between the Black Forest and New York, and Rudolf continued to devote his attention to his many business interests, but they did not escape all personal sorrow. On August 3, 1888, a third little boy was born, but Harold Gottlieb was not well and lived only until February 14 of the next year. Two selections from Ada's memory book cast a certain warm and personal light upon the sad experience:

> Harold was the darling of our girlie's heart. After God took him from our earthly love and care, little Ada watched me with memorizing affection. No sooner did she perceive the shock on my face than she was in my arms, petting me, stroking my face, and, looking into my eyes with an infinite look of confidence and trust, whispered gently but firmly, "God knows best, Mamalimooli!"

> Rudi's love of country is so strong it will require all our love and patience to help him to be patriotic in the noble sense and not narrow-minded as he is now, and which his tender years make pardonable. His most ardent wish was to have his baby brother Harold wrapped in the American flag as a shroud. I explained to him that to be buried in the stars and stripes, one must first have earned the honor by some great illustrious action for the country whose highest emblem it was.

The children grew and prospered, and Ada feelingly recorded many childish episodes.

During our absence in Canada, Adalibooli, then three, was ill and wanted kind Tante Bertha to rock and sing to her. Unfortunately, Tante Bertha possesses not the gift of tune, and unfortunately the rocking chair squeaked. Baby stood it awhile and then asserted: "Mama doesn't sing that way!" And, at last: "Oh, Tante Bertha stop! You sing like the rocking chair!"

And this:

Whilst in Holyoke visiting Aunt Nellie, she crocheted a pretty white Angora wool cap for Baby that elicited warmest admiration. When they were driving out one day to allow Aunt Nellie to purchase the small quantity of wool she needed to finish the wonderful cap. Baby heard about it and asked: "Mamalimooli, what will Papibooli say when he sees my new cap?"

"He will say it is very pretty and just the thing for his little girlie."

"Oh, Mamalimooli, but what will the *horsies* say when they see me in it?"

In those pre-auto days, *horsies* were an integral part of life, and little Ada had absorbed a special love of those noble animals from her mother.

When little Ada was five, mother Ada tells about a time when she and her daughter were in a doctor's office, waiting to be received: "Adalabooli complained of a loose tooth which was annoying her. I persuaded her to let me play dentist, fastened a thread around it, and the next instant to her surprise the tiny pearl was dangling in the air. We examined the pretty little thing, then Baby was so pleased she ran with it between her fingers up to a cage of parakeets, and showing it proudly to the stupid looking birdies, she asked them what they thought of it. They cocked their green heads, looked sideways at the innocent child, made some sort of a sound which she claimed to understand was their expression of admiration, and Baby came away quite content and happy!"

When Baby was a little older—perhaps seven or nearly eight—her mother recorded another small happening that she thought revealing. "Papi was in a playful mood, and he tickled Adalabooli as he held her close. Pulling herself away from her father, she said firmly: 'Papi, that is no way to treat a young lady!' "

Ottocar also provided his mother with little stories to tell:

> Yesterday Ottoli pinched a little girl in school. I talked with him, telling
> him how very naughty and cowardly it was for a boy to hurt a girl and
> persuaded him to take her some bon-bons the following morning and
> tell her he was sorry. Upon his return the following noon he hunted
> me up, found me at the piano, came and nestled his head upon my
> arm.
>
> I asked him if he had given the bonbons and told the little girl he
> was sorry? After much hesitation he said yes, he had given the bon-
> bons and said twice he was sorry. I patted him on his head and told
> him he was a good boy and I was proud of him. I do not know whether
> my praise or kisses hurt his conscience, but be that as it may, he raised
> a very grave face and a pair of sad blue eyes and said: "*but she didn't hear
> it, Mama!*"

When Ottocar was younger, Ada wrote about his favorite poem: "Ot-
toli's favorite poem was 'Polly put the kettle on.' The precious little
fellow used to look very shy, then commence 'Polly, put the kettle on,
Polly, put the kettle on,' and continue thus until interrupted by a word
or a smile, then with a jubilant voice he said: 'and let's drink tea!' "

Years later, when Ottocar was a successful businessman in New York,
he introduced an admiring little midwestern niece to "a song that you
can sing as long as you want to." That little girl was captivated by her
imposing uncle's baritone rendition of "The Bear Went over the Mountain," and her later repetitious singing of it prompted her grandmother
to caution her that "so many *yards* of that are enough!"

So for the Martinsens life went on. In the spring of 1891 New York musical circles were agog in anticipation of the grand opening of Carnegie
Hall, which would take place in May. Tchaikovsky would be there to
direct the orchestra in one of his own compositions. Rudolf was excited
that he would get to see his noted countryman in such a distinguished
setting.

The event was widely advertised; from May 5 to May 9 a Grand Festival
would be held at the newly completed music center for which Andrew
Carnegie had provided construction funding. The hall had taken a year
and a million dollars to build, but it was not located in the familiar

downtown entertainment area; it was located at Fifty-second Avenue. Many people thought that its uptown location would be disastrous because fewer would attend, but it was not so, and after the opening festivities, the New York Times reported that "it had stood the test."

Tchaikosvky would be in New York throughout the five days of the Grand Festival and would conduct on each of the nights, but Rudolf and Ada made plans to attend on the first night, May 5. When the gala night came, they spent a little extra time in dressing for the occasion. Rudolf was impressive in a new dress suit, and on the left lapel of his jacket he placed the red carnation corsage that Ada had given him.

Ada wore a spring green silk gown from one of the better dressmakers in New York. The diamond ring from Tiffany's was matched by diamond earrings that Rudolph had given her for her birthday the February before. To ward off the chill night air Ada wore a short fur jacket.

It was a beautiful evening, and as they drove along the lighted streets of the city, their carriage was caught in a line of similar conveyances also going to the great hall. When they arrived they left the carriage with the aid of a uniformed doorman.

The lobby was filled with other finely dressed patrons, and the Martinsens stopped several times to visit briefly with persons they knew before making their way to their box seats. There was a steady hum of conversation among the audience members as they waited for the concert to begin, but after the orchestra members had taken their seats, quiet quickly took hold.

When the time came for Tchaikovsky to do his part, the world-famed musician was greeted with a standing ovation from the expectant crowd. The entire audience was delighted as he conducted his Festival Coronation March (Marche Solanelle), but for Rudolf—and for Ada—the event had an especially deep emotional impact.

Rudolf, though he had chosen citizenship in the United States, was still a Russian at heart. His business career had taken him away from the country of his birth, but the bright first impressions of his youth were never erased. Through her devotion to Rudolf, Ada had absorbed much of his love for all that was Russian. It became an integral part of her being.

They left the concert on a plane of high excitement, and for Ada the evening would never be forgotten. Years later she told a wide-eyed granddaughter that she had actually seen Tchaikovsky and heard him conduct at Carnegie Hall! It was a happening that her music-loving granddaughter could only try to imagine.

Rudi was quite caught up in his parents' enthusiasm for America. Another excerpt from Ada's memory book is descriptive and meaningful here:

In the latter part of 1890, Rudi brought his United States history book home and was reading the lesson for the following day aloud to me in the library, after the gas had been lighted. It was about Washington, his hero, but not of the past, his living, breathing hero, of his last days, etc. Suddenly his eyes filled with tears; he rubbed them hard, complaining of the light. I suggested: "Step back, dear! Let the light fall over your shoulder, then it will not pain your eyes."

Soon he came to Washington's last words: "It's hard to die; still I am ready to go." A great sob, and the next instant Rudi was nestled on Mama's breast, weeping as though his heart would break. No longer the light to blame; it was his living hero passing away. I did not reason with my patriotic boy; I only felt for him, cuddled him closer to the mother-heart, and picking up the history, continued, as if nothing had happened, to read from whence he had taken off.

In January 1891 I crossed the stormy Atlantic to join my beloved husband in Holland. Amongst the passengers was a West point officer, to whom I related the above. His eyes shown with feeling, and when I had finished, he begged me to send that boy to West Point, saying: "The country needs boys who at this date could shed tears of real grief over the Father of our country's death."

Ada was happy to be on her way to Holland to join her husband, and she was anticipating a certain event with considerable excitement. Rudolf had received an invitation to attend a reception to be held in Amsterdam for the new emperor of Germany, Wilhelm II (1888–1918).

Wilhelm was young and impetuous. He desired to rule on his own, free from the omnipresence of his prime minister, Bismarck. In an attempt to woo workers from the Socialist Party, which was gaining in strength in Germany, Bismarck had been able to pass laws establishing national health insurance and old age disability and retirement insurance. Both were funded by mandatory deductions from wages. These laws were passed in Germany almost fifty years before similar legislation was passed in the United States.

Kaiser Wilhelm chafed under the political accomplishments of Bismarck, which made him feel that he played second fiddle to his underling. A dynamic young man, he did not wish to be so overshadowed by Bismarck, and in 1890 he forced Bismarck to resign. It was a decision that proved to be a mistake, for Bismarck's Democratic Party would continue to expand dangerously in its power.

The reception for the emperor was carried out on a grand scale. Wilhelm II appeared in a brilliant red-and-gold uniform accompanied by the empress, who was dressed in the finest fashion of the time, as befitted her exalted station in life. Rudolf and Ada—and especially Ada—enjoyed the grandiose formality of the event.

After the reception they dined with friends, then spent the early evening walking contentedly together, hand in hand, through the beautifully planted grounds of their hotel. They were happy, for the whole day had been a pleasant change from the busy routines of their lives—a needed change for both but especially for Rudolf.

It was late when they at last decided to return to their room, and although the stroll in the pleasant night air had been refreshing, they both felt the need for rest. The grand quarters the hotel had supplied, including the ornately carved bed dominating the room, seemed inviting.

Rudolf was already abed when Ada finished her nightly tasks and joined him. The feelings that had filled her being when they were first married had not changed; Ada still loved to cuddle. Rudolf opened his arms to her and pulled her close—very close to his heart.

In her happiness Ada thought sleepily about the young man whom she and Grandmother had met aboard the *Bavaria*, and she wondered if ever before Chance had brought such unexpected good fortune to anyone. Ada Martinsen was entirely caught up in her happiness.

9

A Family Is Broken

Es ist bestimmt in Gottes Rad, dass man vom liebsten,
was man hat, muss scheiden, ja scheiden . . .

Goethe

FOR THE MARTINSEN FAMILY, 1892 had been a felicitous year. The children were doing well in school. Papi had spent most of the time at home in Gernsbach. His business travel had been mostly to places in Europe, and on some of those trips the family could accompany him. Because of Rudolf's many international interests, the family had done a great deal of traveling between homes in Europe and the United States; in fact, by the time little Ada was eight, they had crossed the Atlantic fourteen times in ships that still relied upon sails.

Because of their lifestyle, the children grew up speaking three languages: English, German, and French. One can imagine how youngsters might, especially when they were excited, mix and confuse the languages. As a result, there was a rule in the Martinsen family that any one sentence must be completed using only one language, which led often to humorous situations. But the rule persisted, and Rudi, Ottocar, and Ada all learned to express themselves in whatever language they had chosen. In any one sentence, that is!

Little Ada loved their home in Germany, and she felt particular friendship for the people who lived in and around the village. She especially noticed how the peasant families chattered together and sang their lovely folksongs as they went about gathering firewood for their stoves or fireplaces. They lived in very small houses and had very little in the way of possessions, but they seemed happy. Ada wondered about this, for in her own family they had so much.

Ada had a surprisingly natural and friendly relationship with the village children who were her schoolmates. At the noon hour she often traded her own fancy French rolls spread with real butter for the black bread covered with goose grease that the peasant children brought for their lunches. During free periods, she joined with the girls as they lined up, each braiding the long hair of the girl in front of her. For Little Ada, the time spent in school was happy, and her memory of the years at Vrohmberg would stand as a bright beacon for the rest of her life.

Early in the spring of 1892 Rudolf gave up all of his positions in the United States except for that of president of the Consolidated Coal Company of Wyoming. In the late summer and fall he learned of business problems in the United States that might soon demand his personal attention. Although he did not comment or complain about his troubles, his wife and children had noticed that when he sat down at his piano, there was a melancholic plaintive note in his meanderings over the keys. Rudolf was plainly troubled.

One late November evening he asked Ada to go out for a walk with him on their grounds. Both donned light coats, for the weather had changed and it was very cool in the evening. Hand in hand, they walked on the tile floor and through the high archways that led out of the house. Without speaking for a time, they strolled among the tall trees and over lawns on which the grass was not clipped short but allowed to reach a comfortable length. The hammocks had been removed and stored for the winter. Rudolf and Ada sat down together on a bench beneath the trees. Then he spoke.

"Ada, my dear, as you may have guessed from the many cable messages I have received and sent in the past few days, there is a problem in America that I must handle. It is simply imperative that I go very soon to New York, and this time I do not think you and the children should go along. Their school attendance is important, and it is so near to the Christmas season. I want you to be in our home at this time. You know how I shall miss you and how much I love the things we do at Christmas. But this year I may not get home in time for the holidays."

Did his voice shake a little as he spoke? Ada thought that it did, and she wanted to know more about why it was so. "Oh, Rudolf, is someone trying to interfere in your business again? Those ruthless men? Oh, please tell me; I need to know what is troubling you so much. When, dear, do you think you must leave? Why could you not take us with you? The children, and especially Baby, will not think it is really Christmas without you!" As kindly as he could, Rudolf told her that it was not possible for them to go along.

The next few days were filled with the sending and receiving of cables, and the preparations for Rudolf's departure seemed more troublesome than usual. Normally Rudolf's leaving on a business trip was casual, and the family routines were not overly upset, but this was different, and his mood was unusually somber. When he sat down at the piano in freer moments, Little Ada sat as near to him as she could, and the music he played did not make her happy. "What is the matter, Papi?" she asked.

Leaning over to her and lovingly patting her cheek, Rudolf would respond, as lightly as he could, "Papi just has some business things he must take care of. Do not worry, Baby dear; everything will be all right."

Rudolf's business problems did not go away, and one evening in mid-December as the family sat at dinner, he announced that he was leaving soon for New York and said again that he would not be back in time for their Christmas celebration.

"But," he said, smiling mysteriously, "there are presents for all of you that I have hidden away in my closet upstairs." Smiling again at Rudi and Ottocar, who were not missing a word, he added, "Now don't you fellows go looking for the presents. They must not be touched until they are put under the tree on Christmas morning. Remember that!" Almost in unison, Rudi, Ottocar, and Little Ada broke in, "Papi, we have presents for you, too! Will you take them with you?"

"No, just keep them here for me. When I return, we shall have another Christmas—a very special one! While I am in New York, I will think about the fun we shall have. And remember," he smiled warningly at Rudi and Ottocar, "don't you try to find the packages I have left for you. They must be a surprise on Christmas morning."

"We promise, Papi! We promise!"

In normal years, how they all looked forward to the Christmas season! There was excitement for days, even weeks, before the big day, but the decorated tree never made its appearance until Christmas morning. Gathered around it, they had a light breakfast, after which the parcels placed all around the tree were opened. Usually it was Papi who acted as St. Nickolas and handed the brightly wrapped packages to the eager recipients. Colored papers, hastily torn from presents, soon were strewn across the floor of the living room, and when the packages had all been unwrapped, Maria came and gathered the ribbons and the papers and took them away.

But Christmas would not happen that way this year.

The morning came when Rudolf would leave Vrohmberg, and the family had gathered in the entryway to bid him good-bye. Ada looked admiringly at her husband. He was, she noticed with warm satisfaction, wearing under his suit coat the dark red sweater she had knitted for him. "A fine figure of a man," she thought, "that is what Grandmother would have called him. And that he is."

During the thirteen years of their marriage, Rudolf had matured no-ticeably. Well filled-out, but not overweight, he was no longer the slim young man she had married. "Really," Ada mused, "he looks better this way. My husband is a very impressive man, and, oh, how fortunate he has made me! He has given me the world."

Ada was not thinking of their big houses, their servants, or her own fine clothes. She enjoyed all those things and felt a great pride in them, but a new thrill of realization was coming upon her. She felt the depth of his soul, of which she was becoming a part.

Now that he was forty-one, Rudolf's once-dark hair was now almost entirely white, and it fell in waves, blending with the sideburns that had become more full about his face. To Ada's great satisfaction, the rest of his face was beardless: this enabled her to see his shapely lips, which Ada thought were the most beautiful she had ever seen. They reminded her of the happiness he had given her and of the emptiness she would feel while he was away. It was always so for Ada Ernst Martinsen.

Wearing a dark overcoat and carrying his top hat, Papi hugged the two boys, then shook each boy's hand, saying, "While I am away, you will be the men of the family. Be sure to take good care of your mother and your sister!" Then he took Little Ada—who at eight years was not quite so little any more—up in his arms, hugged her soundly, then put her down, patting her gently on the cheek. "And you, young lady, you must be brave and happy while I am away. Remember that!" He cautioned his family that they must have a very happy Christmas, as he would try to do in New York. "But I shall miss you . . ."

Ada said nothing about the carefully wrapped package she had put in one of Rudolf's bags; he would find it when he arrived in New York. It was from all four of them, and when he opened the parcel and saw what they had chosen for him, he would realize just how very much he was loved.

Before Rudolf left, he looked tenderly into his wife's eyes, took her in his arms, and kissed her, but he said little, except, "You know that I love you dearly. Take care of our family and my beloved wife while I am away." Ada thought he was more emotional in his goodbyes than usual. She wondered, "Is he especially worried about business, or is it just that he dislikes leaving us at Christmas-time?" After a moment's thought, Ada chose the latter explanation.

Gerhardt, their servant of many years, had driven up outside, and Rudolf turned and left quickly. Little Ada cried when her father put on his top hat and walked down the long row of steps to the drive and the waiting carriage. It was snowing lightly, and he reached for the iron railing to keep from slipping on the many concrete steps. As he entered the vehicle, they watched as Gerhardt closed the door, stepped in, took his place in front, and then urged the horses forward.

When the horses gingerly made their way down the snowy driveway and passed through the front gate, Baby left the group gathered in the foyer of the house and ran, sobbing uncontrollably, to her own room upstairs. There she threw herself down on the bed and gave way to her sadness. It was not long until she heard someone enter her room, and she looked up, expecting to see her governess. But it was not Maria; it was her mother who lifted little Ada up in her arms. Mothie's cheeks, too, were damp with tears.

"Papi has a lot of difficult troubles, dear Adalibooli; he would not leave us at this time for any other reason. We must do the best we can without him. That is what Papi wants. Come downstairs, dear daughtie, and let's see if Herta does not have something extra tasty for us in the kitchen." Rubbing her eyes, a sorrowful little girl did as her mother had asked.

Rudolf traveled by train, with changes, to Hamburg, where he boarded a steamer bound for New York. During the ocean crossing, he felt mildly ill, but by the time he reached New York on December 14, he seemed fully recovered.

On December 20, after a series of business meetings, he went to the St. James Hotel for dinner with friends. At dinner he complained that he felt sick, and by ten o'clock he was seriously ill. A doctor had been called for him and was in attendance, but he could do nothing. Far from home and the family he loved, Rudolf Martinsen died at the St. James Hotel two minutes before two o'clock in the early morning of December 21, 1892. His brave, strong heart had simply given up.

When Ada received the cable from New York, it was late in the afternoon of December 21. Ada and the servants had been busily cooking, cleaning, and doing many tasks to prepare Vrohmberg for the Christmas season. Young Ottocar answered the door, and when the cable delivery man asked for Frau Rudolf Martinsen, he hurried to call his mother. It was not unusual for a cable to arrive at Vrohmberg, but Ottocar could not escape a feeling of dread about this one.

Ada hastily read the brief cable. First she felt only total disbelief, then shock, and finally she burst forth in tears. The three children and the servants hurried to her side, and she read to them the cruel message. It was a crushingly sad moment for them all, but Ada knew that she could not let her feelings take over entirely, not this time. It was clear to her that they must leave for New York with all possible haste.

Ada went up to the room she shared with Rudolf and began to put a few articles into a suitcase. The children, aided by their governess, Maria, did the same. Somehow they all made it through the night, and early the next morning four sorrowing Martinsens walked down the stairway from their home to where Gerhardt waited with the carriage, ready to take them to the train station.

In 1892 a fast steamer took more than a week to make the transatlantic crossing, and we may be certain that this journey was not at all like the fun-filled voyages they had taken in the past. At those times Papi, with his warm and affectionate nature and his special awareness of the beautiful things in life—music, art, and literature—had always made the world seem wonderful to little Ada and her brothers.

On those voyages, holding Papi's hand as she stood beside him on the rail of their liner, Adalibooli had seen through his eyes the amazing beauty of the ocean as it rocked and tossed the ship. Through the limited perspective of her childhood, which was just beginning to merge into the wider horizons of adulthood, she always felt the beauty of the sunsets and marveled at the display of stars over the great ocean at night. But her beloved Papi was not on this trip, nor would he ever, ever be again. How can the feelings of a broken-hearted eight-year-old girl be described?

All four of the Martinsens appeared tired and drawn when they arrived at 58 East Fifty-fourth Street, near the corner of Fifth Avenue, their New York home. It was now a place of sorrow and of loss. On the day of the funeral, the cold, gray sky suited perfectly their feelings. They all managed to survive the traditional and well-intentioned services in their Lutheran church, and when they were over, a horse-drawn hearse and several carriages took the mourners to the cemetery.

In the cold dampness of the graveyard, the bereaved family stood huddled together. Clutching her mother's hand, little Ada barely heard the traditional words spoken by the pastor, which were intended to bring comfort and hope to the sorrowing family. For her, no words could have been of any comfort.

When the time came for the gleaming, brass-bound mahogany casket to be lowered slowly into the snow-covered grave that had been dug for her Papi, little Ada was so overcome by the horror of it all, that for a moment she wished she could jump down into the wet earth and go with her father. She did not do that; instead, she and her brothers stood silently beside their black-veiled and grieving mother. It was a tragic time for the whole family, and for little Ada the loss of her beloved Papi and the desperate sadness she felt would remain with her throughout a long lifetime.

Ada learned from her advisers that Rudolf, so knowledgeable in financial matters, had provided well for his family, and they also assured her that her fears of a remaining business problem were unfounded.

The probate estate was shown to be quite small, for Rudolf had wisely placed most of his assets in trusts. Among those assets were bonds and stocks in the Maxwell Land Grant Company, the Missouri, Kansas, and Texas Railway, and the Wyoming Consolidated Coal Company.

Confident that she could carry on and manage the family affairs with the substantial fortune Rudolf had left, Ada informed her financial advisers that she and the children would return to Vrohmberg as soon as matters were completed in New York.

10

Back in Vrohmberg

Sprich, o trauend Herz, was willst denn du?

IT WAS EARLY SPRING when the family finally arrived in Gernsbach. Small patches of winter's remaining snow could be seen here and there in the dark pine forests. In the warming soil of the gardens of Vrohmberg, a variety of bulbs were awakening, for intrinsic in their nature was a subtle awareness that spring was coming. Permeated with a wordless faith that to live and make beauty is worth all the effort it may take, bulbs and seeds sprouted and pushed their way through the cool soil, reaching for the sunshine above, and they were soon followed by the chirped rejoicing of finches and other winged ones. To Rudolf's grieving family, it seemed wrong that the outside world should continue as though nothing in particular had happened, as though the family's center had not been cruelly snatched from them.

Gradually, almost imperceptibly at first, the returning springtime had its warming effect upon the family. Even little Ada began to sing as she played with Ottocar or Rudi in the gardens of Vrohmberg. The hammocks were once more tied between tall trees, one for each child, and little Ada tried to recapture the happiness she had always felt when she lay in one and allowed it to swing back and forth. Still it was not the same.

Torn as she was between the sorrow she felt and the emotional pull of the returning springtime, little Ada found release in the words of a folksong she had heard the young peasants sing in the Black Forest. It was about Die Frühlingszeit, the springtime: "Weiss nicht was ich will;

möchte weinen still; möchte jubelnd wandern immer zu. Sehnsucht lockt hinaus, Sehnsucht zieht nach Haus; sprich oh trauend Herz, was willst denn Du?"

Young Ada's heart was troubled, and she, as the folksong expressed, did not know whether to weep quietly or wander far and wide, rejoicing. Longings she could not understand lured her to go far away; more longings urged her to stay. It was not an easy time, for little Ada was beginning to have more than childish feelings. She was beginning to grow up.

All three of the children were considerably behind in their school work because of the time they had been absent, and it took extra studying to catch up, but Rudi, Ottocar, and Ada were all good students, and they received help from Maria and from their mother—when she was at home in the evening.

For young Ada, Mothie's all too frequent absences during the time when the children were home in the evening was increasingly disturbing. It seemed to her that their mother was out socializing more and more in the evenings, and Adalibooli and her brothers relied more and more upon their governess for the mothering they still needed.

Ada was only thirty years old when her husband died, and being alone is never easy for such a young woman. Rudolf had been warmly companionable, and his bright spirit invigorated Ada. Together they had enjoyed the social life that was everywhere available to them. Now, although she was single, she was still invited out often.

Ada did truly miss Rudolf, and at first she was reluctant to accept any social invitations, but her loneliness and her need for companionship gradually lessened this reluctance, and Ada was soon once more taking part in the society of her peers. She was better off personally because of this, but her little daughter and her sons missed their mother.

11

Richard Scholz

ADA HAD MET RICHARD SCHOLZ two or three years before he began calling on her. Scholz was a German painter of unusual talent; both his portraits and his outdoor paintings revealed a sensitivity that Rudolf and Ada together had admired. He had first come to see Ada shortly after the family's return to Vrohmberg, as a friend who wanted to express his sympathy for the loss of Ada's husband, and Ada appreciated his kindness. Together they spoke of Rudolf and of his untimely death, at which times Richard did what he could to calm the confused and highly emotional Ada.

On one occasion Ada was unable to control her feelings, and she burst forth with conviction, "Oh, Richard, his heart was broken by the unethical methods used by the men he was in business with. He simply could not stand it any longer. I am sure of that!" To show that he understood, Richard took her hand and held it in both of his.

Scholz soon found that he was sincerely fond of Ada's three children, but he was particularly attracted to little Ada. He was also quite taken with the elder Ada, and he made no effort to conceal the way he felt about her. As for Ada, fine art was one of her great loves, and Richard was a manly, if not dashingly romantic, social partner. She came to enjoy and look forward to the times she and Richard spent together.

One evening turned out to be particularly eventful. They attended a concert given by a young baritone who was accompanied by a young woman pianist whom Ada thought especially remarkable. After the concert Richard suggested that they stop in at a small restaurant for a glass of white wine, which had made a Gernsbach winery well known.

Seemingly tireless, and never ready for a pleasant evening to end, Ada agreed, and they were soon seated at a small table offering the privacy Richard wanted.

The two visited about the concert and some of the people they had seen there, then chatted briefly about the local affairs of the day. None of those topics was what Richard wanted to talk about, nor was it what Ada wished to hear.

Most European restaurants had some kind of music, and this establishment, small though it was, boasted a strolling violinist who dressed in a German peasant costume. When he came to their table, Richard asked him if he would play Schubert's "Serenade."

Something about the request seemed to delight the young man—or did he perhaps anticipate a generous tip from the fine gentleman who had asked for that piece he played so well?

However that may be, he immediately set forth with great vigor in a passionate rendition of the serenade, even at times adding in a deep German voice certain romantic words from the song. "Leise flehen meine Lieder, durch die Nacht zu Dir," ending with a passionate "Liebchen, komm' zu mir!" The latter phrase was performed with much feeling, for he was an emotional young man, and Ada's feminine charms had not escaped his notice.

When he finished the last sweet tones of the serenade with a flourish, the young musician bowed politely to the lady and her escort. Ada applauded enthusiastically, and Richard's tip was not disappointing.

The enthusiasm of the violinist had set the tone he wished, and Richard felt that his moment had come. Reaching both hands across the table and taking Ada's two hands in his, he looked earnestly into her eyes.

"Ada, these past few weeks with you have been very happy ones for me, and I hope they have been so for you too. Ada, we have so much in common; there is so much real understanding between us. We both love art and music, and I have many exciting friends in Dresden who would love to meet you. But most of all, dear and beautiful Ada, I do love you. We are both alone, and I am sure that you are as lonely as I. Ada, will you marry me?"

Ada did not speak at once, and Richard continued his plea: "You have not seen my home in Dresden. It is a good, solid home—not as fine as Vrohmberg but very comfortable. And, Ada, Dresden is such a wonderful city! How happy we could be there together! I am sure, dear Ada, that if you were with me all the time, I could be a much better painter, and I am sure that I could make you happy. Oh, Ada, you should be happy! You should not be alone. You should have the protection of a man who loves you as I do."

Ada had not thought of her relationship with Richard as more than a friendly change from the loneliness she had felt after Rudolf's passing. She had not allowed herself to anticipate a proposal of marriage, and what Richard said came as a surprise to her. She was even more surprised at her response, for she did not refuse him. Drawing her hands away from his grasp, Ada answered him calmly, and her words carried with them a hint of feeling not unlike his.

"Yes, Richard, I do think we could be happy together, and you know how truly I admire your artistry. But we must not be in a hurry. Don't you think we should talk to the children first and see how they feel about it?" Ada did not miss the look of disappointment in Richard's eyes, and she hastened to soften the effect of what she had said: "I know that the boys and little Ada like you. I will talk to them soon."

Her marriage to Richard Scholz made it necessary for the family to move to Dresden. It was not easy for Ada to take—perhaps to wrest—the children and herself away from the home they had so dearly loved, away from all the memories of happier days that Vrohmberg held within its beautiful grounds. Her years with Rudolf Martinsen had been more than happy. His strength of character and the stability he brought into their lives had fostered in Ada an increasing maturity and a sense of her responsibilities as a parent.

Now she realized that they must push forward with their lives and that the burden was largely upon her to make certain that Rudi, Ottocar, and little Ada had the advantages that a center of culture could provide. Rudolf would have wanted no less for his children, and Ada believed that Dresden offered what they needed.

She was right about Dresden. The boys were soon enrolled in schools for young men, and for Ada they chose the Hoehere Toechter Schule. Like her father, who had a pleasing voice and who so often expressed himself by way of the keyboard, Ada loved to sing. As she grew, her small, childish voice grew with her, and she often raised her lovely voice in song as she went about the house.

Ada had been aware of her daughter's love for music and liked to hear her singing, but she did not arrange for voice lessons. She decided that the violin would be a suitable instrument, and, after some basic instruction, her discussions with the violin teacher convinced her that little Ada had ability that merited continued instruction.

That professional appraisal encouraged her mother to arrange for more advanced lessons with Joachim Petri, a well-known virtuoso and teacher in Dresden, whose son, Egon, later became a world-famed pianist.

Little Ada would need a better instrument, Maestro Petri insisted, than the simple German violin on which she had begun her training. With the help of M. Petri, Ada Scholz found a violin at the shop of Richard Weichold in Dresden that had a German-made back and an Amati front and which was declared adequate by the maestro. It was an instrument well above the ordinary, and a bow was chosen that matched the capabilities of the violin. Little Ada was delighted.

Dresden was well known as an artistic and cultural center, and Ada Scholz soon found herself involved in the society of the city. As one result of this preoccupation, the children—especially little Ada—felt that they were denied the full-time affection and the tender personal care that other children they knew—their school friends, in particular—received from their mothers.

Little Ada talked about this matter more than once with her girl friends, and she learned that, indeed, not all mothers were as caught up in social affairs outside the home as was her own mother. Many spent more time with their children. Little Ada was so distressed that upon more than one occasion she vowed, "When I grow up and have babies of my own, I will take care of them myself!"

Ada was not aware of any neglect of her children. In placing them in the care of a governess whose qualifications she had investigated, she believed she was properly providing for their needs. After all, she did love her children—all of them—and did she not spend many hours with the children, when she was home?

Meanwhile, Ada Scholtz was still quite young, and she was sought after socially because of her outgoing and pleasantly dramatic personality. Richard Scholz had become an established artist in a city that appreciated artistry, and his father before him had been equally well known.

Grandfather Scholz's home was the scene of many cultural soirées, and Ada took pride in the importance of certain of the guests. She learned that on one evening at Grandfather Scholz's home the popular pianist-composer Robert Schumann had been a guest, and it was there that he met for the first time another talented pianist-composer—Clara Wieck, who later became his wife. Ada told her daughter this bit of news, and later, when little Ada had children of her own, she related the serendipitous happening to her own daughter. And so the story lived on.

After a time, a son was born to Richard and Ada, and he was given his father's name, Richard Scholz. He was from the first day unlike his half-brothers and sister, but they loved him. Rudi and Ottocar liked to make funny faces accompanied by silly sounds in an effort to make Richard gurgle and laugh.

As often as she had the chance, little Ada held him gently in her arms and sang softly to him the little sleepy-time songs her father had sung to her. Richard Scholz was a kind stepfather to Ada, and she did like him, but Papi was always in the back of her mind, always in her heart. Adalibooli could have only one father.

It was when the family was living with Richard Scholz that Ada decided she wanted to have her own first name. She loved her mother, of course, but in her own emotional makeup she was so different from her mother that she did not want to be known by the same name. She had thought about this very often since her father's death, and one day she found the name she wished to have as her own. Just how she came upon the name we can only imagine, but she did make a definite choice. As soon as she made this choice, she waited for a time when the family was all together. Everyone was at table for dinner that evening, and little Ada announced to her mother, her stepfather, and her brothers that her name was no longer Ada; it was Mona.

Young as she was, she did not ask permission to change; she merely stated her intention, and for some reason there was little objection to her wish. This most unusual young lady was from that moment on Mona—Mona Martinsen.

Richard Scholz had painted a strikingly beautiful pastel portrait of Mona when she was ten years of age. In the portrait her earnest young face, framed by masses of wavy blond hair falling to her shoulders, looks directly out from the center of the picture, and her large, wide, Russian eyes follow the viewer. Her dress is a soft pink with a wide lace collar, and a pink ribbon is in her hair. Near the bottom of the painting in broad, black strokes is the word "Baby," followed by "R. Scholz" and the year, 1894.

Evidently very fond of Mona, Scholz did another portrait of her when she was thirteen. This time he used charcoal as his medium, and Mona's face is seen from the right side. There is the same thick, wavy blond hair falling to her shoulders, and full bangs cover her forehead almost to her eyebrows. Again, her right eye—the angle of the picture allows only an impression of the left eye—is shown as large and wide. It is the same girl, but her increased maturity is evidenced in the strength of the nose and chin. Her appearance leads one to think that this portrait might have been made near the time when she changed her name to Mona.

Brothers Rudolf and Ottocar were doing very well. Both were sturdy fellows, were quite successful in their schoolwork, and in general were growing into husky young men. Richard Scholz did his best to be a father figure for them, but both remembered Papi and the strong influence he had on them. They remembered his smiles and his strength.

Mona's health was excellent. The Høehere Toechter Schule that she attended was considered one of the best from the standpoint of educational instruction, but it did more than merely teach. The school attempted to mold its young women in the German—perhaps the worldwide—societal model of the time. It sought to prepare them for the life roles it was assumed they would follow as educated and cultured wives and mothers. They were prepared to be the homemakers of the future, and little or no thought was given to possible careers. It would be their noble task to care for and inspire the next generation and, above all, to be loving and self-effacing wives.

This well-intentioned but somewhat crippling curriculum did have its effect upon all the girls, but it could not negate the spirit of self-sufficiency and purpose with which Mona's young nature was endowed. It would have been apparent to anyone well acquainted with Mona that in mind and spirit she exhibited an overall independence uncommon in her time. Was she perhaps an early feminist?

Although many of the teachers at the School for Higher Class Daughters were middle-aged or past, there was one young man, Herr Adolph Schmidt, who caused considerable excitement among the girls whenever he entered a classroom. If one of the young ladies whispered to her seatmate "Herr Schmidt kommt!" they were all alerted. Hands were quickly raised and shaken a bit, so that when they were lowered they would have a smooth white appearance. Cheeks and lips were pinched to make them rosy, and the girls assumed erect and lively postures. All these preparations were intended to attract the admiring attention of the fortunate Herr Schmidt, and one can have little doubt that he was aware of that fact.

Ada could not be entirely happy in her second marriage, nor was she entirely unhappy. Richard Scholz was a good man, and he was kind enough to her and her children, but the marriage seemed doomed. Ada could not be what he wanted her to be. Richard thought his wife should be a regulation German *Hausfrau*, and no doubt he believed that he was entitled to no less. If he discussed this dilemma with his friends, we can be sure they all agreed with him. "A wife should be a real wife," they no doubt pronounced in no uncertain terms.

There was, however, precious little of the *Hausfrau* in Ada's makeup—little or nothing at all. Rudolf Martinsen had known this from the very beginning when he first had met her aboard the *Bavaria* so many years before. For Rudolf, what Ada did have was all he wanted. He understood her highly emotional makeup, delighted in her vitality and zest for living, and he found her dramatic ways quite enchanting.

On evenings when they entertained, as he watched his wife sweep gracefully into a guest-filled room, Rudolf thought her entrance much like that of a beautiful sailing vessel gliding into a quiet harbor. Ada warmed and decorated his world, and, having been born to a life of culture and wealth, he never doubted that she was what he needed and wished to have. Rudolf could afford servants, and they could do all the other things that a *Hausfrau* should do.

Ada's thoughts turned more and more to Rudolf and the devotion they had felt for each other. They had married, she mused, for one reason only: they loved each other. It was not habit, nor was it unwelcome loneliness that brought them together; it was just that they could not live without each other. She remembered the newness of the love she learned on their honeymoon, his mastery and his tenderness.

They had traveled to many places on that trip, but it was the same wherever they were, for the days were filled with adventure, and the nights—oh! the nights!—the nights, she remembered, were filled with love.

Ada had learned love and caring in a new and a deep way with Rudolf, and she had found passion. She had felt overwhelming passion based upon love and caring for another person. She did not have this with Richard, and she feared that it would never come to her again. "And never," she thought, "never is a long, long time."

Richard and Ada gave much thought to their problem and they spent considerable time trying to think of a solution, but the gnawing feeling of dissatisfaction in their marriage only grew worse. It seemed there was no good or happy solution, but finally they both—Richard only reluctantly—agreed that divorce was the path they must take. They were divorced, and Ada was granted custody of son Richard and of her own children.

Ada moved her family back to Gernsbach, to Vrohmberg, the home they all had loved. But it was not the same—not the same at all.

12

Mona Martinsen

IT WAS NOT LONG BEFORE Ada became convinced that she must take her family back to their New York home, but young Rudi, who had formerly expressed so much interest in the United States, would not return with them. He had made many friendships in Germany, and even though his family was aware of these attachments, his decision to remain in Europe came as a shock to his mother and his siblings. He expressed his feelings when they first discussed returning to New York.

"Mother, I want to stay here, at least for the time being. I hope you will understand my decision. After all, I am nearly twenty-one. You have helped me get a good education, and I feel sure that I can make my way here. I will write you often, and as soon as we are able, I promise you that I will come to New York to see you all. Please understand me; I feel at home here, and—well—I just want to stay here."

Ada noticed that he used the word "we," and she thought of the pretty young girl he had taken out a few times in Gernsbach. "But," she told herself, "he could not be serious now." At first her motherly feelings urged her to advise him that he was far too young even to think seriously about a girl, but she thought better of such a warning. She remembered all too well that she herself had been only seventeen when she thought seriously about a young man. "Certainly that was not a mistake," she reassured herself, "for Rudolf brought me nothing but happiness."

And so Ada just wished young Rudi well and hugged him—but not without the tears they both understood so well.

As for the rest of the family, places they had formerly enjoyed in

Europe now seemed bleak and unfriendly without their beloved Papi. Ada experienced this feeling as well, but she also believed that Rudolf would have wanted them to return to America and that the children would benefit from the many opportunities that awaited them there. She remembered that it was because he believed so firmly in the future of the New World that he had made certain that their children were born in America and that he had become a naturalized citizen of the United States.

So it was that the Martinsen family made ready to go home to New York. Ada sold the beloved Vrohmberg to a Russian jeweler, and all the fine, hand-carved furniture she and Rudolf had collected to make their home together disappeared by way of the auction block. As each familiar piece of furniture was sold, the children—especially Mona—stood by in silent helplessness. Mona never forgot the sorrow she felt as she saw these last material vestiges of life with Papi disappear.

New York presented an entirely new way of life. Ada had kept the home at Fifty-fourth Street near Fifth Avenue, and they returned to it. Without Papi, it seemed at first cold and almost unfriendly, but gradually it became home again for all the family, even for Mona.

On the first floor of the home was a gracious living room and also a dining room for entertaining, and the family bedrooms were on an upper floor. The kitchen was in the basement, and on one wall a cabinet stood that housed a substantial dumb waiter. At mealtimes, the dumb waiter was filled with steaming bowls and platters, and it was sent up through a boxed-in area to the dining room above. This convenience made repeated stair climbing by the servants unnecessary.

Ottocar was ready for college, and they chose Harvard as a suitable school because he showed interest in following his father's business career. Ada decided that a boarding school would take care of Richard's needs and would be best for him. The poor young fellow had no choice in the matter, and he was not entirely happy about it. The plan for Mona was that she should attend a suitable women's college, and Bryn Mawr was the most likely choice for her.

Mona was growing up. She was now quite as tall as her mother, and the golden blond hair that had framed her young face had darkened slightly. She no longer let her hair fall, slightly curled, to her shoulders but wore it up in back so that her face and entire head were framed in its softness.

Was she pretty? Some might have hesitated to call her that, for her well-modeled face had a strength that one does not customarily associate with prettiness. But Mona, with her tall, lithe figure and her graceful ways, was good to look at. When she smiled, which was often, her whole face was transformed by a radiance that a viewer found beautiful. Yes, that was it: Mona was beautiful.

She applied herself seriously to whatever she was doing, which included her studies in school and her attendance at the nearby Lutheran church. Mona had come to know Pastor Guenther Schaibel well, for he directed his attentions in a fatherly way to the younger members of his flock. In return, the good pastor was respected and loved by many of the young people. Pastor Schaibel had noticed in Mona a natural spirituality and a naively uncompromising honesty, characteristics he welcomed.

Mona was sixteen in the year 1900, and she considered this circumstance something of an achievement, a landmark in her life. It was assumed that at sixteen she would confirm her membership in the Church, and Mona had already attended a series of meetings intended to prepare her for that most important step. These instructional meetings were conducted during the evening in the parsonage.

After the serious part of each session was over, Mrs. Schaibel often came into the room with fresh-baked cookies, strudel, or some other treat for the young people. Marianna was a good foil for the rather serious-minded pastor. An attractive, brown-eyed blonde, nearly her husband's height, she usually had something witty to say to the group, although the pastor thought her witticisms were as often confusing as they were entertaining. Nevertheless, her uninhibited gaiety and good humor brought many a somber instructional evening to a pleasant close.

Mona had taken an active part in the sessions, but there was one matter in the teaching that so troubled her that she knew she would have to talk to Pastor Schaibel personally about it. One Sunday, after members had participated in a communion service, Mona decided that she would go to see the pastor the very next morning.

When she reached the doorway of the pastor's office, she could see the good man seated at his desk, shuffling through a stack of papers.

Schaibel was in his mid-sixties, although Mona and her friends thought of him as much older. His full head of hair, slightly ruffled, was only partly gray, but his short, trimly cut beard was completely white. His well-lined face bore a tired expression, and for a moment Mona thought she should not disturb him. But just as she reached the doorway the pastor looked up and smiled. He did not look nearly so tired when he smiled.

Mona spoke in a low, soft voice, and Guenther Schaibel could see that it had not been easy for her to make her way to his office. "There is something I must ask you, Pastor Schaibel, for it disturbs me very much . . ."

Again smiling warmly, the kind man invited her to come in and motioned that she should take a chair near his desk. "Now, what is troubling you, my dear?"

"I don't know how to begin . . ." Mona managed to say.

"Just begin, Mona, just *begin*. Just tell me what troubles you." The pastor's gentle urging gave Mona the courage she needed.

"Pastor Schaibel, if I join the Church, do I have to believe, must I really believe, that the bread you break at communion and give to us is actually the body of Christ and that the wine is really his blood?" Mona's expression and a tenseness in the language of her body made it clear to Schaibel just how unpleasant, how entirely unacceptable, was her literal understanding of the words.

There was only one response to her question that the Church permitted, and Schaibel gave that answer firmly: "Yes, my dear, you do have to believe it. Yes, you must believe that."

Mona braced herself, sat up very straight, and, looking directly at him, expressed the difficult and troubling decision she had reached.

"If that is so, Pastor Schaibel, then I cannot join the Church."

This statement, so simply and honestly given and with such courage, had not been anticipated, and Guenther Schaibel at first did not know how he should rightly respond. He sat quietly for a time, looking straight ahead at a painting of the man who, nineteen hundred years before, had broken the bread and drunk the wine at supper and had told His followers as they sat with Him that the bread was His body and the wine His blood. Then He had lovingly instructed them that they must continue to do this in memory of Him. All this, and even more, Guenther Schaibel pondered.

When the pastor at last turned to the earnest young woman, he saw that her head was still held erect, but he knew that the sheen that brightened her gray eyes was caused by tears. He did not rebuke her when he spoke, and his voice shook slightly with the strength of his emotion and the tenderness he felt for this vibrant young person.

"I wish, dear Mona, I only wish that my own daughter were as sincere as you are."

That is all he said; that is all he knew to say. Yet, the expression of caring and tenderness that dominated the serious expression on his face was reassuring to Mona. Neither spoke; they just sat quietly, each sensing a gentle understanding in the other. When Mona rose to leave, Guenther Schaibel followed her to the door of his study, and as she turned to bid him good-bye, he held out both hands to her. Silently she took his hands in hers, kissed them, then turned and hurriedly left the church.

Life went on day by day in the handsome brownstone, and the family gradually felt once more at home there. Mona liked to visit the downstairs kitchen to see what Cook was doing. Anna, a comfy, warm-hearted woman much like the peasants they had in their employ at Vrohmberg, was always very friendly to Mona. When Cook was making bread, Mona on several occasions had taken a chunk of dough and molded it, idly, in her hands.

One morning Ottocar came down the stairs to see what she was doing. Mona admired and loved this manly, six-foot-tall brother of hers, and today she coaxed him to sit on a stool for a few minutes while she tried to make the dough look like him. When she was satisfied that she could improve the likeness no more, she held the dough figure up, and both she and Ottocar gazed at what she held in her hand. To Mona's delight, and to Ottocar's great surprise, the former chunk of bread dough did have the appearance of a young man. It *was* Ottocar!

Mona put the dough on a small plate and dashed up the stairs to find her mother. The two almost collided, for just then Ada was coming down from her bedroom on the upper floor. She was dressed in a riding habit, and Mona could see that she was going to the stable near Central Park where she kept her big black gelding, Hector. Ada rode several times a week.

Mona's excitement as they met surprised Ada. "What on earth is the matter, Mona?" Mona held up the plate bearing the chunk of dough that had somehow become the head of a young man. "Look, Mothie! Look what I have made! Does it not look like Ottocar? He thinks it does. Cook does too!"

Ada took the plate holding the dough sculpture from her daughter. She held it up at eye level and turned it around, seeing it from all sides. "Why, it does look like Ottocar. Mona, how were you able to do this with just a chunk of bread dough?"

"Oh, Mothie, I go down in the kitchen often, and I have been trying, just for fun, to make something with Cook's bread dough. This is the first time I got it to really look like anyone. Ottocar helped me a lot."

Mona was pleased that she had impressed her mother. It gave her a feeling of closeness to her mother that she needed. As for Ada, she did not say very much more at the time, but for the rest of the day, even while she was riding in the park, her thoughts kept returning to the little ball of dough that Mona had shaped to look so much like her son. She had been not only surprised but truly impressed at the likeness Mona had formed with such a lowly medium. Ada could not deny her growing belief that Mona had a special talent that should not be neglected.

A few days later, while her knitting needles were busily clicking as she put the finishing stitches on a pink-and-white scarf, Ada came to a decision: Mona should be given lessons in sculpting. She had met the director of the Metropolitan Museum of Art in New York, a Mr. Elwell, who was quite well known as a sculptor, and she had heard that he also took pupils. Ada decided she would speak to him, but first she would have to talk to Mona about her idea. While she was knitting and thinking, Ada heard the front door open, and Mona came in from a walk around the neighborhood.

"Mona, please come here. I want to talk to you about an idea I have."

"What is it, Mothie?" Mona was interested. She came into the living room and sat down on the ottoman near her mother's chair.

"I have been thinking about that head of Ottocar you made with some of Cook's bread dough. Mona, you have a special ability, and I think we should do something about it. How would you like to have lessons in sculpting? Some time ago I met a fine sculptor who is director of our Metropolitan Museum of Art. His name is Edwin Elwell, and he does take students. What do you say, Mona? Shall I try to arrange for you to study with him?"

Her mother's suggestion surprised Mona. "Oh, Mothie, that is a wonderful idea! But what about college—what about Bryn Mawr?"

"You could still go to Bryn Mawr, dear. That would be no problem. Mona, I don't think we should forget what you have done, the ability you have shown. I am sure that Papi would want us to see about sculpting lessons for you." That statement convinced Mona, for Papi and his ideas would never cease to be an important influence in her life. "Mothie, I should love to do something like that, to learn about sculpture. Do you really think that is possible?"

"Of course it is, Mona. I will make an appointment to see Mr. Elwell and talk to him about you." Ada was able to arrange a visit to the sculptor, and a time was set for her to call at his office at the museum.

As the years had passed Ada, too, had matured. Slightly fuller in her body, she had lost little of her youthful attractiveness. Dressed in the handsome fashions that were available to her in New York, she portrayed with a certain ease the elevated station in life that she now took quite for granted. On this day, she was wearing a two-piece suit of a brown tweed material. From the belt at her middle hung a small purse, and over the suit she had swung a fur cape. A smart pillbox hat completed the attractive picture.

To get to Elwell's studio Ada rode one of the small, two-wheeled, one-horse cabs that waited along the avenue. The passenger compartment was partially enclosed, and the driver sat up high at the rear, leaving the view toward the front of the compartment open. A ride in such a vehicle was quite pleasant.

When she arrived at Elwell's studio the master was working on a large equestrian statue. Ada introduced herself, and Elwell said that he remembered having met her—somewhere. He suggested that they go to his office, which would be more suitable for a visit, and the two sat down together there. After a few opening pleasantries had been exchanged between them, Ada came to the point of her visit. She told him about Mona and asked if he would consider taking her as his pupil.

Director Elwell thought Ada Martinsen a most impressive lady, obviously not entirely unacquainted with art, and he gave a calmly measured but polite response to her request.

"Mrs. Martinsen, at one time I did try to teach young women who wished to be sculptors. Eventually, however, problems arose which led to my decision that I would take only men as pupils. However, what you tell me about your daughter is most interesting, and all I can say today is that I should like to meet her. Can you arrange for her to come in and see me?"

Ada assumed from what he had suggested that Mr. Elwell had formerly had some unfortunate experiences with women students, but such problems were not new to her, and she did not let this knowledge discourage her. After talking about the matter for a few more minutes, Ada and Mr. Elwell set a time for Mona to come to the museum and meet with the sculptor.

In the slightly foreign manner that had become natural to her, Ada thanked Mr. Elwell for his time and for his consideration, after which she rose to leave. Director Elwell conducted her to the door of the museum and then to a cab that waited outside.

Mona arrived at the museum promptly at the appointed time: eleven o'clock in the morning on the following Monday. She wore a simple but dressy full-length dark skirt with a long-sleeved, rose-colored blouse topped by a high collar that complimented her neck with its softness. Mona had her hair neatly done up, and she wore no earrings in her pierced ears. Leather gloves, matching in color her comfortable walking shoes, covered her hands.

Although it was almost unthinkable in those times, Mona refused to wear a corset, in spite of her mother's insistence that she would one day regret it if she did not do so. One not caught up in the customs of the day might well have agreed with Mona and noted that her slim, strong figure did not need artificial restraint.

Director Elwell had given some thought to Mona's desire to study with him, and he fully intended that any instruction he might decide to give to her should be based upon a proper understanding between them. With this end in mind, he met Mona at the door of his studio as she entered and spoke firmly to her. We quote his own words from an article he later wrote:

> There is no sex in the studio. The moment you fall in love with me or try any feminine tricks, out you go. There is no reason to fear anything in this world, least of all the clay you are working with. *See* with your own eyes, and *make* what is in your own mind, regardless of what others have made. Fear is the beginning of the end in an artist's career, and the cause of woman's mediocrity.
>
> Do not fear your master, do not set him up on a pinnacle to worship, in a stupid, feminine way. . . . When you chop clay or wash the floor, remember that it is to be as well done as your modeling, so that you get into the habit of doing work thoroughly, and not shifting your real hard work on to some assistant, and letting him do the brain and the labor work.

At first Mona was taken aback by the tone of voice and the harsh content of the sculptor's words. She had not known what to expect from him, but she undoubtedly did not expect him to speak as he did. He had simply and firmly put her on notice of what she should and should not do if she were accepted as his student. Never before had Mona been spoken to so roughly; she was, however, built of far sterner stuff than Elwell had assumed would be the case, and she took his words well.

"I understand, sir. What you say will be no problem for me."

Director Elwell guided a subdued and serious Mona into his studio and showed her the large equestrian statue he was creating. One of the boots of the rider was unfinished, and he told her that if she could finish the boot to his satisfaction, he would consider taking her as a pupil.

"I am going out to meet some friends for lunch," he told her, "and when I return we shall see what you have done." With those words, Elwell picked up his coat and hat and left Mona alone in his studio.

Mona removed her gloves, and, setting to work immediately, she found that the well-prepared clay was much easier to work with than bread dough. The clay was smooth and firm, and her attempts at modeling remained intact as she had made them, and did not ooze back into the living dough, as they had done in the kitchen at home.

A couple of hours later, Mona had just put the finishing touches on her boot when the master returned. She stood expectantly and somewhat fearfully aside while Elwell examined, critically, the boot that she had completed. Mona hoped he would agree with her that it matched the other boot rather well. After he had looked for some time at what Mona had done, he turned to her but made no comment about the completed boot. Instead, he simply said, "Come back tomorrow at eight o'clock, and wear something suitable for work."

Ada was a little surprised and very happy when Mona told her about the day's session with Mr. Elwell. As for his rather rough words to her daughter Ada explained that she had felt when she first went to talk to him that the sculptor had previously had unfortunate experiences with young women students, and that he did not want them repeated.

"But, Mona dear, you are not at all like that. You have never been silly, and you really want to learn, don't you?"

"Oh, yes, I do! I told him that!" was Mona's quick response.

"Then, daughtie dear, don't let the way he speaks bother you. He is only trying to teach you something about art. He thinks you have to be stronger than most girls—more like a man. You can do that, I know." Mona agreed, and she promised herself then and there that she would show Mr. Elwell that she was not afraid. Yes, she would most certainly show the master what she could do.

Ada helped her choose something appropriate to wear, and Mona dressed the next morning in the nearest thing she had to work clothes— a simple, washable dress with a low, rounded neckline and short sleeves. She arrived at Elwell's studio a few minutes before eight o'clock and found the master already there.

After another bit of verbal "rough-housing" calculated to drive away what he considered her feminine timidity, Mr. Elwell asked a male art student to show Mona how to prepare clay for modeling. She was given a long, heavy knife and was told to chop a large chunk of hard, dry clay into smaller pieces, which, with the addition of successive small amounts of water, could be softened and mixed with the hands until the clay became workable and ready for use. Any hard bits of clay that did not soften were to be removed and tossed into a waiting pail.

Mona set to work, and while she chopped and softened and mixed, she thought about the course she had taken. She was to be an apprentice to a man who was actually doing sculpture that had a *big* quality about it. She realized that she wanted to get nearer to the artist, to feel his daily life, and to learn something that could not be taught—something that could only be gained from the atmosphere that surrounds a sculptor who is truly honest and sincere in his work. Such an artist, she came to believe, was F. Edwin Elwell.

Elwell knew, as he said himself, that "it would be impossible to destroy the eternal woman in someone so well born," and no attempt was made to do this. The washing of the floor and the pounding of the clay were intended to teach, not to subdue or harass. Elwell was convinced that unless an art student learns to work for her craft, her art, she will never become a true artist.

Mona studied with Elwell for three years. In that time the delicate hands of her protected youth grew larger and stronger because of the work she did so that they could master the clay and make it interpret her own inspirations in a firm and solid fashion. She had learned to do her own thinking and to destroy without hesitation any unsatisfactory work—as well as to create.

Mona was commissioned to do a bust of a New York banker and was paid a substantial sum for her work. She made, at nineteen years, a life-sized statue called "Motherhood," and it was entirely her own creation. The statue represented a woman tenderly holding her baby with her right arm, while her left hand grasps a snake, from which she is protecting her baby.

The sculptor-teacher praised the piece with these words: "Is it not a wonderful statue that teaches, without words, the grandest truth of the universe, 'Motherhood'?" He suggested that the statue was not unlike Rodin in treatment, yet it was thoroughly original. Then he commented that the experiment he had undertaken—teaching a young woman art student—had succeeded and that he, the once brutal master, had become the kind and affectionate friend.

"Think you," he wrote in an article, "that she is any less a lady because she has learned to use the strength and handling of the man, or that she will more easily be led to the evil of life? She has risen to the plane of mental virtue through the 'rough-housing' of the masculine mind; she has a wider view of life and is in no fear of man or her clay."

Elwell was so impressed with Mona's ability and the progress she had made that he urged her to go for advanced study with a great master, and he suggested Auguste Rodin in Paris. He had felt a power growing in Mona's work that seemed to him akin to that of the world-famous French sculptor. Elwell's suggestion was highly complimentary, but it was also a momentous one for Mona and for her mother as well. It would require a drastic change in their plans for her future, which up until that point had been that Mona would attend Bryn Mawr College.

It was not an easy decision, but the soul-filling satisfaction gained from her work in sculpture with Edwin Elwell led Mona to decide against college. She decided that her heart's desire—her real calling—was to continue in her art, and she hoped that it might be possible for her to study with "the Sultan of Sculpture," the great Rodin. Ada was also convinced of Mona's calling, and she told Mona that she would make plans to send her to Paris.

13

Paris and Auguste Rodin

*The great artist's ecstasy is terrifying at times, but it is still
happiness, because it is the continual adoration of truth.*

Rodin

PLANS WERE IMMEDIATELY made for Mona to study with Auguste
Rodin. Mona had been well paid for the portrait bust of the banker, and
her mother was able to put together the additional funds that would be
required for the venture. Mona was ready for the challenge, for she was
as courageous as her grandmother, as enthusiastic as her mother, and
she was supported by the unforgotten wise strength of her father. In
1903, when she was only nineteen years of age, the young sculptress set
out for Paris to learn from the most honored sculptor of the time.

Youthful as she was, a certain maturity had developed in this nineteen-
year-old, along with a noticeable individuality and a strong, if unusual,
faith. The teachings of F. Edwin Elwell had largely dispatched whatever
feminine fears she might have had, and Mona was ready to learn and
achieve her high aspirations. She already knew how to work—Elwell
had taught her that!—and she was ready to work even harder. Mona
Martinsen longed for a career in sculpture.

Paris was not new to Mona; she had been there with her parents
several times. But Paris was always new. How could it be otherwise with
"the city of lights," where so much was always happening?

It might be said that Paris was two cities—the busy, business-oriented
city of the day and the city that came to a different kind of life when night

arrived. The Paris of the night was brilliantly lighted by innumerable gas lights, for the people of the beloved city had placed ten times the number of lights along her streets than had citizens of other cities.

Paris in the early years of the twentieth century was a mecca for students of art, great artists, fledgling and accomplished writers, and any visitor who dreamed of a city of glamour and romance. A visitor to Paris would no doubt miss a great deal that the Parisian boulevardier might enjoy, but that visitor could easily imagine that he was surrounded by famous poets and noted duelists. He could fancy that every well-dressed young woman he saw go by in an open fiacre was a celebrated actress of the Comédie Francaise.

Paris was a city of narrow streets and broad boulevards, where people sat and chatted at marble-topped tables on the sidewalks, under heavily leaved trees. One could not have failed to be impressed by the broad boulevards, with their ceaseless bustle and gaiety.

One might have thought that surely the celebrating boulevardiers would rest after a long night out and that the cafés would be closed and the long passing stream of cabs and omnibuses would stop. One might have thought this in the late evening, but at nine the next morning it would surely have been the same—the same waiters, the same rush of carriages and buses with their fine horses, the flowers in the booths, and newspapers neatly piled around the kiosks.

But carriages pulled by horses were not the only conveyances in Paris shortly after the turn of the century. The automobile had been developed in France in 1895, and Mona saw a fair number of them on the streets of Paris. They did not appear too far removed from the carriage, for they still retained carriage wheels and a carriage appearance in the front. The rear of the automobile was made of steel and was rounded, and Mona thought that the brightly painted vehicles looked like colorful bathtubs as they were driven about the narrow streets.

Mona was fortunate to have had considerable experience in travel and living abroad in childhood, which made it easy for her to find a place to live in Paris and get somewhat settled in student life. She found a small apartment at 15 rue des Bourgeois—a small street, not long, but it was a neighborhood.

The houses had tall fronts with gray slate roofs and flowers in pots in the windows. Some houses had balconies, from which a woman might lean and visit with a friend or neighbor next door or across the street. Mona was soon struck by the fact that residents of a similar street in New York would know little of their neighbors. In New York, the fronts of the houses would tell nothing to the outside world, and they would even seem to frown on each other. But here in Paris, the people lived in their houses or on the balconies or in the windows.

It was possible for a Parisian to know what her neighbors were going to have for dinner; one could see them bringing uncooked food from the restaurant on the corner, with a loaf of bread under one arm and a single egg in hand. If someone was planning a party, the neighbors knew it because they could see the bottles on window ledges and the jams or jellies set out to cool on the balcony. Mona delighted in the intimate, Parisian way of life.

After she was settled in her apartment, Mona's first job was to find M. Rodin. After dressing carefully in a dark suit with matching hat and gloves, she decided to go directly to his *atelier*. As luck would have it, just as she was stepping off the curb into the street near his quarters, she saw the famed sculptor himself walking toward her.

The master was not tall—perhaps not quite as tall as Mona—but his stocky body gave the impression of strength. Mona thought the most striking thing about him was his face; it was a markedly strong face, accentuated by a large but handsome nose and topped by large, piercing eyes and a forehead that slanted slightly to the hairline. His wavy gray hair, cut short at the back of his neck, reached on each side just to the top of his ears, and the long, fluffy sideburns joined with a well-trimmed moustache and a very long beard.

Mona stepped in front of him and excitedly addressed him in French: "Monsieur Rodin, I have come all the way from New York to study with you!" Rodin stopped, took off his hat, bowed, and responded: "Je serais enchanté, Mademoiselle!"

That was only the beginning. It was necessary to convince Rodin that she—such a young person and a woman—had sufficient basic artistic ability and had accomplished enough that he would care at all to teach her. Mona was able to demonstrate that she had ability worthy of Rodin's consideration. She showed him photos of the works she had already done in New York, and she had brought with her a letter of introduction from her former teacher, whose opinion carried considerable weight.

Beyond that, Rodin's wide experience and his intuitive sense of ability caused him to see potential in Mona. He agreed to teach her, and arrangements were soon made. She was to report at his studio the day after next.

The studio to which Rodin had directed Mona was in "l'Hotel de Biron," a residence in a quiet street on the left bank of the Seine. Built in the eighteenth century as the town house of a powerful family, it was later the home of the Convent of the Sacred Heart. In Mona's time, it was occupied by several tenants, among them Rodin. A very beautiful dwelling, its rooms were large, with high ceilings, and it was paneled in white, with mouldings in white and gold. Rodin's studio opened through French doors into a garden that, though neglected, grew flowers each spring—a source of pleasure and inspiration for Rodin and, as it would turn out, for Mona as well.

Mona later learned of another of Rodin's *ateliers*. To reach this particular studio, one had to go down the long rue de l'Université, near the Champ-de-Mars. There in a large, grassy courtyard were blocks of marble indicating the sculptors that had been honored by the State. Along one side of this courtyard was a row of a dozen *ateliers* used by various sculptors. Rodin occupied two of the rooms in this little artist colony.

When Mona entered Rodin's studio in l'Hotel de Biron, she saw nude models just walking around the studio in a relaxed manner, stopping now and then to rest. Rodin was already at work, but when he saw Mona, he stopped and went to greet her.

Mona was wearing one of the loose-fitting, round-necked dresses she had used at Elwell's studio in New York. Seeing that she was dressed to begin at once, Rodin showed her to a small area in the corner of his studio, where he said she might temporarily set up a modeling pedestal. He advised Mona that she would need to find a studio nearby, where there was adequate light for her to work.

Rodin most likely had very definite words of introduction for his new student as he explained to her how his teaching would take place. She would work in her studio alone, and—perhaps once a week or less—he would examine what she was doing, point out any mistakes, and make suggestions.

Following the master's direction, Mona found a small, skylighted studio near the Boulevard Montparnasse that delighted her and that she promptly outfitted with a pedestal and with tubs of clay.

During the course of her apprenticeship to Rodin, Mona would become familiar with many of the great sculptor's techniques, his way of thinking, and his spirituality. With regard to technique, she learned that a sculptor must *look and see*. She must not just glance at something; she must see it fully.

One day, early in her association with Rodin, he took her to one of his smaller studios, where a number of busts lined the walls. "Pick the one you like," he said, "and study it. I will be gone for about half an hour, when I shall return."

Mona chose a bust of the head of a young man with strong, but handsome, features. She studied it carefully from all sides until the master returned, asking, "Have you looked at the head carefully?" When Mona replied that she had done so, Rodin led her to a small studio that contained only a pedestal and several tubs of clay that had been prepared for use.

"I want you now to model from memory the piece that you have been studying. This clay is very strong, and you will not need an armature to support the bust you make with it. When you have finished, let me know, and I will see what you have done."

Mona set to work at once, and the fine French clay worked well beneath her strong fingers. Her mental picture of the sculptured head she had chosen was clear enough that its basic outline soon became visible in the mass of clay she put on the pedestal. After she had achieved the first general outlines of the head, Mona set to work completing and refining it, and the young man's features as she remembered them began to appear in the clay.

From her first "sculpture" of her brother's face in bread dough 'Mona had possessed a special ability to capture a likeness in the clay. This talent, which she referred to as something of a "knack," stood her in good stead as she worked from memory. After some time—perhaps hours—had passed, she felt that she could go no further without referring to the original model. She went at once to Rodin and told him that her bust was far from finished, but she could do no more from memory alone.

The master returned to the small workroom and examined what Mona had done. His severe look of appraisal softened as he turned to his pupil and said, "It is not bad, but perhaps we should return to the model and you can see what mistakes you have made." This was Mona's first introduction to Rodin's insistence that his students work from memory. He favored carefully made drawings of a model but strongly discouraged sketches.

Another of Rodin's methods was his habit of having nude models moving around the studio as he worked. The approach more commonly used by sculptors was to have a model sit and take a certain pose, but Rodin wanted to see how the muscles, ligaments, and bones acted under the outer skin while the model was moving.

When he noted a certain movement or pose he liked, he might ask the model to hold that position, and he would begin to make a figure. He made many models of parts of a body—an arm, a foot, a leg—which gave him valuable practice for future pieces.

Over and over he emphasized the act of modeling, and he once remarked:

> The science of modeling was taught to me by one Constant, who worked in the atelier where I made my debut as a sculptor. He counseled, "Always remember what I am about to tell you. Henceforth, when you carve, never see the form in length, but always in thickness."
>
> This principle was astonishingly fruitful to me. I applied it to the execution of figures. Instead of imagining the different parts of a body as surfaces more or less flat, I represented them as projectures of interior volumes. I forced myself to express in each swelling of the torso or of the limbs the efflorescence of a muscle or of a bone which lay deep beneath the skin. And so the truth of my figures, instead of being merely superficial, seems to blossom from within to the outside, like life itself.

On one occasion a sculptor friend had compared his work with that of Rembrandt, and Rodin immediately retorted that to compare him with Rembrandt was sacrilege. Then Rodin added in partial acknowledgment, "But you have concluded justly in observing in my works the stirrings of the soul towards that kingdom, perhaps chimerical, of unlimited truth and liberty. There, indeed, is the mystery that moves me."

On one occasion he asked Mona, "Are you convinced now that art is a kind of religion? It is very necessary to remember, however, that the first commandment of this religion, for those who wish to practice it, is to know how to model a torso, an arm, or a leg!"

Mona realized, as fully as a young person could, the great worth of the opportunity she had been given. A doorway had been opened for her to achieve not only an understanding of sculpture and art but also a spiritual development.

Mona was so deeply impressed by Rodin, and so caught up in her own work, that she disliked taking time for such ordinary tasks as eating. A favorite snack or meal for her was to take an egg or two, crack them into a cup or glass, stir well, pour on some French wine vinegar, then drink it quickly! A nourishing meal, and no time was lost!

But when she was not working, she did find time to associate with other young art students she met. Also studying in Paris when Mona was there were the Italian painter Modigliani and the Mexican Diego Rivera. Of course, there were many others, and Mona came to know some of them, in spite of the passionate dedication she felt toward her studies.

A fond habitué of Paris has said that it is the only city in the world that the visitor refuses to take seriously. The visitor may have come to Paris to study art, he said, but "no matter how serious his purpose, there is always some part of each day when the visitor rests from his labors and smiles indulgently and does as the Parisians do."

This was true for Mona. She was attractive and young, vibrant and full of life, and it was not surprising that more than one young student whom she met invited her to go with him to see the night-time show-places of Paris.

A favorite spot for many Parisians was the Café of Aristide Bruant—the contemporary Francois Villon—on the Boulevard Rochechuart. Bruant was a young man and a handsome one, and the songs he performed were based on poems that he had written. He dressed with great individuality in brown velvet, his trousers tucked into high boots, wearing a red shirt and a broad hat. His café was small. It was barred and dark outside and guarded by a man dressed to look like a policeman.

When a visitor arrived at Bruant's establishment, he had to rap on the door, and eventually he would be admitted, perhaps even by the owner himself. The interior was filled with long tables and decorated in a fantastic manner. Once inside the woman visitor was greeted by one melody, the man by another. When guests left Bruant saluted them as they departed, and he paid special attention to pretty women. Mona did not particularly like this restaurant or its proprietor.

With friends Mona visited a finer and more pretentious café called the Black Cat. Originally a gathering place for journalists, artists, and poets, it was at the time only a show place but nonetheless a most interesting one, with an immense fireplace and massive rafters. The room was arranged to appear odd and bizarre, but Mona and her friends noticed with approval the drawings and the watercolors on the walls, which had been done by some of the best artists in Paris.

Three times a week a performance was held upstairs, in which poets of the neighborhood recited their own verses or someone told a story, standing on the floor in front of the audience. Mona found the performances enjoyable, and although the performers were usually young men, she thought that she might like to take part sometime.

Other favorite spots were café chantants for music, and perhaps the best of these was the Ambassadeurs'. Substantially a roof garden on the ground, it had benches instead of chairs and gravel instead of wood flooring. At the back was the restaurant, where visitors could sit and dine. There was a stage for the entertainers, and at night, when all the gas jets were lit, it was a very bright and happy place. Mona went there more than once with her friends.

Unlike New York or other cities with which she was familiar, the whole of Paris was lit at night. Mona thought that it would be difficult to feel gloomy in a city so brightly lit that she could sit in a window of her home and read a newspaper by the glare of the gas lights. In Paris there were no slums, no dark alleys. As in any city, Paris had its bad people, of course, but if a man wished to commit a criminal act, he would have to accomplish it on a brightly lit street or boulevard.

There were many things about the life in Paris that made Mona feel at home and that she truly loved, but she did not entirely approve of what she regarded as a lax way of life. She felt that the conduct of many art students as well as many Parisians bordered on immorality. Her work with Rodin was a source of great happiness to her, but in her personal life, there were problems. One might have considered Mona worldly because of the varied experiences she had had before moving to Paris, but she still was not comfortable with the relaxed manner of life in the city. Mona was strongly dedicated only to what she felt was truly good, and this uncompromising characteristic remained unchanged throughout her life.

Mona had been in Paris for more than two years when she met a music student from America, a young woman who would become a best friend. Her name was Olga Currier. The manner of Olga's first meeting with Mona could only be characterized as most unusual, and her story of that meeting is so informative of certain occurrences in Mona's life that its telling takes a burden off the shoulders of the narrator. Let us, then, allow Olga to tell her story.

Olga Currier's Story

I came to Paris to study music. My family in Boston was comfortably situated, and my parents were convinced that my love of music and the ability I had shown warranted sending me to France to continue my studies. Like many other students, I chose to live in the Latin Quarter, and, although my study was mainly in music, my daily life did bring a pleasant association with an assorted group of fellow artist-students. I learned from one of them, a young painter, that the funeral of a student from Luzern, Switzerland, was being held at a certain time in a small, vine-covered church not far from my home.

I had only the most casual acquaintance with Martin Darmstadt, but I had noticed him in the company of several young men when I occasionally took a late dinner at the café of Pere Lunette, or at another of the many restaurants in our Quarter. M. Darmstadt was tall and fine-looking, even handsome, but it was more than his good looks which attracted my attention. His bearing and his quiet manners placed him,

I thought, well above the usual run of students who gathered in the evening to dine and listen to the music that was everywhere in Paris.

The funeral was a topic of conversation among other students, and I knew that some of them would attend, but I decided only at the very last minute that I would go. I was alone, and, arriving after the service was well under way and wishing to be as unobtrusive as possible, I chose to sit in a pew near the rear of the rather dark sanctuary. Soft music played by a bearded young man seated at a small organ blended imperceptibly with the quiet sorrow which seemed to emanate from the group assembled there, who in the main were young people like myself, and with the scent of flowers which filled the air.

The service was in French, which I had scarcely mastered at that time, and the small, white-haired pastor in his unimpressive, somber black suit alluded only briefly to the young man who was his subject. It seemed entirely possible that Pastor Gaston DuPres had not personally known Martin Darmstadt, and those who attended the service learned precious little about that young man or his life beyond that which they already knew. The intent of his service seemed directed more toward warning his young audience of life's vagaries and the resultant inescapable punishment, than of memorializing their friend, the young artist who had been taken from their midst.

The spoken service was barely over, and the organist had just begun his final selection—Bach's *Jesu, Joy of Man's Desiring*—when I noticed a young woman walking quickly down the aisle toward the rear where I was sitting. She wore a dark suit, and a dark veil covered her face, but I could sense that she was weeping. For a reason that I did not fully understand, I rose and followed that sorrowing young person out of the church.

She was slim and tall, and she walked so swiftly that I needed to quicken my normal pace in order not to lose sight of her on the crowded walks and the narrow street. Near the corner of Rue du Chateau and Rue Vercingetorix, she entered a smaller, short, tree-lined street known as the rue des Bourgeois, and at Number 15 of that street she turned, went up a few steps to the vestibule of a small building, and entered, closing the door behind her.

I hesitated, standing near a linden tree in front of the building for a few minutes, before I found the courage to go to the door and knock. When I did so, the door was soon opened, and I found myself looking into several small rooms. The young woman for whom I had felt such a remarkable attraction now stood in the doorway. She had removed the jacket of her suit and was wearing only its black, shoe-top-length straight skirt, topped by a full-sleeved pink blouse with softness about the neck.

Gone were the black hat and the veil, and her darkening blond hair was done up high on her head. She wore no jewelry of any kind; no earrings hung from her pierced ears. As I looked slightly up to her I was impressed again that something in the way this stranger held herself bespoke quality. There was no hint of affectation in her manner, yet something about her presence gave me the unmistakable feeling that this young woman belonged to a family of some standing. Because of my own rather proud Boston background, I felt a closeness to this young woman.

As I looked at her, I was once more aware of the sorrow, which, as she hastily left the church, had hung like a cloud about this person I did not know. The strongly-modeled but softly rounded face still showed traces of the tears, and her gray eyes—unusually large and wide, I thought—also revealed her grief. I could not help being surprised by the upward rush of sympathy that I felt for this stranger. It did seem that my feeling was quite out of place, directed as it was toward a person I had seen for the first time. "Even so," I thought, "I do feel for her, and I want to know more about her."

Her greeting was warm and friendly: "What may I do for you, my dear?"

I was somewhat at a loss to respond, but I did my best. "My name is Olga Currier. I came from Boston to study music here in Paris. I was at Martin Darmstadt's funeral and was sitting in the back of the church near the aisle when I saw you hurrying out before the service was over. For some reason, I have followed you here."

She reached out and took my hand in hers, drawing me into the room. "Do come in, my dear. I am Mona Martinsen from New York City. I came to Paris hoping to study sculpture with M. Rodin, and he accepted me.

What a remarkable man! I have been studying with him for two years, and I am learning more than I can say from him."

She paused and looked directly into my face. For a moment Mona seemed quite withdrawn, and her eyes took on an intense, impersonal stare with which she seemed to look deep down into my very being. That piercing look left her face almost as quickly as it had come, and when she saw the discomfited expression on my face, she quickly explained:

"Forgive me, dear; I am quite under M. Rodin's spell. You see, he urges us, his pupils, to gather into our minds all we can of the shape, the details, the essence of how a model looks. Then we are told to re-create what we saw from memory. But I did not want to embarrass you, as I see that I have done."

Once again I felt Mona's remarkable warmth as she asked:

"I was just going to brew a pot of tea. Will you join me?" I agreed eagerly, and she proceeded to heat water in a tall brass pot, which she then poured into a copper teapot on a round copper tray, on which a small pitcher and bowl holding cream and sugar had also been placed. After we had sat down together in her living room, we drank the tea from china cups decorated with a Greek key pattern.

As we visited, the strangeness between us passed, and I felt that I had known Mona for much longer than the short while since we met. Mona must have had a similar feeling, for she told me more than I should have expected her to tell me about herself and the happenings of the twenty-one years which led up to our shared moment.

"Music has always been one of my greatest loves," she confided, "even though I hope to make sculpture my career. I learned to play the violin while I was in school in Dresden, and I did so want to study singing as well. And the harp—oh, how I do love to see a young woman singing while she plays the harp! But I did not get to do that."

"I love music, too, and only music, so we have a lot in common," I responded, and again I was aware of something like the opening of a spiritual passageway between us. Thinking that she might welcome the release, I turned the conversation to Martin Darmstadt's funeral. Mona opened up to me, and what she told me about her relationship with that young man did much to explain the sorrow that had impressed me so vividly when I first saw her.

"Martin was a very gifted artist from a fine family in Luzern. He understood so well—and truly believed—the things that are important to me. I thought of Ruth and her belief that one should be able to say about the man she chooses to marry: 'My God is thy God.' We planned to marry as soon as he had recovered enough from his illness. He had suffered for some time from consumption."

Mona was silent for a time, and she seemed far way, looking out a little window onto the rue des Bourgeois. Then she turned again to me, and I hoped that the softening I observed on her mobile face was caused by the sympathy I felt for her.

With a little sound that was part moan, part sigh, Mona shook her head from side to side, looked directly into my eyes, and included me in her feelings. "Oh, Olga, I was holding him in my arms when he died! Martin was alone in Paris, and so I had to arrange for everything—even his funeral."

For a time she sobbed softly as she gazed out the window at a linden tree that stood near the building, and I yearned for the power to comfort her. Mona soon regained her outward composure and said, "As I was walking home just now, the thought came to me that I should try to recapture Martin's beautiful spirit, his gentle courage, in a piece of sculpture."

Again Mona fought back her tears, and it seemed to me that she would not be able to continue, but she pulled herself together once more and finished what she wanted to say. "I think the piece should be called 'The Fallen Hero.' I shall try to make it."

It was a few weeks before I visited her again, and when I arrived, Mona asked me to accompany her to her studio, saying she had something to show me. We walked together, arriving soon at the little studio near Montparnasse. She uncovered for me what she had been working upon. It was a damp, finely modeled clay figure—it should be called a model, I think—of a young man lying lifeless upon a raised base, his fine head cradled in the arms of a woman. "This will be what we talked about before. This will be 'the fallen hero,'" she said.

I looked a long time at the model, for it expressed so beautifully the heartache of young love lost forever. "And he died in your arms," I murmured, "I can hardly imagine what you went through, but I do feel for you. My heart goes out to you, dear Mona. I hope that this beautiful memorial you are creating will make the pain lessen or go away. Don't you think it may do that?"

"But, oh, Olga," said Mona, trying not to weep, "this is the second time I have lost someone I loved. A little more than a year ago a man I admired ever so much was killed in Africa in the dreadfully unsettled times after the Boer War. Will it ever stop for me?"

"Yes, Mona, I am sure it will. We are both young, and we have many years ahead of us. You must keep on working, but you should also relax more—go out with me and your other friends. There are so many exciting places to visit in Paris. We must go to the Chateau Rouge and the Opéra. We must go to the opera—we must!"

"Oh, Olga, I have gone to those places, but not much since Martin died. It will be enjoyable to go again with you. I am happy that we met, for I needed someone like you. We shall be good friends." Mona brightened as she spoke, and I noticed something in her that would become familiar to me: her face, her wonderful face was illumined when she smiled, as if it reflected the light of a lamp.

Mona stayed on at her studio to work, but I needed to leave. She gave me an affectionate little hug when I left, and as I walked slowly along the narrow, bustling streets to my home, the strange emotion that I had felt for my new friend did not leave me. "What a gentle but strong person she is," I thought, "she is not like anyone I have met before. We shall be true friends, I am sure of that. I must stop by Mona's place again—and soon!"

14

Italy

True realism is in spiritual qualities, not in physical attributes.

Lilian Whiting

FOR QUITE SOME TIME Mona had experienced a growing feeling that she needed to go to Italy. Her teachers and even a few of her fellow students had spoken often of the works of art there, particularly those in Rome and Florence, and of the inspiration that seeing and studying the treasured pieces of classic sculpture would bring to her as a student of the art. In addition to this, she had come to a place in her studies where she needed a break from the routine and would welcome the encouraging effect of new vistas.

She had written to her mother about it, and Ada had been encouraging, but she urged Mona to avoid as much of the Italian winter as was possible. "It does not become exceedingly cold in Italy, for the climate is similar to that of our American Southwest. Many, many people from Germany, France, and the United States winter in Italy, but it is damp, and it is chilly. The mountains around the city are white with snow, and the views are always beautiful. In Old Rome there are few sidewalks, and the streets are paved with small stones, so it is muddy when the heavy rains come.

"I know how you love to walk, dear, but at least in the older part of the city, walking would not be a pleasure in the winter. Be sure you are there in the early spring, Mona, for in the springtime Rome is simply bewilderingly beautiful. A number of years ago, when Papi and I were in Rome, we were invited to the salon given by the Queen Mother—the Regina Madre—and we enjoyed the affair very much. Her palace is built of pink marble, and there were many talented people—artists, writers, musicians—at the salon." In a postscript, Ada added, "Tell me, Mona, who will travel with you?"

Mona had not yet made any plans for the trip, and she had no particular traveling companion in mind, now that Martin was gone. While he was alive, they were planning a sojourn to Italy. One day, quite out of the blue, it struck her that her new friend, Olga Currier, might be interested. Olga was near her own age, and she would be a sympathetic companion on a venture that Mona anticipated would be both enjoyable and instructive. She felt sure that Olga would be as serious as she about learning, and Italy was as important for music as it was for sculpture. With this in mind, Mona decided to broach the subject the very next time she saw Olga.

The idea was not new to Olga. Like most foreign art students, she had from time to time thought she would enjoy a trip to Italy and learn from it as well. First, she told Mona, she would have to see if a time away from Paris could be fitted into her musical and financial schedules. "I really need to visit Italy, Mona, and you know I should love to go with you. I promise that I will tell you as soon as possible when I could get away; then we may plan when you and I could both go. Oh, I do hope we can go together—and soon!"

They left Paris in mid-March on a mid-morning train to Rome that gave Mona and Olga an early spring tour of the lovely French country-side. The two had given considerable thought to their adventure and had decided that time and finances would be best served if they went only to Rome and Florence. Limiting the places they visited would make it possible for them to do at least partial justice to the opportunities the two cities had to offer.

They were not entirely ignorant of the history of Italy and its rich tradition of art and music, for they had read about Italy, had heard exciting things about it from friends, and Mona's mother had told her something of her experiences there. Mona and Olga were ready to enjoy its every facet; they were ready to absorb and to learn everything that Rome and Florence had to give. And that, they felt confident, was plenty.

The railway station in Rome was bustling. It seemed that everyone in Europe was arriving and many from America also. Mona and Olga had to satisfy customs officials, and they knew that the crowded station would make the ordeal time-consuming, but it was over sooner than they had anticipated and they were free to be on their way. Not far from the station, they could see the great ruins of the Baths of Diocletian, and as they drove toward their pension, they went along a street named for its four fountains. They would soon realize that Rome was a city of fountains, with water spraying into the air and the pleasant sound of water falling everywhere.

A friend in Paris who had recently been in Rome had directed them to a pension on the Via Sistina, which was situated in a beautiful neighborhood. They were fortunate to arrive just when two other guests were leaving; otherwise there might not have been room for them.

The first evening at the table d'hote dinner, they met two American women—two older ladies from Philadelphia. Marguerite Stanley and Helen Brown were founts of information about the history of Rome and the artists who had lived there and whose works were everywhere to be seen. When they learned that it was Mona's and Olga's first visit to Rome they offered to be of any assistance to make sure the girls did not miss the important sights.

"We are walking a bit this morning," Marguerite said. "Would you two like to go with us? We can show you the famous Spanish steps, and then you may go on your own way."

Olga and Mona accepted eagerly, and the four went out together. They walked along the Via Sistina a short distance to where it joined the Via Gregoriana, then proceeded past the Church of Trinita de Monti, and beyond that they saw a large group of ilex trees that were twisted and bent and clipped in the fashion followed by Italian gardeners. The trees made a pergola that shaded the sunny street leading to the "Hill of Gardens."

They stopped at the garden and all sat upon a stone wall above the Piazza del Populo, from which they could see much of Rome spread out below them, beautifully bathed in the brilliant sunlight. Helen made the scene real: "There," she said, indicating the direction they should look, "you can see St. Peter's Cathedral and the Vatican buildings—a

Rudolf Martinsen shortly before his
untimely death in 1892.

Ada Martinsen in New York, about
the time she took Mona to the
New York Museum of Art to begin
sculpture studies.

Mona's childhood home in Gernsbach,
near Baden-Baden, Germany.

Mona during the Paris years.

John and Mona in the early years of their marriage.

(*Opposite top*) Mona sculpting the
bust of John, ca. 1909, Bancroft,
Nebraska.

(*Opposite bottom*) The Bancroft home,
1909–20.

(*Above*) John made Poet Laureate
of Nebraska, 1921.

(*Above*) Mona during the St. Louis period.

(*Opposite top*) The Branson home.

(*Opposite bottom*) Mona in the prayer garden
at their Branson home, with her sculpture.

(*Opposite top*) Mona in the Branson
studio built for her by John.

(*Opposite bottom*) Nicholas Black Elk
and John, ca. 1945.

(*Above*) Their Skyrim farm home in
Columbia, Missouri, 1974.

Mona and John at Skyrim.

city in themselves—which lie to the right, while way out on the western horizon you can see Janiculum Hill. See, if you look carefully you can make out the outline of the great equestrian statue of Garibaldi. You must go there and see the statue, for it is glorious!"

After a few quiet moments in this spot, they strolled back through the blooming shrubbery to the Square of Trinita de' Monti and down the famous Spanish steps. Great, wide steps they were, and so many of them that Mona soon stopped counting as they went down. Marguerite told them that the Spanish steps were of warm yellow marble. As they made their way down them, she pointed to a small yellow house. "That is where the poet Keats spent his last days. We must walk over to it." As they approached the building, they saw a tablet that declared that in this house the "rare spirit of Keats had outsoared the shadow of our night."

At the bottom of the steps they met vendors of fresh, springtime flowers—men and women selling roses, lilies, daffodils, frisias, anemones, and long sprays of peach and almond blossoms. Although it was still not yet mid-morning, there were many visitors already engaged in the tourists' sport of trying to bargain with the flower vendors.

At the lower end of the steps was the Piazza di Spagna, which gave the stairway its name, and in the Piazza rose another sparkling fountain. Mona and Olga were overcome with the beauty of the whole scene, and they thanked Marguerite and Helen for guiding them to it. The American ladies had a trip planned for the day, and the new friends bid each other good-bye.

Olga had left her guidebook back in their room, so she and Mona walked back to the pension. Inside, they found a number of young Italian women—nicely dressed and with their shining black hair neatly combed—busily cleaning and making beds. Preferring not to hamper progress in such important matters, they left the pension once Olga had retrieved her book. On Helen's recommendation, they decided to make their first trip to Janiculum Hill.

They soon found a young Italian who would take them there in an ancient hack. The Hill rose abruptly from the plain below, and it seemed to be of such great height that they hoped it would give them a view of the city. Indeed it did, although the hill was actually only a few hundred feet high. Mona was impressed by the statue of Garibaldi, and she spent some time examining it from all sides, memorizing its beauty.

She recounted to Olga her experience with the unfinished boot on Maestro Elwell's equestrian statue when five years earlier she had gone to his studio in New York. They both laughed about Mona's first tense meeting with Elwell, from which she had so completely recovered, and Olga stated, "I imagine, Mona, that your boot was almost as good as Garibaldi's left boot up there!" With that loyal comment, Olga took a seat on the ground nearby and waited until Mona joined her.

In the clear air of that crisp, bright day, they could see much of Rome—the old and the new city—spread out in front of them. On one side lay the vast city of Rome, and on the other were the mountains—blue first and then white, where the snow lingered on the peaks. The sky was blue, such a deep blue as the girls had rarely seen, but they would come to know it as Italy's usual spring and summer sky.

The guidebook informed them that in the area below them—known as Trastevere—beautiful villas had once stood, but it was then the home of working people. The local inhabitants claimed, possibly with some right, that they were the direct descendants of the ancient Romans. Mona and Olga were filled with the relaxed happiness both needed as they gazed on the world below them.

After an hour or so on the hilltop, they decided to return to their room at the pension. They would need time to formulate an overall plan for their stay in Italy, and surely their first day in the Eternal City had introduced them to a new and fascinating land. The young Italian driver took them quickly back to the Via Sistina.

Mona's choice of a person to accompany her to Italy proved to be most fortunate indeed. Although Olga was interested in visiting places or events that would further her music studies, she did not need to feign interest in the art that Mona wished to see. Nor did she feel at any moment that Mona lacked interest in the musical events that she desired to attend. Both students believed that exposure to true art added as much to the understanding of music as opening the soul to fine music increased one's appreciation of paintings or pieces of sculpture. A lasting friendship between Mona and Olga grew out of such mutual understanding.

As soon as possible, both girls wanted to visit the Villa Medici, the French Academy of Art, where twenty-four students were supported for several years at the French government's expense. They were students of painting, sculpture, music, and architecture who had shown special abilities in their fields. Although trams were waiting at the Piazza di Spagna near their pension, Mona and Olga walked together along the little Via Condotti, a street that has been called the rue de la Paix of Rome.

Referring often to Olga's guidebook, they climbed the steps to the Convent Church of the Trinita di Monti and walked across the Piazza di Trinita, then along the brow of the hill and the low stone parapet. The view from that point was strikingly beautiful. Silhouetted against the blue Roman sky were the commanding dome of St. Peter's, the domes of other churches, and the new white marble buildings of the Law Courts. In the distance they could see again the statue of Garibaldi. As they walked a little farther on, they entered the gardens of the Villa Medici

The Villa Medici was a handsome building with two towers and an imposing entryway with tall round columns. "What a beautiful spot this is!" Mona exclaimed. "How I do love formal gardens!"

Her guidebook in hand, Olga added, "Yes, and we are looking west, and there is the Janiculum and the Monte Mario, and down there is the Piazza di Spagna and the Piazza del Popolo. Remember? We went there."

They walked in the gardens on narrow paths paved with gravel, and everywhere it was very damp. Olga consulted the guidebook again. "Those bushes are boxwood, and this is called the real Italian idea of a garden. Just look at all the broken sculpture lying along the paths. It is all so weather stained; it must have been put there ages ago."

"And," Mona broke in, "another gushing Roman fountain." Then she added: "I think the students are very lucky to be chosen to attend this school, and the building is certainly lovely, but I would not trade one week of study in Paris with M. Rodin for years and years here! I am in the real world there, and that is where I want to be! I am so glad that I chose study in Paris over college!"

"And I too am glad to be in Paris," Olga agreed.

They had seen enough for one day, and on their way back to the pension, Mona purchased a small bouquet of roses to make their room feel like home.

At table that evening, Marguerite and Helen talked excitedly about the experiences they had had during the day. Experienced travelers as they were, they still found Rome exciting. The two ladies were also interested in hearing about Mona's and Olga's walking tour, and they insisted that the girls absolutely *must* go with them to St. Peter's for the upcoming Gregorian ceremonial, held on a Monday in mid-April.

If, of course, they were fortunate enough to find the right tickets! White tickets for general admission to the church were not hard to come by, but the yellow bigliettos that assured a place in the tribunes where the ladies of the audience sat were indeed scarce. Mona asked if a note of introduction that M. Rodin had given her would be of any help in getting the precious tickets. "Possibly, possibly," Marguerite replied, "I shall ask some of my friends."

Much as she enjoyed their sightseeing in the great city Mona did not forget the real reason she had come to Italy. In every free moment, she had been gorging herself on the great classical and modern art for which Rome was justly famed. She visited the Sistine Chapel many times and stored up in her memory the sublime works of Michelangelo and of Raphael. She and Olga went to St. Peter's, where she gazed with rapture on Michelangelo's *La Pieta*.

For Mona, the works of Michelangelo were the best of all. "When I look at one of his pieces," she told Olga, "an emotion stirs in me that is like no other. It is like a warm merging of my own spirit with that of the Great One, and it leaves me with a feeling of both joy and inspiration."

They made a point of visiting the studios of their fellow American, Franklin Simmons. Mona found in Simmons' *Mother of Moses* not only beauty of form but a representation of maternity that to her was an inspiring achievement. One evening at table, Marguerite told them about the famous salons that Simmons and his musician wife had once hosted in their spacious palace apartments. Mrs. Simmons had died in 1905, and the salons disappeared with her. Mona was disappointed. "How I should have loved to attend one!" she said.

Mona stored in her mind all of the consummate skill and sublime inspiration in the great works they saw for later reference. Just to know that she would remember their greatness made her feel rich beyond any material wealth she had known.

A day or so later, Mona and Olga were slowly returning from a little shopping expedition when Marguerite stopped them near the front door. "I don't know how it could happen," she announced breathlessly, "but I have yellow bigliettos for you two for the festival at St. Peter's. It will be on April 11. Do you wish to go with us?" Almost as one voice, Olga and Mona responded, "Oh, yes, we do want to go!"

"Then come to my room, and I will tell you all about it." They followed Marguerite eagerly.

Until the big day of the ceremonial, Olga and Mona continued their sightseeing—or, perhaps, artseeing. They purchased only a few small things, for neither placed much value in physical mementos, knowing that the stored memories of Rome would remain bright forever. Mona did, however, purchase a small plaster plaque with a sculptured figure on it and the important word "Rome" stamped at its lower end.

At evening table on April 10, the talk was all about the next morning's ceremonial, and Marguerite and Helen, who had attended the event on a previous year, gave full instructions to Mona and Olga. Clothing, they said, must be both dignified and respectful, for it was an important religious event. Although they were not Catholic, neither Mona nor Olga would have considered dressing otherwise. However, both took the instructions in good humor and made sure that Marguerite knew that they would be properly respectful.

Neither girl had brought a long black gown of the kind that Marguerite had suggested they wear, so Mona chose the long-skirted dark suit in which Olga had first seen her, and she wore a high-necked blouse of her favorite color—a rosy pink—under the dark jacket. Olga dressed similarly in a dark blue skirt and matching long coat. Both wore small hats with veils and tight-fitting gloves. As Marguerite requested, they presented a charming and yet respectfully dignified appearance.

They joined Marguerite and Helen promptly at the appointed hour— just before eight o'clock—and the four ladies set out in a waiting carriage that took them toward St. Peter's. When they reached the Piazza Rusticucci, there was already a long line of carriages waiting, so they left the carriage and started on foot. Above the very wide Piazza, the weather had managed one of Italy's best days, with skies of an indescribably deep blue. Maderno's magnificent fountains were vying, each to throw its spray higher than the rest. Mona and Olga were completely captivated by that Roman morning.

St. Peter's was awesome in size. "I have never seen such a tremendous church!" Mona exclaimed. "The courtyard is simply filled with soldiers and people—so many people!"

Olga agreed. "And the soldiers and guards are wearing ever so many different uniforms. I wonder who the people are with blue, green, and purple gowns?"

Marguerite explained, "Yes, the soldiers wear different uniforms so that their group is recognized. I cannot name them all. But the people in brightly colored gowns are seminarists—students in the church."

When they reached the top of the steps leading to the vestibule, they turned to look back upon the throng below—a great, heaving crowd of happy people. How many were they? Helen ventured a guess: "Inside the walls there may be fifty thousand!"

Mona and Olga pulled their veils over their faces, and following closely after Marguerite and Helen, they walked to the sacristy, then through a marble doorway, past Romano's statues of St. Peter and St. Paul, and finally to the tribunes in the transcript. They were shown to their seats, which were only a few rows back from the front.

"Oh, Mona, have you ever seen such a beautiful place?" Olga was quite overcome. Mona agreed: "Yes, it is just—it is just magnificent!"

Other visitors had described the scene in this way: "Rich silk hangings draped the stone walls and columns, those behind the papal throne being embroidered in ecclesiastical designs. The throne was placed in front of the ancient Chair of St. Peter, and between our seats and the throne was a great high altar, ninety-five feet in height, with its bronze canopy and graceful spiral columns of Bernini, double spirals richly gilded."

They found themselves almost surrounded by Swiss guards wearing the uniform that Michelangelo had designed. Then there were the Pope's guards in handsome black and white uniforms with headpieces topped with red plumes. Mona thought the most beautiful costumes of all were those worn by the chamberlains. They were Spanish dresses of dark velvet with velvet capes over one shoulder, lace cuffs and collar, and a large ruff around the neck. Gold cords and chains hung overall.

The view in every direction was so interesting to Mona and Olga that they did not in the least mind the long wait before the ceremony began. First, a detachment of Swiss guards came along the central aisle, now wearing cuirass and iron helmets, and lined up by the papal throne. Mona felt an almost breathless hush over the entire audience, for the people sensed that something was about to happen.

Everyone looked at the eastern door, through which the procession was beginning to enter. The Guardia Nobile came first, then the abbots, the bishops and the archbishops in capes and mitres of white and gold, and then the patriarchs and cardinals, who wore long capes of gold cloth over scarlet robes.

The procession continued with the canons and monsignori in lace and fur, then the prince in attendance on the papal throne, followed by the secret chamberlains bearing tiaras and mitres covered with gold and jewels. The triple crown was borne on a cushion, for it was so covered with brilliant jewels that it was too heavy for the pope to wear. Whispering as much as dignity would allow, Marguerite and Helen kept the girls informed of the proceedings.

A blast from the silver trumpet announced that the Pope was coming, and they soon saw him seated in the ceremonial chair, carried very high by members of the household, who were dressed in scarlet cloth. The Pope was rather pale and seemed uncomfortable; it was said he disliked being carried into the church. He was borne very high and very slowly, and his carriers stopped every once in a while to make sure that everyone would have a chance to see their Pope.

It was all most impressive, and everyone in the huge crowd of onlookers was silent and reverent. The Pope turned from side to side, giving the blessing, and when they reached the apse, he stepped down from the chair and knelt for a time in prayer by St. Peter's chair. During the service that followed, Mona and Olga listened to the Pope's voice as he intoned the Gloria.

Pope Pius X had desired to make Gregorian chants an important part of services, and the chants were echoing beautifully in the great basilica, when suddenly the silver trumpets sounded from Michelangelo's dome overhead. The long line of soldiers lowered their arms resoundingly upon the stone pavement, and the huge audience bowed or knelt. There was nothing but stillness in the vast church. Later the sound of the audience rising was like a great wind in the trees.

The service had much antiphonal singing, and Olga whispered to Mona that she could hear the Holy Father's voice taking part. The choruses were glorious, with some twelve hundred voices joining in song. After his benediction was read by the Cardinal Bishop in a loud voice, the Holy Father once more stepped into the chair and was carried out, once again giving a blessing from right to left.

Helen commented that the Pope appeared much relieved as he left the church when the service was over. Placing one finger on his lip, he signaled the crowd not to make loud applause.

Everyone was quiet as he requested, but after the Pope's chair was carried out of the church on its way back to the Vatican, the crowd burst into talk, friends cheerfully greeting friends. It seemed that every English or American person in Rome was in attendance, and the widespread chattering was accompanied by loud laughter. "What a relief to be free to talk!" Marguerite remarked, expressing Mona's and Olga's feelings after the hours of respectful silence.

All four ladies were glad to be out in the open at last, for the fresh air and the brilliant sunshine were most refreshing after the hours spent inside the church. The ceremonial had been an impressive experience and one that they would remember for a long time, but all agreed that on the next day they would wish to do something very different.

The "something different" Olga and Mona decided upon was a trip to the capitol, for they had not yet visited that most important site. Electric trams encircled the building, but Mona and Olga were advised to drive to the Piazza del Campidoglio at the rear so that they would not need to climb the many, many steps leading up from the street below.

Since they did not climb the steps, they missed the first view of the great statue of Marcus Aurelius, but they did marvel at its beauty later. They walked through the museum, taking in its beautiful bas-reliefs of classic scenes, the great statue of Emperor Hadrian, and the many other fine pieces. As the noontime approached Olga somewhat wearily stated, "I have looked quite enough for one day, Mona. Let's see about something to eat. I'm hungry!"

Mona was a little hungry too, and she readily agreed, adding: "Yes, let's eat. Anyway, if we don't take a breather once in a while, we will only decrease our pleasure. We need to let our experiences settle in our minds. Say, here's a good place to eat!" It was a cozy little Italian eatery, and the food was good—especially the salads. Mona loved salad.

It was dark and rainy throughout the week before Easter, but when the day arrived, it was once more bright and sunny. In the morning they went with friends to the English church on the Via del Bambino, and later they visited the Pincio, which was magnificent with Judas trees, wisteria, roses, and anemones. On Easter Sunday, all Rome was out and about. They were able to see the king and queen driving in their gilded carriage, and they thought that the queen looked quite pretty.

Well-to-do people were drawn up in their carriages, and those less well off were on foot on the walks and beaches. Soon they arrived at the place where the band was playing, surrounded already by a good-natured, cheerful crowd. The people all seemed unusually happy—more light-hearted, Olga said, than the crowds she had seen in Paris. Students from different colleges were playing ball on the meadows. Everywhere was gaiety and joy, for on this day of the feast of feasts, the Italians and their guests were enjoying themselves.

Standing in the midst of that unrestrained and happy crowd, Mona could sense that Olga shared her exhilaration. "What a perfect way to spend a beautiful afternoon! We all need this kind of joy—such a feeling of freedom everywhere! In New York we don't express happiness in quite the simple, free way these Italians do!"

"They certainly do know how to be happy!" Olga agreed.

During their stay in Rome, Mona and Olga had driven only a time or two on the Appian Way, and they had not visited the Catacombs. There was much that they would not have time to visit, for to see Rome entirely would require years, not weeks. If they were to see Florence and all that the City of Flowers had to offer, Mona and Olga knew they would have to leave Rome.

Even though she had been reveling in the great artworks she had been seeing, Mona was beginning to feel the need to finish her own neglected pieces that she hoped to exhibit at the salon in Paris. Olga too could not avoid thinking of all she should, or would, be doing were she back at her studies. But they did want to see Florence.

They collected their belongings, and as they did so, they were glad that they had brought relatively little with them and had not purchased many souvenirs in Rome. They sent their larger bags on ahead of them so that they might stop over a few hours or a day in the small towns between Rome and Florence. Marguerite and Helen had enlarged upon the quaint charm of those villages, and their descriptions had appealed to the girls.

After paying for their stay in the pension and tipping its various employees, Mona and Olga took a cab to the railway station, a place that had seemed so strange when they first arrived but that now presented a friendly, almost familiar appearance. The train was nearly on time, and when they were seated in its second-class section, both Mona and Olga felt a small thrill of excitement: they were on the way once more.

Their train arrived in Florence when it was nearly dark, and since they had not made a reservation at a pension, they asked a cab driver to take them to the nearest hostelry. As he drove them along, they were able to see, now and then, the shining river and bridges, and they could make out a dark line of mountains beyond.

The pension to which the driver took them was not particularly inviting, but it was right on the Arno River, and when they were taken to their room, they were pleased that its windows opened on that stream. Hungry and tired after their journey, they ate lightly and went immediately to bed. The sound of the Arno's rushing waters, fed by springs in the neighboring hills, made sleep come easily

In the morning they were able to see what a beautiful city was Florence. As they looked out the windows, they could see the city that Elizabeth Barrett Browning loved, with its many churches and palaces. In front of them, they could see past the heights of San Miniato to the many hills shining so beautifully under the deep blue Italian sky. They had planned the evening before that they would on the next day look for a more satisfactory pension, but when morning came, neither Mona nor Olga wished to waste time looking for one.

Confident that their guidebook would serve them well, they set out on foot, wandering through the Loggia del Lanzi, with its many statues, then across the Piazza della Signoria and by the Struzzi Palace. The palace was a relic of the middle ages and had no doubt been an impregnable fortress when war was a chief occupation of the people of Florence.

From there they went to Thomas Cook's office to check for any mail that might have reached them. They were rewarded with letters from home, and Ada's letter was full of her eagerness to hear about Italy. On the same street as Cook's office were many cafés, souvenir shops, and confectioners' shops that brightened the dark presence of the old Struzzi palace.

It seemed to Mona and Olga that all America had traveled from Rome to Florence, and Olga jokingly commented that "it would be just downright exciting to see some people of Florence once in a while, or even some real Romans!" Mona recalled Marguerite's statement that "Romans never travel. Like Parisians, they find their own surroundings quite satisfactory." It was not so for Americans.

Before many days had passed, they did find a better pension, and they were delighted to discover that the food served there was excellent: strawberries with cream, asparagus, and even fresh sweet peas! Mona and Olga appreciated the change, for they had grown rather tired of artichokes and fennel.

In spite of the fresh fruit and vegetables, they feared that they would soon become tired of the other guests at the evening table d'hote, especially one elderly gentleman who managed to be something of a pest, particularly to Olga. He spoke only Italian, which neither Mona nor Olga had studied, and upon the slightest provocation he would indulge in a long, fast flow of conversation that they could only partly understand.

The gentleman's otherwise annoying interest in Olga had one advantage; he saw to it that the choice dishes were passed to her and Mona. The preponderance of women over men in the pension was surprising, and they were mainly widows with young daughters, although some were wives with husbands at home. The few husbands who were traveling with their families gave at times the impression of being bored. Bored in Florence, Italy?

Both girls had a love for fine poetry, and they decided that while in

Florence they must see the grave of Elizabeth Barrett Browning. They set out to find it, having only the slightest idea of where the Protestant cemetery was located. Fortunately, thanks to their guidebook and repeated questioning, they found the cemetery lying just outside the Porta Piuti. The cemetery was once enclosed by walls, which had been removed, and it stood in the open in the middle of a dusty highway, with noisy trams loaded with tourists passing over it. When they got inside the enclosure where Elizabeth's grave was located, the scene changed; there were trees and shrubbery and roses blooming.

They stopped for a brief rest in the shade of a tree and then walked on to find the poet's grave. A branch of a cedar tree leaned over the grave, and there were many roses all about. As Mona and Olga stood beneath the tree, a bird sang from an overhead branch, and the whole scene made them realize how suitable it was for Elizabeth Barrett to rest there, in the Italy she loved, instead of with her husband in a vast abbey in England.

At the time of Mona's and Olga's visit, Italy was still a young country, with less than forty years as a united nation. When one spoke of Rome or of Florence, so different from each other, one spoke of separate entities, not of towns that were part of a united country.

Just as the cities differed, so did their inhabitants. The society of Florence was characterized by music, art, philosophic culture, and learning in all fields of research. Florence, like Rome, could not be experienced in full in only a few weeks, but Mona and Olga could not arrange for more time. They would do their best to assimilate as much as possible of the beauty and culture of Florence before they had to return to Paris and their studies.

Mona and Olga started out to view the city. They walked across the Arno by means of the Ponte Vecchio, a passageway that linked galleries on each side and that was lined with paintings of royal personages from long ago. Half-way across the passage there were large windows in the bridge. After consulting their guidebook, Mona exclaimed, "Look, Olga! Those are the heights of San Miniato we see there on one side, and next to them the Arno River is winding along. How beautiful it is!"

After crossing the bridge they climbed a stairway to the salons of the Pitti Palace. Here Mona recognized many pieces of art that were familiar to her from photographs and engravings: Raphael, Del Sarto, Murillo, and at last Fra Bartolommeo's *Marriage of St. Catherine of Siena.*

As Mona gazed intently at the beautiful composition, drawing, and relief of the work, she was quite shocked to hear the adjective used to describe the work by a fellow viewer: "Rather *nice*, is it not?" The speaker was not an American, as she at first feared it might be; it was a young British woman.

Mona's thoughts turned increasingly to the work she needed to do on her next pieces of sculpture, which she hoped to have accepted for the salon. Even though the two young women were having a good time in Italy, both Mona and Olga found that they were experiencing a nervous eagerness to get back to their work in Paris. They decided to return to that city as soon as possible.

When they told their hostess at the pension that they would be leaving, she warmly and volubly wished them the very best of luck on their return to their studies. One of the guests at the pension had at one time been a member of the chorus in an opera company, and she and Olga had become rather good friends because of their mutual interests. They exchanged addresses and agreed to write each other.

The packing all done, the two young ladies took a cab to the railway station, and even before mid-morning, the area was all a-bustle with cabs arriving and departing and travelers eager to check luggage, purchase tickets, and depart for their various destinations. Mona and Olga were able to arrange for their larger pieces of luggage to go directly to Paris, and without much trouble they found the train that would take them there.

The return trip was quite unlike the earlier one that had brought them to Italy. Both girls were feeling the need to return to their studies in earnest, and they felt none of the eager expectancy that came naturally when they had embarked upon their visit to Italy.

Early spring in the Rhone Valley had been so vibrantly lovely, and now it was well into the summer. As they looked out the windows Olga pointed out many equally beautiful, warm-season views of the Rhone Valley as their train made its way back to Paris.

Once back in the great city Olga and Mona gathered their belongings and hired a cab that first took Olga to her lodging and then deposited

Mona at 15, rue des Bourgeois. The little apartment showed neglect from the preceding weeks.

"No matter," Mona thought, "a bit of dusting and some re-arranging here and there, and it will be home again!" She set herself directly to that task, and soon all was in order. Mona was happy to be home, and her thoughts were on the next morning, when she would see Rodin and return to her studio and her work.

There was not much in the way of food in the apartment, so it was necessary for Mona to go out and purchase something for her supper. She found just the right loaf of bread at one shop, then some cheese at another, a few pieces of fruit, and finally eggs for next day's lunch.

Wine might have completed a tasty meal, but Mona had a glass of cool water to accompany her light meal of cheese and fruit. She hoped that an early bedtime would assure a bright and early morrow. Getting back to serious work was uppermost in her thoughts.

15

The Grand Salon, Paris

It was just becoming light outside when Mona set out for her studio on the Montparnasse. Shopkeepers were busily getting ready for the day, and men in lumbering wagons were making morning deliveries. A familiar flower lady was arranging her fragrant wares, and Mona chose a small bouquet to brighten her little studio.

When she reached her building and walked up to her skylighted workplace, she was relieved to find that the partially completed statue that she intended to show at the salon as well as some other, smaller pieces were moist under their cloth coverings. An artist friend had agreed to care for the sculptures during her absence, and he had most faithfully kept his promise.

Mona removed the damp cloth from the life-sized figure "Vierge," her most important effort at the time, and stood back from it, viewing it from various angles. That is all she did for a long time, for a new feeling had come over her. She was seeing details and the underlying formation of the sculpture more fully, more deeply, than she had before.

Wondering how this could be, she came finally to the conclusion that this larger, clearer way of viewing was the result of her experience in Italy. For weeks she had feasted on the greatest of past sculpture, and she had absorbed some of that greatness. It was like an unexpected gift, this upsweep of inspiration, and the very thought of it ran warmly through her very being. Mona eagerly set to work.

As she modeled and smoothed the clay, she did not forget Rodin's admonition that a piece of sculpture should have "thickness" and that from the very beginning the sculptor should keep in mind the underlying bones, muscles, and ligaments of the represented figure. "Vierge" gained greatly from Mona's careful work during the succeeding weeks, and finally the sculptress felt that she had done all that she could with that young lady. She sought the opinion of her master, whose guidance had been so helpful during the creation of the piece. Rodin agreed that "Vierge" was now ready for submission to the jury of the salon.

Mona had also completed two busts, already cast in plaster: the commissioned heads of a Cuban sugar planter and of a Swiss lady who was related to Martin Darmstadt, the deceased friend of Mona's. She planned to submit these two busts to the jury along with the larger piece.

The casting of "Vierge" would be a much larger undertaking than that of the busts, for the two halves of the plaster cast would be large and heavy and not manageable for one person. She knew that many of her fellow students would hire professional persons to do the casting of larger works, but Mona wanted to do the work herself, so far as that was possible. She asked for help, and two of the more experienced students among her friends—two strong young men—volunteered to assist.

After oiling the entire surface of the sculpture, Mona carefully stuck flat pieces of metal into the middle of all sides of the sculpture, forming a wall several inches in height that would prevent the plaster from forming into a single mold. They would thus be able to separate the halves of the mold.

Now that the oiling of the piece was done, and with the metal "wall" in place, they placed plaster that had been mixed with water to form a heavy paste over the entire sculpture, and additional applications followed until the resulting mold was thick enough to be strong. Because of the size and length of the mold, during the plastering process armatures were placed vertically along the mold to give it the necessary rigidity.

After the plaster had hardened sufficiently, which took several days, the two parts of the mold were carefully separated and placed on a rack with the inner sides up. When the mold was sufficiently dry for her work, Mona painstakingly cleaned the reverse, outside-in impressions, correcting any slight damage or imperfections, then carefully applied a coating of oil to the entire inner surface of the molds.

The "Vierge" was life-sized, so a brace was necessary to give the plaster figure stability. The brace was carefully established vertically down the middle so that it would not show in the final figure, and the two halves of the mold, edges carefully oiled, were placed together in their original upright position, secured, and then braced from three sides. Through a hole in the top of the mold they poured some plaster that had been mixed into a thinner paste until the mold was entirely filled and they were sure that no air pockets existed.

Later, when this plaster had become firm and fairly dry, they carefully removed the two halves of the mold. One can only imagine the tense excitement that prevailed at this juncture in the casting process, for if it proved unsuccessful, many months of work would be destroyed in a moment. The eager sculptress controlled herself well, but she was almost breathless while the mold was being removed.

Good fortune and careful work had brought success. Gone was the somber gray clay figure; the "Vierge" now stood erect and beautiful before them in her pristine white plaster body. So well had Mona done her job in repairing small imperfections in the mold that there were few spots that needed to be smoothed in the final plaster version.

It was a time for celebration, and Mona invited her two helpful friends to wine and dinner at a nearby café. The two young men drank the good wine naturally, but Mona had to exercise restraint. Wine always made her feel shaky in the knees!

It was not easy to be invited to exhibit at the Salon in Paris. The Salon Jury was generally thought of as something of an ogre, whose extremely challenging qualifying standards all too few young artists were able to overcome. With this well in mind, Mona had worked toward excellence in both subject and modeling as she created the pieces she wished to exhibit.

She had sought and profited well from Rodin's instruction and suggestions. When the final judgments of the jury were made public, Mona was successful, almost beyond her most optimistic expectations. She was accepted! *Vierge* and the head of a Cuban sugar planter were chosen to be exhibited at the Salon!

The catalog of the Société National des Beaux-Arts de 1907 au Grand Palais (14avril–30juin) contained the following under sculpture:

Mlle Mona MARTINSEN (née at New York, habitant 15, rue bourgeois Paris XV no 2020: Vierge (platre)

no 2021: Portrait d'homme (platre)

Musée Rodin in the Hotel Biron in Paris also has this information in its archives.

Mona's mother Adah (she had recently added the "h" to her first name) and brother Ottocar came to Paris to attend the exhibition and to rejoice with Mona over her success. Together the three toured the Grand Palais and spent a few evenings at dinner in some of the places familiar to Adah. Although her mother and brother entered into the festivities, Mona could not escape the feeling that all was not well in New York. When Adah told her daughter after only a few days in Paris that they must leave, she also intimated that there were financial problems at home in New York.

Adah had recently made a bad investment with the money left to her by Rudolf. During this period the automobile was being developed in America, and in connection with it, there were many individual inventions striving for recognition. One invention in particular had caught Adah's attention through its promoters, and she became very much caught up in its development. It was an automobile wheel that did more than merely support and carry the body of the auto by turning on an axle and it was popularly called "a wheel within a wheel." The device appears to have attracted considerable interest from automobile fanciers of the time and from inventors in several countries.

Adah was taken for a drive in a vehicle equipped with four of those remarkable wheels, and she was impressed with the comfort they provided. She was surprised and quite amazed that the vehicle could be driven over a substantial bump in the road, or even over a curb, with the occupants of the vehicle barely aware of the occurrence.

The object of the invention was to provide a resilient wheel for motor vehicles that would have the advantage of a pneumatic tire's comfort without the tire's disadvantage of wear and punctures. The device included an outer wheel and an inner wheel with resilient springs that would absorb the jolts received from the unevenness of the road. The "wheel" would not require an expensive pneumatic tire; it would need only a rubber pad around its perimeter.

Adah Martinsen was won over by the demonstration, and she listened to the promoters, who urged her to invest in the "Wheel" and convinced her that it would be successful. Adah's financial counselors were of a different opinion, and they tried to discourage her from risking her financial security by participating in the promotion of such an innovative device.

"It may very well be a good invention, Mrs. Martinsen, but that alone is not necessarily enough to make it successful. We have witnessed a number of new designs that failed in spite of the fact that they might well have been desirable. In your case, one of the Wheel's advantages may well lead to its downfall.

"The wheel-within-a-wheel requires much less rubber than a conventional pneumatic tire, and the rubber interests will kill it. You may be sure of that! We do not want to see you go out on a limb to back this product, for, Mrs. Martinsen, you would be doing just that: you would be taking too big a chance. We fear that you could lose the estate left you by Mr. Martinsen, which is quite adequate to keep you in comfort the remainder of your life."

Adah listened to her advisers but not well enough. She was entirely convinced that the "Wheel" was a valuable innovation and would be successful, and the promoters built upon her enthusiasm by encouraging her not to lose the great opportunity that the invention represented. She could, they urged, easily double or triple her investment. Adah thought about what she could do with all that income! Perhaps she also was tempted to think she had absorbed some of Rudolf Martinsen's business ability.

Ottocar was then just getting started in business, and in spite of his youth, he was cautious, and he tended to think as his mother's advisers did. He agreed with his mother that the "Wheel" was remarkable, but he was concerned that it would not be a wise investment for her. As firmly as he could, he told her just that, but Adah had become too convinced about the merits of the invention to listen to warnings.

In the end those warnings proved correct. Adah, along with the other promoters, lost her entire investment. She was left with a small portion of the Martinsen fortune, and—bravely—she set her thinking to what must be done in the future.

16

The Little Book that Went to Paris

I want to build true love an altar ere I die . . .
"The Last Altar"

MONA MARTINSEN HAD reached a highly respected and difficult-to-achieve level of recognition in her profession, and Rodin told her that only the failure to work could prevent her from achieving great success as a sculptor. Orders for portraits were coming in, and she was busy for long hours in her studio on the Montparnasse, immersed in the work she loved.

But, hovering still above the happiness that these successes brought to her and weaving itself in and out of her consciousness, was the still-painful tragedy of her lost love, Martin Darmstadt. Now the additional problem of the lost family fortune added to the thoughts that weighed heavily upon her.

From time to time she recalled a letter she had received earlier in the year from her mother. At a reception held in the home of one of her New York friends, Adah had met a young writer from the most unlikely state of Nebraska. He had written poetry that was considered "very frank" at the time but was of such power and spiritual insight that Amy Lowell and other poetry enthusiasts in New York had become interested in him.

At the reception, Adah was entranced. John Neihardt's athletic and manly young presence and his dynamic recitation of the poems were unlike anything Adah had experienced before, and she had been so moved that she wrote to Mona about the young poet.

"I have met such an interesting young poet from the West today. He is small, Mona, with a great shock of blond hair that reminds me of our Slavic dreamers. His home is near Omaha, a very lonely place for a man of literary aspirations, I should judge."

"A young poet, lonely in Omaha," Mona mused. Then a thought that she had been suppressing came to her. "Sometimes it seems that I am a bit lonely too."

It is not surprising that Mona was so intensely involved with her exhibition at the Grand Salon and with her own personal problems that she soon forgot all about the young poet and his lonely life in far-away Omaha.

Late in December 1907 Mona was once more reminded of the poet, for she received another letter from her mother about him: "Do you remember the young poet I wrote you about? John Neihardt, from Nebraska? I am sending you a volume of his poems. He admires your work very much, dear. I told him about you when I met him in New York."

Just published, the book was entitled *A Bundle of Myrrh*, and Mona was enthralled by its unusual contents. She was also surprised, for she found in the poetry of that far-away young man a deeply moving expression of many of her own thoughts and yearnings.

In her heart she felt even more than that. Mona was overwhelmed with the growing realization that a great, yet unexpressed need in herself had been met and that she had become aware of someone she very much wanted to know.

What young woman—and especially a serious young artist—would not be charmed by these words from "The Sound My Spirit Calls You"?

> I would I knew some slow, soft sound to call you,
> Some slow, soft syllable which should linger on the lip
> As loath to pass because of its own sweetness

or

> It would be as a rose leaf becoming vocal,
> As a honeycomb talking of sweetness,
> And it would pass slowly and gloriously as a sunset passes,
> Gloriously and lingeringly it would die away,
> To be like fragrance remembered!

She recognized certain basic life instincts within herself as she read—
at first she almost peeked at—the poem "If This Be Sin":

> Can this be sin?
> This ecstacy of arms and eyes and lips,
> This toying with incomparable hair?
> (I close my dazzled eyes, you are so fair!)
> This answer of caress to fond caress,
> This exquisite maternal tenderness?
> How could so much of beauty enter in,
> If this be sin?

and then . . .

> Although we be two sinners burned with bliss,
> Kiss me again, that warm, round woman's kiss!
> Close up the gates of gold! I go not in—
> If this be sin.

On a spiritual level, urgent emotional needs of the young sculptress
were once more answered in this stanza from "The Last Altar":

> And I have left mine ancient fanes to crumble,
> And I have hurled my false gods from the sky;
> I wish to grasp the joy of being humble,
> To build great love an altar ere I die.

She had seen among many of the art students conduct decried by the
poet:

> O many a night has seen my riot candles
> And heard the drunken revel of my feast,
> Till Dawn walked up the blue with burning sandals
> And made me curse the east!
>
> For my faith was the faith of dusk and riot,
> The faith of fevered blood and selfish lust;
> Until I learned that love is cool and quiet
> And not akin to dust.

Mona had witnessed something of a riotous way of life, although she had not been a participant, and she had grown to detest it. She too wanted "to build great love an altar ere I die," and she realized that never before had she felt so truly close to another person as she did to the young poet she had never met.

Mona told her good friend Olga about the letter from her mother and showed her the book of poems. Together they read them all, and Olga soon was as enchanted as Mona with the words of the young Nebraskan. They shared the book with others, and the little volume was passed around among many of the art students in Paris. One evening at the Black Cat Café, they had gone up with some of the young people to a higher floor in the café, and Mona had read a few of the lyrics to her friends.

Something happened in the group when she read the youthfully impassioned "Let Me Live Out My Years."

> Let me live out my years in heat of blood!
> Let me die drunken with the dreamer's wine!
> Let me not see this soul-house built of mud
> Go toppling to the dust—a vacant shrine!
>
> Let me go quickly as a candle light
> Snuffed out just at the heyday of its glow!
> Give me high noon—and let it then be night!
> Thus would I go.
>
> And grant me when I face the Grisly Thing,
> One haughty cry to pierce the gray Perhaps!
> Let me be as a tune-swept fiddlestring
> That feels the Master Melody—and snaps!

The words that Mona spoke with considerable feeling were those of a young person's prayer, and as she read, she spoke directly to her youthful audience, touching their hearts. One young man in particular—an Italian student of painting—was so struck by the poem that he came up to Mona, took the book from her hands, and, with accent and passion both highly Italian, declaimed the last two lines:

Let me be as a tune-swept fiddlestring
That feels the Master Melody—and snaps!

Years later, *Modigliani*, a biography of the Italian painter, revealed that he was in Paris at the time when Mona studied there, and the book's *New York Times* advertisement quoted those same two lines in this manner: "I want to be a tune-swept fiddlestring that feels the Master Melody and snaps—Modigliani." Apparently Modigliani had come to think of the young American's passionate outpouring as his own, but when queried by the publisher, William Morrow and Company, about the matter, his biographer was unable to explain how the famed painter came to be credited with the lines. That he first heard the poem from Mona would explain the mystery. However that may be, after that stirring evening in the Paris café, she had no little trouble keeping track of the "Bundle"; so many of her friends and acquaintants wished to read the poetry.

As for Mona, she found herself opening the pages of *A Bundle of Myrrh* very often, and as the days passed, her thoughts turned frequently to the young man living in a small town in America whose heart and soul seemed so akin to her own. She talked to her friends, and especially to Olga, about the feelings that were becoming so much a part of her waking thoughts. The advice received from all was much the same: "Write to him and tell him what you think about his poetry. He will be happy to hear from you."

One day Mona did just that. She sat at her desk and spoke earnestly to the man she had never met. She wrote about art and life, and she wrote much about his poems and what they meant to her. She closed her letter with the simple expression that she would like to hear from him, and she signed: "Sincerely, Mona Martinsen."

Mona had never done anything even remotely like this before, and it was not easy for her actually to post the letter, but she did so. She walked to the post office in her department of the Latin Quarter of Paris and purchased the correct postage for her letter. Once more she examined the envelope she had carefully addressed:

Mr. John G. Neihardt
Author of "A Bundle of Myrrh"
c/o Outing Publishing Company,

New York, New York, USA
Please Forward

Satisfied that the address was correct, Mona posted her letter. As she did so, she softly breathed these words: "Dear God, let him not be married!"

2

An American Pioneer Family

17

John Gneisenau Neihardt

IN EARLY OCTOBER OF 1880 a battered covered wagon pulled by a rather unlikely team—a big, buff-colored Missouri mule and a slightly shorter but heavily muscled black mare—rattled its way along a dirt road just west of Coal City, Indiana, in the United States of America.

Lured by the thought of land free for the taking, settlers had driven thousands of such wagons west during the preceding years to Kansas, Oklahoma, or some other western territory to find a new life. This particular wagon was not heading as far as the others had, and it would not have attracted much attention from other travelers.

However, for our story the wagon was of considerable importance, for it carried young Nicholas Nathan Neihart, his wife, Alice, and their two daughters, Lulu and Grace. They had left the Neihart family farm near Coal City, where Nicholas had grown up with his parents and sixteen older siblings, to travel west, and their immediate hope was that they might get settled in a new home in Illinois before winter set in.

They had learned of a farm on the road from Taylorville, three miles west of Sharpsburg, that was for rent and that might provide a home for their family and the chance to earn a living. There was no future for Nickolas on the family land near Coal City; there were just too many young Neiharts for one farm, and most of the boys realized this and went their separate ways.

The Neiharts had become acquainted with the Cullers after the latter family moved from Ohio to Indiana, and Nickolas was quite smitten with young and vivacious Alice May Culler. She too found the vigorous young Nickolas attractive, and the two were married in 1876—the year of the Custer Massacre out in Montana—in Bowling Green, Indiana. He was twenty-three, and she just seventeen.

Nick, as he was familiarly known, was a sturdy fellow. He was not tall, being somewhat under medium height but "by the cut of his jib," as a local saying went, it was obvious that he was strong. His shoulders were unusually broad, and his chest deep, and as he held the reins of his well-kept team lightly in his right hand, something in the way he sat—all casual and easy—on the spring seat gave the impression that he could move quickly, if he were of a mind to do so. He was dressed in the denim overalls of a farmer, for that was his occupation, but something about the far-away look in his blue eyes seemed to suggest he was not entirely dedicated to that calling.

Alice was small and blond, and one would find it quite easy to call her pretty. Just twenty-one years old, she was trim and neat, wearing a homemade dress of an inexpensive but nicely flowered cotton material that matched the bonnet on her head.

Alice had just returned from the rear of the wagon, where under a cover of heavy canvas stretched over wooden bows fastened to the sides of the wagon, her two little girls were sleeping. In the wagon, the young couple had packed all their worldly belongings, and that cramped space would serve as their home while they traveled. All four slept in the wagon, but cooking and other homemaking activities were done outside, with little regard for weather conditions.

As they made their way along a dusty road that wound slowly past farms and through fields and wooded areas, Alice's thoughts turned to her pioneering parents, George Washington Culler and Catharine Hott Culler. "How different," she said to Nick, "was Ma's and Pa's trip from ours. They traveled by covered wagon just like us, but we at least have a road to follow. Ma and Pa had to make their way across open prairie to claim their land in Kansas. And when they found it, it was just empty land—nothing else."

"And just think of all the work they had ahead of them to make a home out of nothing. I tell you, Alice, I don't envy them a bit," Nick commented, hoping to bring Alice down off of what he saw as a rosy cloud.

"But it was their land, their own wonderful land! Oh, Nick can you just imagine how exciting that was for them? Just think! They had to leave everything—everyone—behind, and they did not even know exactly where they were going.

"They could not have known what it would be like out there in that land where only Indians lived, and they just had to have been afraid they might not make it. But the land! Oh, it must have been exciting when they found a piece of land they wanted and knew they could actually have it!"

Nick managed a somewhat gruff "Yeah, I guess so." Alice saw he did not wish to talk, even about anything as wonderful as land that was there for the taking. She kept on thinking about the land in Stockton County, Kansas, where her Ma and Pa were homesteading, and she wished—oh, she wished—to be there with them.

As they drove, Alice checked regularly to make sure the two girls were safe and comfortable. This time she found three-year-old Lulu playing with her beloved rag doll, while curly haired Grace, not yet two, was sleeping soundly, lulled by the steady, monotonous bouncing and rattling of the wagon on the dirt road. Satisfied that all was well, Alice cautioned Lulu to "be a good girl," then returned to the front of the wagon.

As she mounted the seat beside her husband—a bit carefully for one so young—one might have suspected that another child was on the way. Nick glanced at Alice as she slid in beside him, but he did not speak, and his wife's expression assured him there was no need to do so. Those who knew Nick well called him "a taciturn cuss," for he never had much to say. In this respect, the two were not well matched, for Alice was communicative. She seemed always to have something to say or a story to tell, and often she brightened sullen silence with a joke or a teasing comment.

They were both descendants of German immigrants. Three Neihart brothers had immigrated to the United States in 1737 from Zweibruecken, in the Palatinate of Germany—Frederick, George, and Michael. Fourteen Neiharts later fought with the colonial armies during the American Revolution, and Nick's great-grandfather, Christopher, a soldier in Washington's army, was killed in the Battle of Long Island.

Nick's father was a quiet man with china-blue eyes. He was soft-spoken, never hasty, and he was known for his kindness and good judgment. Nick's mother was a Roxbury, born in Stüttgart, Germany, whose family came to America not long after the Revolutionary War. Mrs. Neihart was widely known as a "character," as a "general" who ran things in her own way, and she was stockily and powerfully built, having exhaustless energy. Seventeen children were born to her, mostly boys, and she let it be known that she did not particularly like girls.

A revealing story is told about this woman who lived into her eighties and was reputedly never sick a day in her life. It seems that she heard, after one child was born, that she was not expected to be at an especially important quilting bee to be held on the following day. She would show those busybodies! Undaunted, Grandmother Neihart was there, and so was the baby!

Alice's family, the Cullers, had also come from Germany, but Alice was only part German. Her mother, Catharine Hott, was the daughter of Irish immigrants. Alice had a bright personality—and a temper, which upon occasion could be quite challenging. For the most part, however, she was of a happy disposition, and her sense of humor served to brighten many an otherwise dull day.

Such was the state of formal education in their home area of Indiana that both Nick and Alice had taught in backwoods schools, in spite of the fact that neither of them had more than a fifth or sixth grade education. With careful frugality, they had saved enough from the small income they had earned from these and other efforts to buy their team and a good used wagon from a neighbor and have some money left over to make their search for a new home possible.

Nick had been hesitant about the unlikely team. "I never worked a mule and a horse together, and they sure do look funny!"

"Nick, they're a good team; they work good together, and as long as I've had him, Jack ain't never balked on me," the neighbor assured him. "Then, too, Jack really likes Maude. You won't have no trouble with fighting, like you'd be almost sure to have with two geldings or two mares. And, Nick, you know I'd have to charge a lot more for a matched team. Come spring plowing time, Nick, when you have the reins looped over your back and you have to hang onto those plow handles with both hands, you will be glad that they know their 'gees' and 'haws.' Yeah, Jack and Maude are a really good team!"

So far, Nick had not been sorry he bought the pair. They did pull well together, and they didn't fuss at each other. Teaching them to turn right when he said "gee" and left when he called out "haw" for plowing would wait for the springtime.

Everything Nick and Alice possessed—covered wagon, cooking utensils, clothing and bedding—was common and ordinary and suitable only for the most basic needs, and yet it represented for Alice and possibly also for Nick much more than that. Dusty and commonplace as it all was, their covered wagon was the means to achieve a goal; it held their most fervent young hopes for a home and a good life. As they drove along on that bright, blue-and-gold October day, hope and fear intermingled, for they could not know what chance might bring in the days ahead. They could only hope.

Nick calculated their journey from Coal City to Sharpsburg, Illinois, to be in the neighborhood of one hundred fifty miles and that it would take a week or ten days to accomplish. Twenty miles a day was considered quite good for a heavily loaded wagon with a two-horse team, and on this, the first day of their journey, they decided to make camp early. Nick stopped at a farm near the Illinois border, where they had the good fortune to find a friendly owner who said they might camp on his property and directed them to a wooded site by a small creek.

Nick had fastened water casks to each side of the wagon, and a rack on each side provided limited space for hay and feed for the horses. After Nick had unhitched Jack and Maude, he tied them on one side of the wagon and gave them each some hay. Then he helped his wife make a small fire. Alice soon set about preparing a meal for the family, all the time keeping a watchful eye on the two little girls.

Lulu and Grace, released from the confinement of the wagon, laughed and squealed happily as they played among the trees. The older sister ran like a little gazelle over the grassy ground, but toddler Grace found it not so easy to keep up. Tumbling often as she ran, she quickly got to her feet without any complaint. It was all great fun, and they had much playing to do before it was time for bed. After they had eaten their supper—good fried potatoes and some eggs the farmer's wife gave them—four weary people prepared for bed. Mother Alice was grateful for the water in the small creek, which made it easy for her family to "wash up" before they retired. That was important to her.

On the eighth day of their journey they passed by Taylorville, Illinois, and Nick began to inquire about the location of the farm he hoped to rent. It was a few miles farther west, he was told, so he and Alice decided to camp just outside of Taylorville and proceed on the next day to their new home. They had been most fortunate on the trip that each afternoon or early evening they reached a farm where they were allowed—even invited—to camp for the night, and each morning before they left the campsite, they showed their appreciation by leaving the spot clean and undamaged. Nick carefully covered the ashes where they had cooked, and Alice saw to it that no trash was left.

The land in that part of Illinois was flat as far as the eye could see, and the crops, which had not yet been harvested, vouched for its fertility and gave promise of a good yield. Nick was unusually excited. "Alice, I am sure I can make a go of it here! This is real farming land—quite a bit better than we had in Coal City! Oh, Alice, I can hardly wait to find our farm!" Alice responded with enthusiasm equal to her happiness that Nick was pleased. She shared his appreciation of the land and the soil, but she thought also of what their new home might be like. "I do hope the house is a good one, Nick. Oh, I do hope it will be what we need!"

It was around mid-day when they found the farm, and Nick drove their tired team down the overgrown but still visible road that led to the homesite. Nick and Alice got down from the wagon seat, and with the two little girls between them they stood at the dilapidated front gate and looked at their new home.

To one side there was a small barn in only partial disrepair and a couple of other smaller outbuildings. Miscellaneous trash of all sorts lay about between the buildings, and weeds hid what they suspected was more trash left by former occupants. If the promised farming equipment was there, it was hidden by eight- or ten-foot weeds. One encouraging thought struck Nick: if the height of those weeds was any clue, the soil was fertile enough!

Up from the barn was a very small house—or should it really be called a cabin? Or perhaps only a shack? Was this their new home? It was small and dingy, and much in need of paint. When Nick tried the unlocked door and they went inside, Alice gasped in disappointment.

The one room of the cabin was fairly large, but it was only partially finished, and the floor—there was no floor; it was just plain dirt! There were four grimy windows, and some of the panes were broken. It was obvious that the place had been empty for some time, and Alice thought that even when it was lived in, its occupants had been people without pride or hope. Overwhelmingly disappointed at first, then angry, Alice tried to regain some measure of composure. She could see what shock and disappointment her husband was feeling.

"Nick, oh Nick! At least it will give us a roof over our heads! But there is a lot of work to do! First of all we must do something to the floor! When winter comes, we can't possibly keep warm without a floor! Water will come in, and it will be muddy and cold!"

The matter of a floor was soon settled. After removing the small, rusty cookstove that stood at one end of the room, Nick found some old hay in the barn and put a layer all over the dirt in the room, pressing it down to make it level and as flat as possible. Then, at Alice's request, he removed the canvas from the wagon. It was dirty, but it would serve the purpose she had in mind.

Spreading the canvas on the ground outside the house, Alice swept and cleaned it as best she could. She had noticed that in the yard around the house were a number of black walnut trees, and fortunately the squirrels had left a few of the unhulled nuts on the trees and lying about the yard. With the help of the little girls, who thought it was all great fun, they gathered walnuts.

Alice removed the still damp hulls and dobbed the canvas all over with their staining juice, making an attractive overall design that resembled a real carpet. Looking at her hands Alice saw that they were stained quite black from the walnuts. Small matter—the stain would wash and wear away in a few days! When the walnut-stained figures on the canvas were quite dry, they carried the fine new rug into the house and carefully placed it over the foundation of hay. Nick cut small stakes from lower limbs on a nearby tree and sharpened them so that they could be driven through the canvas and into the dry ground. That would hold their rug in place.

With nervous intensity, Alice set about washing the windows. More than once of late she had felt a movement inside her—a little kick which warned her that the time was drawing near when there would be a third child to care for. Somehow she had to make this dreary little shack into a home for her family. She had used the word "shack" to herself. Alice hated even to think what that word meant, but her practical nature forgave her the insult. It *was* a shack, and they would have to make it into something better than that.

Even though the tall trees in their yard had already been left leafless and stark by the advancing autumn, the world outside looked better as the cleaner glass of the windows let in more light. The bright October sunlight cast wiggly patterns on the opposite wall as it made its way through the old panes. Alice was encouraged, and she began to think up ways to bring some happiness to the discouraged little house. Curtains! That would help! She knew they could not use any of their precious little supply of cash to buy such luxuries, but she thought of a way to make some curtains herself.

"Nick, can you go to Sharpsburg and find some old newspapers? Or just any kind of paper?" "Paper?" Nick asked, "*Paper?*" That is all he said before he went out to the horses, put a bridle on Maude, and rode off. An hour or so later he returned, carrying under one arm some old newspapers that he had somehow been able to find. Nick was like that.

Alice laid the papers out on the carpet and began cutting. She took the measure of each window, and interrupted her cutting many times to plan the curtains. When she at last put down her scissors, the newsprint had been fashioned into curtains that had quite a bit of style, with pleats and even the appearance of ruffles. Nick helped her put them up over the four newly washed windows. The transformation was amazing, and the room took on a much more civilized and even homey appearance. Lulu and Grace danced gleefully about the house.

If they could just keep it warm enough in the winter, it could be home for four—even five—Neiharts. Together Nick and Alice looked at the one stove—a small cookstove. That one little stove could not heat the whole room. Then, while they entertained that disturbing thought, Nick noticed a small board tacked on one wall in the middle of the room. It covered a round hole that must have been the opening for a second stovepipe. "But, where is the stove?" Alice asked.

Apparently the former tenants had left in the summer when the stove was not needed for heating. Nick found a small pot-bellied stove in one of the outbuildings, almost hidden by miscellaneous "stuff" that had been tossed in front of it. It had never been a handsome stove, but it was in usable shape, and after Alice gave it a good dusting, it did look better. Nick soon had it set up in the main part of the room. With a thought about safety, he made a foundation and a hearth for the stove with some flat rocks that he found lying about the place. He made a mental note that they would need to keep an eye on the two stovepipes, for there was no chimney, and the pipes went right out through holes in the wall.

The only item of furniture they had was a bed, and they created other pieces—tables, chairs, and closets—with boxes. Nick gathered boards that were lying about and fashioned little beds for the girls. Scraps of cloth made the furniture "pretty." Alice did like "pretty."

There was much to be accomplished before winter set in. With axe and crosscut saw, Nick set about making firewood, and Alice, in spite of her condition, took one end of the saw when the logs needed to be cut into stove-length pieces. Nick split the chunks and stacked the firewood neatly near the kitchen door. Meanwhile, provisions had to be laid in for the winter, and Alice busied herself with that necessity, all the while doing what she could to make the house more pleasant and, if possible, more comfortable.

Christmas came and went, and Alice was glad that the two girls were so young that just a very little satisfied them. They did have a small tree—a little pine that grew in the barnyard—that Alice managed to decorate, but they had little more than that.

At this particular time, this year, the emphasis was on something other than a holiday. Alice knew that her time was near, and she was doing all she could to be ready. Nick had asked around, and they had learned of an old German woman in the neighborhood who had a reputation as a reliable midwife and who was generally known as "Old Herta." She agreed to come to their home and help Alice when the time came.

It was a very harsh winter, and during the first week of January the season seemed to redouble its efforts. Snow and wind battered the little house, and even though the heating stove was kept going around the clock, it was not equal to the task of keeping out the cold. Parents and children alike wore several layers of clothing even when they were inside.

In the early evening of January 7, Old Herta arrived, carrying on her back a small featherbed, for she knew the Neihart house would not be warm. Alice was already in labor, and she was having a very difficult time of it, made worse by her concern that there was little food in the house and by her feeling that Nick could not manage the problems. Old Herta was kind, and as she went about her business, she did what she could to reassure Alice.

It was not until nearly noon of January 8 that the baby finally came. It was a boy—a strong, healthy little lad who announced his entrance loudly, much to the relief of midwife and mother. "Sie haben einen schoenen Knabe; you have a little boy!" Herta whispered to Alice, and after she had cleaned him with great care, Old Herta laid the baby upon Alice's breast.

Perhaps only one who has experienced new motherhood can realize the happiness Alice felt when she saw that this eager, blue-eyed, curly haired little person was complete with the proper number of arms and legs, of fingers and toes! She was radiant as she showed him to Nick, and she was crushed by his unfeeling, harsh comment about the bright-red little creature. Nick was like that, and you just had to know how he really felt. They named him John Greenleaf Neihart. For some reason, in that pitiful little house, in such financially near-hopeless circumstances, Nick wanted his son named in honor of the famed American poet, John Greenleaf Whittier, and Alice agreed.

The young Neiharts had not been favored by Lady Luck in many ways, but the children were an exception: they were—all three of them— healthy and inclined to be happy. Alice was a good mother, and, with Nick's somewhat sporadic help, she somehow managed to do what would seem impossible: she fed and clothed all three and—as an expression of her innate pride—saw to it that they gave a presentable appearance

Nick had found a workable one-bottom plow and part of a harrow that were hidden by the tall weeds, and when spring came, he plowed and prepared the good Illinois soil and managed to get enough seed corn to plant thirty acres. Alice made a garden near the house, which grew and thrived under her care.

During the summer, the garden provided the family with a goodly supply of fresh vegetables, and Alice canned and stored as much as possible for the winter to come. They had fresh milk from a cow Nick had bargained for, eggs from Alice's chickens, and meat from the plentiful wildlife in the surrounding countryside. Nick was a good hunter; hunting was one thing he really liked to do.

Even though he had grown up in a farming family, Nick was not happy as a farmer. When they first arrived at the farm he had told Alice that he was determined to "stick with it" and make a success for her and the kids. To his credit, he did try to do just that for nearly four years, but farming on the limited scale his circumstances allowed was disappointing. Prices for crops were low, and his efforts to find jobs to supplement the family income met with little success. Nick became increasingly dissatisfied with his lot, and finally he convinced himself and Alice that things would be better if they moved to a city.

Discouraged, they gave up the farm in 1885, packed the most valuable of their belongings in the wagon, hitched up their older and rather tired team, and moved to Springfield, the capital of Illinois. Just how he managed to accomplish it is unclear, but Nick was able to open a small grocery store at Fourth and Oak. The family had living quarters in the back of the store, and life was better there for a while.

The store was about two blocks from the grounds of the Illinois capitol, which was just then being built. John remembered seeing the great marble columns for the capitol being dragged up the street on rollers by many teams of horses. Nick began to pay more attention to the young boy and took him for walks about the city. John in later life had no memories of his father before this time; his father seemed to have almost not existed before they moved to Springfield.

Five-year-old John was deeply impressed by the size and beauty of the capitol building, and in later years he commented that the sight of it gave him his first impression of greatness. On one of their excursions, Nick and John walked through a tunnel that led from the basement of the capitol to the grounds. As they reached the street, Nick heard newsboys shouting the news, and he told John that a great man, General Grant, had just died. Of course, young John did not know who General Grant was, but the way Nick told it made the news impressive to the lad. Father and son often walked by the Lincoln Monument and Lincoln's home, which was only a few blocks from their store-home. Abraham Lincoln's widow was still living there, and John often heard his father talk at home about her and her eccentricities.

Two other occurrences during this period made a lasting impression on young John. The first was a love affair with a little girl his own age who lived just past the railroad bridge on the way from Fourth and Oak to the capitol. John never forgot little Etta Stadden. He told about it later: "She was dark, charming, and graceful, and as I remember her, she was the most beautiful little girl I ever knew. I remember her mother as a gentlewoman with graceful manners and soft speech. She encouraged our 'affair,' as did my mother also. I remember with something of a thrill how she used to come to our store and kiss me through the screen door."

John's other memory was of a very different hue. Nick had taken little John to an encampment of soldiers on the Sangamon River near Springfield, and the little boy was impressed with his father's admiration of fighting men. John had mixed emotions as he watched long lines of soldiers running—stark naked—to a deep pool and diving in. He remembered how abashed he was that grown men should run naked, but he also never forgot the feeling of admiration for them that he absorbed from his father.

John's mother, in the meantime, had been working any odd-time jobs she could find to supplement the inadequate income from their little store. Once more Nick decided it was a hopeless situation, and Alice, equally discouraged, agreed. They still had the wagon and team from Indiana, and once more they set forth—one of many covered wagon families searching for the good life, and hoping that this time it would happen for them.

The family started out together, but it seemed best for Nick and Alice to go their separate ways—mother and children going to her parents' homestead nine miles south of Stockton in Rooks County, Kansas, and

Nick making his way toward Kansas City. It was the same as before; Nick seemed always to think he would do better if he moved farther on. Their decision to separate was not lightly made. If they did, Alice and the three children would have the security of a home with her father and mother, and when Nick had found a job and could make a home for his family, they would join him in Kansas City.

In spite of the unfortunate circumstances that had made the separation necessary, the arrival of Alice and her three little ones at the Culler homestead was treated as a happy homecoming. They were welcomed at the two-room sod house that George Washington Culler had created out of slabs of grassy soil cut with a special plow from the surrounding prairie. The walls of the "soddy" were a foot or more thick; the roof consisted of poles and brush covered with more slabs of sod. To cause rainwater to flow off the roof, slate was carefully arranged on top of the sod, and inside the house, muslin cloth fastened to the poles did its best to catch the dirt that fell from the roof as it dried.

Alice was pleasantly surprised when she entered the house. The thick walls provided good insulation from the heat of summer, and it was surprisingly cool in the dwelling. Her father had pounded the dirt floor with a hammer until it had a hard, smooth surface. When wear caused a hole or indentation in the floor, more dirt was brought in and pounded until the surface was smooth enough to be swept clean.

Alice admired the house and her parents' hard work and courageous ingenuity that had brought it into being, but she wondered how it would be possible for all of them to live in it. She and the children made four, and there were already five people in the small house: her mother and father, her two brothers—Charles and George Culler—and her sister, Gertie. Being a loving family, they found a way to make it work.

John recalled in later years how his Aunt Gertie was not an especially able student. He heard her trying to memorize a spelling lesson in sing-song, and it sounded something like this to John: "Sayta cat, doja dog, fayta fat, rayta rat," which, translated, would be: "C-a-t, cat; d-o-g, dog; f-a-t, fat; r-a-t, rat." Many years later, John's own children laughed merrily when he told them about Aunt Gertie.

Signs of the frontier were all around the Cullers. The last buffalo herd had passed over that land only eighteen years before, leaving behind as evidence of their presence numerous "buffalo wallows"—hollowed-out places in the soil where they had rolled on the wet earth. These "wallows" were everywhere and were still deep enough to hold water after a rain.

The Kansas countryside was then as wild as when God had made it—a vast expanse of buffalo grass and little else. Truly it seemed not fit for farming people to live in. As for John, even at that early age the vast prairies gave him a feeling of wonder, and he remembered them later as glorious. They gave him his second awareness of greatness.

The people living in the surrounding area made up as fine a democracy as one might see, for they had so little, and all shared what they did have and respected their neighbors. Among these neighbors living a few miles from the Cullers was a family of "colored people," and they were treated no differently than the other neighbors. Everyone was living too close to absolute reality for that.

Truly, it was a genuine democracy, both spiritual and material. Nobody was rich; nobody was poor, and anyone in need was certain of voluntary help from his neighbors. "Neighbors" were not merely those in one's immediate vicinity; they might live fifteen or twenty miles away in that vast, thinly settled country.

Social life was merry in spite of the hardships all were experiencing. People came from a wide area to the square dances and the "literary societies," which were hardly "literary" in any strict sense. There was much reciting of poems, and everyone who came was expected to contribute to the programs. The evening usually included something like a feast, for the ladies brought box lunches.

John's Uncle George was sought after for his fiddling. If someone could not play the fiddle or sing, he could at least "say a piece." At one social held at the old schoolhouse near his grandfather's farm, little five-year-old John recited this piece taught to him by his playful Uncle George:

> As I came down the new-cut road
> I met a possum and a toad;
> And every time the toad would jump,
> The possum bit him on the rump!

That was John's first speaking engagement, and he brought down the house. He was so surprised and excited that he wet his pants!

In such a society a young boy was bound to get the impression that all people were good. Whenever anybody had an especially big job to do enough men would flock in from all over the countryside to do the job in a jiffy, and the women would see that there was plenty to eat and places to sleep if home was too far away.

When John's grandfather and his two sons were through with the summer's work, they would get in a wagon and go east until they found a place where there was corn to husk, and in that way they were able to get a little money for the winter. Grandfather George Culler was a blacksmith, and a good one, but his work did not always bring in cash. There was not a lot of money to be had in the country, but the grandfather's skill did help to support the family.

John remembered his grandfather's joking comment, made as he wiped off a red-hot piece of iron with his bare, heavily calloused hand: "John, I can make anything except a pig with spots!" No doubt the admiring grandson suspected he could even make the spots.

John was six years old when he witnessed an impressive spectacle—a prairie fire. People were always on the lookout for wildfires, and if someone saw a column of smoke on the horizon, he would leap on a horse and ride to the nearest hilltop to see what it was. If necessary, he would warn his neighbors. A prairie fire was a major catastrophe, for it often destroyed homes. Grandfather Culler kept a wide swath of ground plowed and bare of burnable vegetation around his home, barn, and haystacks to create a fireguard if there was a prairie fire. When a fire did strike, he would go out with his team and plow and increase the plowed protection.

One time a fire arrived toward dusk, and it caused a tremendous and frightful night. The whole Culler family—children included—was out, setting backfires to stop the onslaught of the wildfire and fighting to control the fire with wet sacks and buckets of water carried from the creek. Fortunately for the Cullers, their plowed fireguards were far enough away from house and barns so that nothing was burned around the home, but the heat was intense and the smoke stifling. As they watched its approach, they could see the wind-blown fire reach a deep gulch full of dry tumbleweeds, and when it struck that tinderbox, a tremendous flame leaped up from the gulch to the sky, and there was a terrific roar.

It was a frightful night for all, and for one small boy that fire would be of surprising importance in his store of memories. Years later, he described a prairie fire in *The Song of Three Friends*, one volume of his series on the exploration and settling of the American West.

The people were all living on hope and hard work, hope that commonly ended in failure because of the hot winds, the grasshoppers, and the prairie fires. How often was a springtime field of fine, green corn destroyed by summer's dry winds, or decimated by the clouds of grasshoppers that were a recurring scourge! During the nine years that the Cullers lived in Kansas, grandfather George, in addition to everything else he had to do, was blasting stone from a quarry on his land, splitting and dressing it for the fine house he planned to build for his wife. In that time he had produced quite a pile of stone, almost enough to make that house for "Mother."

Catharine Culler was an excellent housewife, mother, and grandmother. She did what many of today's women would consider impossible; she made their crude sod house seem warm and "homey." It was kept as clean as possible, and when it was not so, she declared it was "glakid and clatty." The very thought of a dirty house made her all "throughother," and she set about to right the condition. In addition to all this, Catharine baked bread and cooked meals on a wood stove or outdoor fire, and she preserved for the winter the produce she herself had raised in her garden during the summer months. She made clothing for her husband, her children, and herself, and she was good—so good—to her grandchildren.

In all of this, Grandmother Culler remained strong and unflinching, and when she had grown old, all the dark hardships they had experienced faded in her memory and took on a brighter hue. Years later, when—widowed—she was visiting John and his family in Missouri, Grandmother Culler remarked, "Oh, John, I wish I was in a covered wagon, going west with Pa!"

John understood: "Oh, Grandma, I can imagine how happy and how filled with hope those old times must have been. Yes, I do understand how you feel, and I only wish I could go with you and Grandpa. How I should love that!"

Unfortunately, the reality of the Kansas experience was that, after nine bad years in which crops were burned by the hot winds or ruined by the grasshopper plague, George Washington Culler was forced to leave, with nothing but his team and wagon and two hundred dollars. That was all he could get for his homestead.

Alice and her children had not stayed to see that happen; when they left, the Kansas homestead was still a place of possibilities. In the spring of 1887 the Neiharts went to Kansas City to join Nick. At first they lived in a rooming house on Fourth Street. Alice took care of the rooming house, and Nick worked at the Boughman Hotel on the northeast corner of Fourth and Main.

It was not a happy homecoming for any of them, and for young John, especially, the contrast between that dismal section of the city and the vast prairies of Kansas was saddening. Even then, when he was six years old, John knew that nothing was right with his family. There was a strained feeling between his parents, and although Nick was never harsh with John, he had something in his nature that was almost brutal, and this unkind streak in his makeup was usually directed toward his wife. It was she and the girls who suffered, but what he saw made John unhappy too.

From the rooming house, they moved to Ninth Street and Vine, where they lived in one room for a while. In 1889, when John was eight, their home was a back room on Vine Street near Bryant School, and it was here that John first entered school. It was while the family lived in the Vine Street room that they had an experience that was not calculated to increase their faith in the goodness of human beings. The memory of that experience returned each year to haunt John throughout much of the remainder of his life.

It was Christmas time, Mother Alice was sick and in bed, and Nick was not at home. The children knew there was not going to be any real Christmas, because their mother was sick and there was no money for such things as presents. On Christmas Eve, the town "Christmas wagon" came around, stopped in front of the house, and distributed gifts to the children there. From their room in the back of the house,

Lulu, Grace, and John could hear a wagon clattering down the street, and when they looked out and saw it was the Christmas wagon, they became quite excited, hoping that they might be included in the gift-giving.

Through the thin walls that separated them from the people living in the front of the house, they heard the driver of the wagon ask, "Do any other people live here?" The heartless answer to the driver's question shattered their hopes: "No, nobody else lives here, nobody at all." The wagon moved on, and there were no presents for John and his sisters. Not that year.

One winter day John, who loved being outside, was standing on a small bridge over a creek on Vine Street, looking at the ice and dreaming. A man came up to John, holding a clock under his arm. "Buddy, have your folks got a clock?" Reminded of how very little they did have, John told the man, "No, we don't have a clock."

"Take me to your mother, and I will show you how she can get one." John did this, and soon the Neiharts were the proud owners of a clock, which Alice undertook to pay for at the rate of twenty-five cents a week. That proved to be something of a burden, but Alice saw to it that they kept the clock. It was a momentous event in their lives, the acquisition of that good clock. Alice was always trying to give respectable status to her family, and that clock certainly helped.

John was growing, and Nick more and more often found it pleasing to take his son with him on his many jaunts about the city and its environs. On a day when Nick was not working, Mother Alice would get the boy dressed nicely—Nick tended to be fastidious about dressing—and, holding one of his father's fingers, John would go off for a new adventure. Nick was a silent fellow, and he seldom let John know where they were bound; he just held out his hand to his son, and they left. Nor did John ask his father; a curious reluctance, both respectful and uncomfortable, prevented the boy's doing so.

John loved those excursions, and memories of them remained as bitter-sweet spots in that part of his life. Some of those memories were life-shaping. On one morning in spring, after heavy rains had caused rivers to run fast and full, Nick took his eight-year-old son on a jaunt that proved to be of the latter type. They came to the banks of the flooding

Missouri River, and as they stood above it, John gazed in amazement at the undulating, muddy mass of water below them. Never before had he witnessed such a sight, for that river was carrying away a great part of North Kansas City. Houses and barns, everything in the way of the mighty flood, were caught up in a mad desire to go to St. Louis. The size and terrific power of the river—its incomprehensible majesty—were thrilling to the boy.

And then, while John was drinking in all that fearful wonder, his father caught him by surprise. Nick took off his shoes and his trousers and dived right into the swirling flood. John saw him come up a few yards out from shore, watched him swim, avoiding the logs and various kinds of trash being carried in the river.

Then, a hundred yards or so downriver, Nick swam to shore and climbed out—soaked and muddy but unhurt. He was smiling broadly as he waved to John, indicating that he wanted him to come down to where he was standing. John picked up his dad's shoes and pants and, trudging through the underbrush, delivered them to his father. In the boy's eyes, the man was some sort of hero; it was a day young John would never forget.

Nick was able to get a job on the cable system of the street railway for a real salary—thirty-five dollars a month! It was before there were electric streetcars and when most cars were drawn by horses. At first, he drove one of the horse-drawn variety. Life was better for the family when Nick had a good job, and Alice found it easier to provide what her children needed. She always kept them dressed well and somehow, in spite of the family's lack of funds, made the girls and John feel they were "quality folk." She even arranged for art and music lessons for the girls.

Sometimes Nick took John with him on his run, and he showed his son how to work the grips on the cable system. John was perhaps nine years old at that time, and the trips on the cable car played upon his growing natural leanings toward things mechanical. As a result, he set up a cable car system in their backyard, using spools, twine, and cigar boxes he was able to acquire from neighborhood storekeepers. He even made tunnels in his cable system, to match the one he had been through on the Ninth Street line. It was all quite impressive and fun.

On one of the "runs" with his father, John was allowed to try to start the car at the end of the line. He did manage to release one of the heavy levers, but somehow it fell back against his head, knocked him down, and raised a considerable goose-egg on his forehead. Obviously a better grip was needed, and John conceived the idea of a magnetic grip to be actuated by small levers that would send a current from batteries around a core and produce a magnet that would force the jaws of the grip together. Then by turning off the current, the spring would be released. John felt that his plan to make the magnetic grip was not at all vague, but there was no money in the house to buy even the minimum of materials that would be needed. He had to give up that notion.

John was a companionable kid. There were other boys in the neighborhood, and for a time he was caught up in adventures with his "gang." During this period the family lived at various locations: Twenty-fifth Street and Park, Twenty-fifth and Wabash, and 2428 Olive Street. John did little except engage in adventure with his pals. The boys played Robinson Crusoe, made caves to "live" in, and swam in Brush Creek. What they did in those times would be quite impossible today; the boys took off their clothes near Thirtieth Street and Prospect and ran naked through the woods to Brush Creek to swim.

During all of this time, Mother Alice was the principal, steady provider for the family needs, working at odd and often demeaning jobs, and the girls, being older than John, helped her in many ways. Although Nick had in his sporadic way tried to be a breadwinner for his family, he met with no lasting success, and some of his efforts were indeed ludicrous.

One time he came home with a motley group of horses, a harness, and an old buggy—animals, tack, and vehicle all in a more or less dilapidated condition. Apparently he had convinced himself that he could make a living with them, but to Alice the motley assortment was little more than an embarrassment, and to the neighbors it was another evidence of Nick's impracticality and inability to cope with life's needs.

It was not the menagerie in the backyard that brought the marriage to a breaking point; it was just everything that had happened to two people whose views on life and whose capabilities were so different. Coloring it all was Nick's darker side—his pitiful attempts to do right always ending in failure and, perhaps worst of all, his capacity for cruel treatment of those close to him.

Alice, herself often a victim of his unpredictably harsh nature, had come to feel the impossibility of their relationship. As for Nick, he was not constituted to be a *pater familias*. He was by nature an adventurer, and he could not lead a conventionally normal family life. His attempts to tame himself ended pitifully; Nickolas Neihart simply could not be tamed. One evening, after yet another of their increasingly frequent arguments, Nick left in a rush of anger. The children were already in bed, but in their small home they were unprotected from the terror of what to them was an unnatural, impossible separation of parents.

John, who had often shared Nick's adventures and who had never felt the brunt of his difficult nature, was deeply hurt. For him the time when they were all together, and when he shared so many outings with Nick, was the family's "golden age," and now it was over. In later years, when John was writing his early memories, he expressed it all in this way:

> But I remember yet, with a twinge of heartache, the angry, terrifying voices that hurt me deep in the middle of my breast.
>
> There was a time when my Father did not come home for several days. Then there was a knocking on the locked door in the night, and a low voice called "Alice." There was no reply. Again the knocking and the voice, but no reply. And after a long silence outside, there was the sound of footsteps going away.
>
> I lay listening to the pounding of my heart and the footsteps until there was only the pounding. Then I had to get up and run to the door and unlock it. The night was black outside and still.
>
> I called "Good-bye, good-bye!"—and his voice came back, like a dimming echo.

18

A Dream Changes a Boy's Life

WHILE ALICE AND HER family were living in Kansas City, her parents, having previously been the victims of drought and grasshoppers in Kansas, tried once more in Perkins County in the Sandhills of western Nebraska. For three years in succession, they were hailed out, and in desperation they moved to Wayne County, Nebraska, where the soil was good and the weather was such that crops could be raised. With their two sons, Charles and George, Grandma and Grandpa Culler lived on a farm seven miles from the town of Wayne.

In 1891 Alice moved with her three children to Wayne, Nebraska, again with help of her parents. They found a house in town but spent a considerable amount of time on her brothers' farm. In the summertime John spent most of his free time on the farm, which was a wonderland to him. He had learned to shoot, and he ran about the farm killing squirrels and rabbits with a .22 rifle and having great adventures in the tall corn and the mysterious valleys, where it seemed to him that no one had ever come before.

There was a small spring creek on the farm, and John dammed it to make an "ocean" for a place to sail his ships. He had gone into the ship building "business" in his playtime, and his creations were mostly warships. The first in John's fleet of warships was named the Constitution, and it had five brass cannon made from shotgun shell casings.

John had a pal, Frank Whitney, who was interested in anything that intrigued John. Frank also built a fleet of ships armed with cannon, and together they had mock naval battles. They loaded their "cannon" with black powder and pebbles and marshaled their fleets on battle lines opposite each other. Then they would take turns touching off their cannons with pieces of punk. When the shooting was over, the fleet that showed less damage to its rigging was the victor.

As a result of this interest in ships, John decided he needed to have a supership that was run by steam. He had read a lot about engines, and he knew he could not make a reciprocating engine, but he hit upon another idea. He would produce steam pressure with an oil lamp under a sealed baking powder can, and from this steam boiler he would run a pipe that would enter the apex of a cone-shaped chamber.

Inside the chamber he would put a shaft with fans graduated in size, the small ones at the point where the steam entered the cone, where the pressure was strongest, and larger ones at the end of the shaft just before the steam escaped. Thus the pressure would be equalized, with the decreasing steam pressure working upon the increasing leverage of the larger fans. John planned to use this engine to run a paddle wheel on one of his boats.

John learned later that his plan was much like that of a steam turbine engine, but when he was designing it in his mind, he was not able to create a model. Although the local tinner might have been able to make one for a few dollars, the family had no money for such things.

Mother Alice was working long hours and succeeded in providing a home for John and his sisters, but there was no money for toy turbine engines. Alice was an excellent seamstress, and she could create a pattern and make any dress that a customer could describe or for which she had a picture. If the material in a customer's dress was in good condition, Alice Neihart could make it over in an attractive style. Her pay for this excellent work was ten cents an hour.

By making dresses and taking any other odd jobs that were available in the town, Alice was able to rent a small home in Wayne and provide food and clothing for her children. Her ability to do so, without help and in those difficult times, is indeed surprising, but she managed affairs so that the girls and John never had to feel they were dressed poorly or were in other ways underprivileged. They knew they were not "rich folk," but they were happy. John recalled being sent upon occasion to the local butcher shop to get "ten cents worth of boiling beef and some liver, please!"

In spite of a lack of material comforts, there was no lack of jollity in the home. Mother's quick wit, her teasing, joking ways, and her appreciation of the natural beauties that were available to all—money or no money—had a buoyant effect on all their lives. Alice was like that.

Up until this time, when John was about twelve years old, his mother and sisters and the other members of the family thought that John would grow up to be an inventor. This was not surprising, considering the inventive nature he had shown on more than one occasion. After the steam turbine engine, he became obsessed with the idea that he could make an airship. He knew he could not make an engine, but he felt sure he could make an airship that could be launched from an upstairs window and that would fly at something like a forty-five degree angle down to the ground.

John's idea was to build a light, cigar-shaped craft that would take advantage of the pull of gravity for its propulsion. A rather large flywheel operating vertically would be on the top of the craft, and the shaft from this large fan would enter the craft and connect by a wooden level gear with a horizontal shaft protruding from the rear. On this latter shaft would be a smaller fan wheel, and beneath the craft he would place a weight of suitable size to hold the craft steady. As it fell, the larger fan above the airship would turn the smaller fan at the rear, giving the craft forward impetus.

This notion fascinated John for several weeks, but then in November 1892 he had a dream that changed the direction of his life. John was an active, athletic youngster, swimming during the summer, skating in the winter, and taking long hikes with his pals just to see how much they would be able to stand. There was nothing morbid in John's nature; he was naturally a happy boy, and it could well be said that there was something harum-scarum about him and his pals.

In those days the family did not see much of doctors, and when a doctor's buggy stopped in front of a neighbor's house, it was thought that someone must be dying. Even when John fell victim to a seriously high fever, a doctor was not called. During his illness John experienced a vivid dream three times.

In each dream it seemed that he was flying outward into space, face down, with his arms extended and his palms down as though he were diving on the horizontal. In the dreams the speed of his flight would increase until the surface beneath him—whether ether or air—became hard and smooth like glass. He flew in this manner in what seemed a vast bubble of the universe, all the while being conscious of the stars and feeling a loneliness that he remembered as both terrible and glorious.

John did not want to go into that loneliness, but he was mysteriously compelled to do so, and with the loneliness was an exhilarating awareness of greatness and strange beauty, of longing and inexpressible sadness. When he awoke from the dream, he reached out to his mother and held her tightly, for he did not wish to return.

Years later, when he told his friend the Sioux holy man Black Elk about his boyhood dream, the old Indian's matter-of-fact response was: "That was your power dream." Be that as it may, at the time there was no apparent connection between the occurrence of the dream and John's change of direction from inventing to writing poetry. But there was a change, and when he was eleven he wrote his first verse called "Your Stubblehaired Boy."

John had done something that upset his mother so much that she would not say good-bye to him when he left for school in the morning. An hour or two later she went to her bedroom, where she found the poem on her bureau.

"In it," she later told a reporter, "John told me how much he loved me, and he made me feel how sorry he was to have acted so that I wouldn't tell him good-bye. I knew then that John was destined for big things, and I knew this time it wouldn't be with copper wires, iron machinery, and such."

When he was on Uncle George's farm, John not only played, he was allowed to take part in the workings of that worthy enterprise, farming. At harvest time, John was permitted to ride the lead horse of a five-horse team hitched to the binder, and after an exhausting ten or twelve hours aboard a sweating horse in the heat of the day, he was dirty, tired, and hungry but proud to have taken a manly part in the work.

Harvesting was a cooperative venture, the crew taking the machinery from one farm to another, and at the end of each day, the women folk of the plot being harvested put on a meal that could only fairly be called a feast. Farming as it was carried on at that time was work of the hardest variety, but, since the harvest was the culmination of a summer's hopes, it became something of a celebration.

Everyday mealtimes were something of a celebration too, for, at least during the summer garden season, the family ate well. John remembered Uncle George's remark after he had hungrily taken the first bite at dinner one evening: "My, that hit the chair!" When earcorn was in season, he would challenge John for a contest. Each would line up his empty cobs, and the one whose cobs stretched farther would be declared the winner. For people who lived without traditional entertainment, they managed to entertain themselves well!

John did not know at the time, nor would he ever know, just why he began writing verses. Poets were not common in that society of intensely practical people whose main interest was—quite sensibly enough—in raising grain and hogs. John's first verses were of little value and showed nothing more than a youngster's desire to learn. His mother and sisters, who seemed to have decided he was going to be a poet instead of an inventor, encouraged him, and to help him in his quest they gave him paperback books they acquired by saving soap wrappers, the first being a copy of Tennyson's *The Idylls of the King*.

John read voraciously, and Tennyson or some other author went with him in a hip pocket always. He read so much that his grandfather in Wayne—and again we quote his mother—"used to storm at him because 'he constantly has his feet up on the table, reading, reading from morning 'till night—*when he should be at work*.' "

A verse entitled "Ambition," telling something of his hopes and plans, was printed in a weekly paper in Bloomington, Illinois. Later, "The Song of the Hoe" was published in *The Youth's Companion*. The poem had been dreamed up while John was hoeing potatoes, and it was written on the back of the hoe. He transcribed it on paper, sent it to the *Companion*, and received fourteen dollars in payment. John, the writer, was on his way.

John's attendance at the public school in Wayne had not begun under happy circumstances. He had arrived at the school without the necessary certificate from the Kansas City schools indicating that he had passed to the sixth grade; the certificate had been lost in their move from Kansas City to Wayne. John's unusually small size and his very young appearance made the principal of the Wayne school doubt John's insistence that he was ready for the sixth grade. He gave the boy a note, indicating that he was to be in the third grade, and John was crushed and embarrassed to join that lowly group. He was alone and lonely in a strange school.

"It was at this point in my history," John wrote many years later, "that my luck changed for the better. Just when I was feeling most lonely, most hopelessly isolated from the mass of my fellow youngsters, a boy whom I had never met before came up and grinned at me with a friendly, toothful grin. He was a little taller than I, huskily built, and about my age. . . . He had thick dark eyebrows that did not take the trouble to separate above the nose, but ran straight across, giving him a belligerent look that belied the grin.

" 'I'll play you a game,' he said. 'Winners keepers, losers weepers.'

"I had no marbles on me, and when I confessed the lack, he said, 'Oh, I'll lend you some, and when you win, you can pay me back.'

"So we made a ring and played. I was fairly handy with a taw, but no expert, and I wondered at the easy shots he missed. I won (or should I say he lost?) and when the bell rang, I paid my debt, and we agreed to meet there by the steps after school.

"Yes, that was none other than John Elias Weston Chaffee, a prince of pals!"

There was more good news. Fortunately, one day the sixth grade teacher came to see John after classes, asked him various questions, and learned about the reading he had done and his efforts at inventing. After he had at her request quite easily recited the multiplication tables, she told John she would be happy to have him in her sixth grade class. Grateful for her understanding and now properly situated, John continued in the public school until he reached the ninth grade, at which time the school for some reason began to bore him insufferably.

Just at that time a new college had been founded in Wayne. Professors J. M. Pile and U. S. Conn of Indiana had started their school in a small downtown storeroom, while the college building was being erected on the hill above the town. They were starting the school largely with faith and enthusiasm, for they were truly bringers of light. Professor Pile's learning was phenomenal, and his dynamic personality soon dominated the community.

John's growing lack of interest in the public school had worried his mother, and when she learned about the college, Alice Neihart took her bored young son to see Professor Pile. They talked for a while, and the professor asked the lad a number of questions, which John, deeply impressed by the imposing personage before him, answered as best he could.

After what was only a few minutes but seemed an interminable time to John, Professor Pile told the ninth grader that he could attend the college and earn his way by ringing the bell for classes. He gave John a silver watch to mark the time, and John's duty was to ring the bell at six-thirty in the morning, and twice every fifty minutes after that until six p.m.

John rang the bell for classes faithfully, both in the downtown location and on the hill after the college building was completed. The learning experience at the college was an inspiring one, and John, remembering in later years, referred to the college as his "hill of vision." The faculty worked all hours, early and late, and if a private class were needed, there would be a private class. The professors were well educated people from the East, and like most teachers, they were eager to help a student who wished to learn.

John had private classes in Latin and in mathematics with Professor Conn. He was particularly interested in reading in Latin, and he studied that course five hours a day. As for the professor, he found it necessary to study in the evening himself, "to keep up with Johnny." At the age of fourteen, John was reading Virgil's *Aeneid* at sight.

During his first year at the college, John had another strange, perhaps psychic experience. Although he was a happy young man, physically quite normal, and regularly hiked or rode a bicycle considerable distances, for a brief period he was given to sleep-walking.

One night something special happened that had a lasting, mystical effect on him. He awoke—or thought he awoke—at about three o'clock on a summer night with a full moon. Wearing only a shirt and giving no thought to whether he was dressed or not, he went out the back door of their home and somehow was able to get out into the street without waking his mother. He had vaguely in mind that he was going to the home of a charming girlfriend to take her bike riding, but he had no bicycle with him.

John tried later to describe to a young friend his sleepwalking experience:

> I never in my life felt more alive or more gloriously awake. I walked in a leisurely fashion, taking in the other-worldly beauty of the night, for although the familiar world was recognizable, it was glorified beyond words to express. There was a deep, thrilling joy in studying the shadow patterns of the trees on the sidewalk, and the trees themselves were more beautiful than any I have seen while awake.
>
> When I arrived in front of the young lady's house, it did not occur to me that I was unclothed. By that time I was so deeply glorified by the experience that I gave up the idea of a bicycle ride and just looked around at the night.
>
> I don't know how long I stood there on the girl's front porch, because I had no sense of time whatsoever; I was just vividly and gloriously alive. I did not knock, and no one came to the door.
>
> The return trip to my home was made slowly, as I remember, but when I reached our front gate, I must have let it click shut, for my mother was standing at the door in front of me, asking what I was doing. When I was really awake the next morning, I remembered my mother as if she were part of the dream.

John was fifteen when in 1896 he finished the Nebraska professional teachers' course, which made him eligible to teach, but he was too young to teach, and he looked even younger than he was, being a small, tow-headed youngster.

It was in 1896 that his first short story was published. He gave it the title "Hot Wind," which gives the impression that it might have been related to things he had witnessed on his grandfather's farm in Kansas. The story was published in a magazine called *The Sunflower*. John was on his way as a writer.

Because he could hardly hope to get a professional teaching position looking as young as he did, John continued in the college and graduated in 1897 with a BS degree from the scientific course. He did not have the four dollars needed for a diploma, and because he did not want to let Professor Pile know this, he left school and got a job in the onion fields at seventy-five cents a day.

Forty years later, when Conn was president of the Nebraska Normal College and its founder, Pile, was dead, John's second daughter attended the school. At a convocation, President Conn was announcing student scholastic standings when he recalled his experiences while teaching Latin to the young Neihardt.

"I found it necessary to study in the evenings to keep up with Johnny, and now his daughter is the ranking student here, and her grade point average is the highest in the school, by more than two points." A certain young, white-blond college girl would never forget what the president said.

Later, in the summer after his graduation, armed with his second-grade teacher's certificate, John was able to get a position teaching in a school about eight miles north of Hoskins, Nebraska. The next spring—1898—he left with his pal John Chaffee to go to Kansas City, where they hoped to find jobs.

19

Searching and Vagabonding

THE SUMMER OF 1898 was a bad one; men were out of work in Kansas City as they were elsewhere, and John and his friend quickly found that the city had no jobs for two young boys. The little money they had between them was soon gone, and they found it necessary to go outside the city and sleep in the fields at night.

One rainy night they decided to go to the Helping Hand Institution, and John later described their experience that night as being "something out of Dante's *Inferno*." They were in a large room with stacks of bunks filled with outcast human beings—the physically, mentally, and morally diseased.

Neither boy had, in the small towns of Nebraska, been in such surroundings before, but Chaffee was a joker, and he made the night bearable by kidding about it. At regular intervals, a watchman came through the room carrying a lantern, and as he passed by with his light falling on the inmates, the swinging lantern made weird shadows on the walls and ceiling.

One night at the Helping Hand was enough, and the next morning they went to an employment office, where they were offered an opportunity to cut hickory wood for axe handles at Sumner, Missouri, near Chillicothe. Having no money to get there, the two boys hiked outside the city, where they managed to get aboard a freight train headed in the direction of Sumner.

At the first stop they were quickly put off the train by a brakeman who came around looking for hobos. It was very dark at that stop, so the boys went around to the other side of the train and got on an oil tank car. Their idea was that if a "shack" appeared on one side of the car, they could crawl around to the other side before he saw them.

It was raining hard, and they sat on the edge of the oil car with their feet dangling over. Finally, at one of the stops, the brakeman caught them. John gave him a very forceful oration about the necessity of their getting to important jobs that were awaiting their arrival in Sumner. The brakeman said "Surely you boys have got something on you." John replied, "I've got a razor." "I'll take that, and you boys can ride."

They rode on, until another brakeman jumped them, and they crawled into an open-top coal car. It was still raining toward morning, when the same unsympathetic brakeman found them and made them leave the train. The sign on the depot informed them they were in Brunswick, and they knew that a branch line ran from that town to Sumner.

It was pitch dark at the time, but they were able to find an empty corn crib that at least had a roof over it. Inside, they found some old grain sacks, and they slept in the crib until morning, when the rain had stopped and the sun was shining. They had nothing to eat, but they started out, walking down the tracks toward Sumner.

They were not sorry for themselves, for both John and his pal liked doing "that sort of thing," and they often hiked long hours with nothing to eat. About half-way to Sumner, they lay down near the tracks and went to sleep in the warm sunshine, and in the late afternoon they awoke and walked on to Sumner. Their experience in that town was not what they had anticipated it would be.

One can imagine how they looked after their night experience of riding in the rain in dirty cars. Both boys were grimy and may well have looked like tough fellows, and their rough appearance, added to the fact that they were from Kansas City, was bound to arouse suspicion in the small rural community. When they inquired about their promised jobs, they found that the hickory timber they had hoped to be hired to cut was standing in several feet of water. There were no jobs to be had in Sumner, and they wanted to leave town on the first train bound for Kansas City.

The train to the city was due to arrive around midnight. It began to rain again, and in the early evening they were lying under the eaves of the depot waiting for the arrival of the train. When it came, they planned to slip onto the blind-baggage car behind the engine. Their plan didn't work; long before the train arrived, the town marshal appeared with two of his deputies.

They were looking for the boys, evidently thinking they were dangerous. A search for guns revealed only a large-bowled pipe in John's hip-pocket, which the marshal at first thought was a gun. John tried to argue the men out of arresting them, but it was no use. They paid no attention when he told them that they were only trying to get out of town, and if left alone, they would soon be gone.

John and his pal were arrested, and the marshal and his two burlies herded them along the main street, where people sitting with their chairs rocked back against the buildings gazed at them as they passed. They were thrown in jail, and the doors were locked behind them when the jailers left. Seeking some kind of revenge for the insult done them, John's pal wanted to do rude damage to the interior of the jail, but John talked him out of it, for he feared such an action might cause them to be kept in jail for a month.

Late the next morning, two dirty, hungry boys were released without any breakfast, and John thanked his jailer profusely for his great "kindness." Between them, they had one dime left, which they had been cherishing, for it would pay their way across the bridge at Kansas City. It took five days to walk back following first the roadbed of a jerkwater line, then the main line up the Missouri River to Kansas City.

Having found no jobs in Sumner, they had no money, save that one precious dime, and during those five days they had nothing to eat except green apples and occasionally some raw potatoes from a farmer's garden. On the way they tried several times to get work, but they were unfortunate in the kind of people they contacted. Several times they were told by an angry woman at the back door, "You don't want to work!" John would say, "We'll work first and eat afterwards. Show us the work!" But the door was slammed in their faces.

On their return trip to Kansas City, they did not wish to run the risk of being jailed again for trying to ride a train, so they kept away from trains and out of towns. Because it was chilly at night along the river and hot in the daytime, they slept by day and walked most of the night. They had kept that one precious dime to pay the toll across the bridge at Kansas

City, but when they reached the railroad bridge at the edge of town, they decided they would try to save that dime for something to eat.

When they arrived at the river they saw that no one was guarding the bridge, and they made a dash for it. They hoped to get across before a train would come, because there was not room on the bridge, except at certain points, to stand safely if a train should pass. Fortunately, they crossed the bridge with no difficulty, and they were soon able to find a pancake joint in the slums where they could get two dishes of wheatcakes for their dime. A big pitcher of molasses stood on the table, and they poured it all on the pancakes in the hope that it would be nourishing. They sorely needed nourishment!

At the south end of Main Street, they found a tombstone shop, and John applied there for employment. The proprietors of the shop needed no one, but they seemed friendly, and that encouraged John to show them his manuscript. It was a long poem called "The Divine Enchantment," which concerned an East Indian religious fable, and John had been working on it for some time. He had carried the manuscript with him, hoping that he might be able to get it published in Kansas City.

That manuscript was the most precious thing John had, and the fact that he had it with him had sustained him. The proprietors of the marble shop were intelligent men, and when they read part of the manuscript, they were impressed. "Someday we'll be hearing from you," they said, and they agreed to give John a job polishing marble.

John's friend, John Chaffee, could find no work, but he was not idle while John worked. They decided that he was the woman and John the man. One would make the money and the other would find food and shelter for them both. Chaffee did manage to find a sympathetic woman who agreed to let them have a room in her attic, and while John worked, he went about the town with a paper sack that he always managed to fill by begging at back doors. When dinner was ready, they would go out in a back lot and eat it, then one of the two would work some more, and the other would get supper.

John's workshop was in the basement, and outside there was a sidewalk that ran diagonally across the window. When he had a little leisure, Chaffee would sit on the sidewalk, swinging his legs and kidding John for working so hard. Then finally he would say, "Well, I guess I'll go get dinner," and he would leave on that important quest.

In this way they soon saved enough money to buy two cattle passes for Omaha.

Armed with their cattle passes, the two boys got on the caboose of the train and rode as far as Atchison, Nebraska. Their cattle passes gave them the right to take charge of two cars loaded with cattle—which, of course, they did not have. While the train was stopped in Atchison, a playful brakeman told them they would have to change cars there, and he indicated where the proper car was standing. While they were off looking for the right car, their train left the station!

They were now again quite out of money, and their prized cattle passes would be of little or no value on any other train. It was night, and it was raining again. They inquired of a passer-by and were told that they should see the train dispatcher. The train dispatcher was a busy man, but somehow they made their way into his office. Busy as he was, the dispatcher did listen to John, who explained as eloquently as he could that they had lost their train, and two cars of cattle would be helpless without their care.

At this, the dispatcher threw his head back and laughed heartily. Then he told them: "There is a passenger train due here at 12:05. As soon as it stops, you boys rush right in past the brakeman, and don't show them anything. When they come to see your tickets, show 'em your passes, say you know that they're no good on the passenger train, but it's the railroad's fault. Tell 'em your story and refuse to get off."

The boys did exactly as they were advised to do, dashed onto the train and sat down in the first car. The train was already moving when the brakeman came. "Let's see your tickets, buddies!" John gave him his oration and showed the cattle passes, adding, "You are bigger than we are, and you could throw us off the train, but we will not go voluntarily, and it's going to cost the railroad plenty if we don't get to Omaha in the morning."

To this the brakeman replied that when the conductor came around, he would probably throw them off at the next stop. The conductor did finally come by, and he heard the same story and saw the same useless cattle passes. "Well, boys, we'll catch up with a freight on the side track, and you can get on it." The train did stop a short while later, and the conductor took John out on the platform and showed him a train that John knew was not theirs and that had no cattle cars on it. The boys refused to get off, and the conductor, quite disgusted by then, said, "Aw, go back and go to sleep!" They did.

They reached Omaha, still without money and very hungry, so they stopped at a back door of a house in north Omaha and asked if they could work for their breakfast. The woman who answered the door had a sweet face, and her reply was kind. "Oh, come right in! I have a boy someplace, and I hope somebody is feeding him!" The breakfast she cooked for the boys was enough for four or five, but they ate it all. Their hunger satisfied for the first time in days, they both thanked the good woman profusely, and when they were told she did not have any work for them to do, they left her house and started for home in Wayne—on foot.

They began walking down the railroad tracks that ran along the Elkhorn River valley. At the town of Pilger, which is ninety-five miles from Omaha, they planned to leave the railroad and walk the remaining twenty miles across country to Wayne. On the way, their hunger returning, they tried another house to see if they could work for a meal. John knocked at the back door, and when a worried-looking woman appeared, he said, "Lady, have you got anything left over that you intend to feed your dog?" She gave the boys four biscuits, but she had no work to offer.

They reached West Point, Nebraska, at about three in the afternoon of the following day, having made seventy-five miles on foot, without any sleep except a couple of hours in a cornfield. It was raining again, and they were reluctant to go into a town, fearing they might be jailed again as vagrants. Near West Point, they caught a baggage car on a passenger train and rode to Pilger, and on the way to Wayne, they were able to get jobs on a farm.

20

The Little Teacher

THE NEXT FALL AFTER the disappointing 1898 trip, John decided to try for a position at a school ten miles north of Hoskins, in the district next to the one where he had taught before. A teacher had already been hired in his former district, for John had told them he did not intend to return. He had high hopes that he would get a fine job in Kansas City and see his book published. Having not found such good fortune, he needed work, and he decided to fall back on his teaching certificate.

The new school was considered a tough one to handle, and when John went to see the director of the school board—a big, uneducated Swede—and said that he wanted the job of teaching at his school, the director looked him all over with an obviously dubious expression on his face.

John was only five-two and weighed a hundred and twenty-five pounds, but he had been training strenuously for several years. The director asked John if he thought he could handle the boys, adding, "What we need is somebody to t'rash 'em out!" John assured him that he could handle the situation, and the board ended up electing him to the position.

It was a curious school, its pupils scattered all the way from kindergarten to high school. The oldest pupil was twenty-one years old, but he was not difficult to handle because he was there to learn. It was the boys fifteen or sixteen years old who were the problem, because they were very husky and strong and considerably larger than their teacher, and they were, as John soon learned, "full of the Devil."

The diminutive teacher had a plan. He was a good wrestler, strong and very fast. He figured that if he could handle the boys and do it as a game, he would be able to control them during learning sessions. At the beginning of the school year, John suggested that they might do some wrestling, and the boys were enthusiastic, for such activities were very popular. At recess, if it was too cold to be outside, the desks were moved into a circle, and John would take the boys on—the biggest and strongest students first.

The teacher had one wrestling throw in particular that he used all winter, and he accomplished it so quickly that the boys never discovered how it was done. As the student approached him, John would use the young man's size to his disadvantage, and he would throw the boy over his head to land on his back, after which his shoulder would hit the student in the chest. Although his intention was to "knock the liver out of the fellow," John would apologize for hitting the boy so hard, explaining that this particular wrestling throw was very hard to control.

In this manner, by wrestling, stick-pulling, and foot racing, John was able to build up his prestige tremendously, and his reputation spread around the countryside, where he became widely known as "the little teacher." Once, on January 8, when John became eighteen, he and some of the boys were having a cob fight in the schoolyard when the little girl who lived where he boarded announced that it was John's birthday. It happened that just then the biggest boy in the school, who had taken the day off, came riding by on his horse. The boys yelled at him: "Come on, Bill, it's Teacher's birthday!"

Bill leaped off his horse, and he, with two other boys, jumped John, who had never wrestled harder in his life. The boys were corn-fed, accustomed to hard work on a farm, and were really very strong. For some time John was able to play one against the other and stay on his feet, but finally they got him down. From his embarrassing position on the ground, John managed to say, "No two of you can do it!" Their response: "That's why we came three." That winter passed rather pleasantly, and John felt that some of the pupils did learn something from his teaching.

In the early part of the year John had heard rumors that the boys were planning to throw him out of the school, as they had done to the young woman who had taught there the year before. They had simply picked her up and put her out a window and locked the door, and she had never returned. John knew who she was, for she had been one of his classmates at college—a sweet young thing who did not know what to do and went away crying. The boys, however, did not try that with John.

21

Becoming a Writer

IN EARLY 1899 JOHN went to Bancroft, where his mother and sister Lulu had moved. Mother Alice was busy with her dressmaking, and for additional income, she kept a teacher as a boarder in her home. Lulu taught in the school. For a time John had no job, but he had many ideas about what he wanted to write, and he was busy working them out on paper. Since people in the village did not see him at work, they assumed he was just living off his mother and his sister.

At times, in darker moments, John himself feared that what they thought of him might be true, but he kept on writing. "The Divine Enchantment" was not yet published, but he continued to write occasional lyrics and some stories. "The Song of the Hoe" had been the first lyric that grew out of his life experiences. At about the same time he wrote another poem out of his personal experience entitled "To a Hatpin," which he sold to *Truth*, a high-class "slick" magazine of the time.

This is the story behind that poem. Across the street from John's home lived a beautiful girl of about his own age. John used to watch her walking in their large yard—a slender, graceful, rather shy creature. One day he saw her walking in the sunlight, combing the long, red-gold hair that hung down to her hips, and even though the Neiharts knew her family well, the girl was an ethereal creature to John.

One winter evening she joined a group of Bancroft boys and girls who were going ice skating. It was a night of full moon, and to John the large, frozen lake was enchanted. Somehow it fell to John to help her learn to skate, and for him that was like associating too intimately with a goddess. It was on that night that he somehow gained possession of her hatpin, and after that the sight of the pin—*her pin*—was so moving to him that he wrote a poem about it. Although the two "had feelings for each other," John had set her on a pedestal, and there she remained.

In addition to his efforts in verse, John was practicing story-telling in prose. One luridly tragic tale, set in India and with an Indian hero, was entitled "Tiger's Lust." Although he knew nothing whatever about the subject matter of the story except the little that he had read, he sold the story to the *Chicago Ledger*, a paper that was sold by small boys all over the country. He received twenty-five dollars for the story, and, since his mother was in need of a new set of teeth, it gave him great satisfaction to use the money for that purpose.

Now that John had decided he was going to be a poet, he did not want his middle name to be the same as the name of another poet. "Greenleaf" had to go, and he began to search for a replacement name that would be more to his liking.

At the same time his interest in family had led him to do some re-search into the background of the family name in Germany. Much to his satisfaction, he learned that the Neidhardts—the name spelled with d—had been given a coat of arms by King Maximilian in Mainz around the year 1497. Their *Wappenbrief* is described in heraldic language as "Three barbed roses, gules (red), on a bend, azure, on a field, gules." Along with the coat of arms they were given substantial estates in the German Rheinpfals, which they unfortunately lost during the Thirty Years' War.

That war, begun as a religious dispute between Catholics and Protes-tants, later became territorial in nature, and it proved to be a monumen-tal disaster for the economy and society of Germany. It has been said that perhaps one-third of the urban residents and two-fifths of rural inhabitants—entire areas of Germany—were depopulated by the war, the movements of armies, and by diseases such as typhus, dysentery, bubonic plague, and syphilis.

Thousands of people fled the area for safer regions. The Neidhardts suffered tremendously, and those losses later caused John's ancestors to emigrate to the United States.

John's research led him first to Neidhardt von Reuenthal, a medieval Minnesinger, and just to know that this person might have been his an-cestor brought satisfaction to the aspiring poet in him. He also learned of Neidhardt von Gneisenau, a German general noted for many accomplishments, although at that time the large battleship bearing his name had not yet been built.

John had found his new middle name! He declared that his middle name was no longer "Greenleaf"; it was "Gneisenau". At the same time, he also assumed the last d in the surname, but not the first, and from that day on his name was John Gneisenau Neihardt.

The young poet was beginning to associate with the Omaha Indians, whose reservation bordered the town of Bancroft. He became acquainted with many of the old Omahas from seventy to ninety years of age, and the memories of the oldest reached back to the 1820s, well into the period of early American history. For some reason John never had any difficulty getting on intimate terms with the old Indians, perhaps because he was genuinely fond of them as people and was eager to learn what they knew.

The need to support himself and his mother never ceased, and John was ambitious in shaping his plans. Having had some success in writing he decided to go to Omaha, where he acquired a job as a reporter on the *Omaha Daily News*.

John's particular type of sympathy for others made him ill-suited to the work, and he often found it difficult to push his way into interviews with persons whose life problems or tragedies made them newsworthy. He was "scooped" by other reporters almost every day, and after a few months, he lost his job on the paper.

Work was necessary, but jobs were scarce, and when he next found employment, it was by way of a "Help Wanted" sign in the window of a restaurant not too far from the *Daily News*. It so happened that John was scrubbing the floor when a few of his former co-workers came in for lunch.

John was intensely embarrassed, and when his rude employer began loudly criticizing the way he was using the unfamiliar mop, it was too much for him. In anger and in embarrassment John summarily threw down the mop and left the restaurant and the city of Omaha as well. He went back to Bancroft.

After his discouraging stay on the *News*, the young writer was able to get employment with J. J. Elkin, who was one of a group of men who were buying and selling Indian heirship lands, leasing Indian lands to white farmers, and lending money to Indians. John kept Elkin's books, did other clerical work, and collected from the Indians when they received their payments from the government.

As a result of his work he was associating with Omaha Indians constantly, both on and off the reservation. He came to know them—both men and women—as people, not merely as "the Indians." The Indian people liked John and trusted him, for they knew he was not receiving any of the money he collected from them but was only making his living at a small salary.

At that time agents who were in collusion with the buyers were selling heirship lands to white men, and this often resulted in the land being sold at prices far below its true value. The Indians were helpless, for they had no experience in dealing with such men.

One day John was present in Elkin's office when an Indian came in wishing to sell some inherited land. When Mr. Elkin asked what he wanted for the land, the Indian replied, "We talk it over, and we say we ask thirty dollars. You no give us thirty, so we take twenty."

If an Indian was in special need of a few dollars, he would come in to borrow. He would get the money, and often he would sign by putting his mark on a note for double the amount received, even though the term of the note might be for only thirty days. In order to impress the Indian with the seriousness of the matter, a mortgage would be taken on his team and wagon, which had probably been mortgaged several times before.

It was not really the mortgage that secured the note; it was the fact that Elkins's crowd could get into the pay-station, while other creditors were kept a quarter of a mile away, where they passed the time playing mumble-peg, horseshoes, and other games along a set line, waiting for the prospective victims to appear. With these creditors the unfortunate Indians would be chased into the brush, and if they had any money left, they could usually be persuaded to pay.

It was different with Elkins's group. A representative would be inside the pay-station, and when the checks were issued, the notes the Indians had signed would be brought out in the presence of the agent. This impressed the Indians that the matter was "official," and the notes were usually paid on the spot.

John's friendship with the Omaha Indian people grew, and he came to appreciate them on a simple, human basis. He visited them in their lodges, drank their soup (which he later described as "god-awful") and played with their babies. They named him "Tae Nuga Zhinga" which translates "Little Bull Buffalo" and commented on the name in this way: "big head, bushy hair, big shoulders, little hips—good name!"

One day Shonga Ska (White Horse), a very old man and one of the last real chiefs of the Omahas, stopped the proceedings at a Saturday night dance in a lodge near Blackbird Hill on the reservation to tell the Indians present what he thought of John. He announced, "This young man here is a white man, but he is a good young man. He has the heart of an Indian."

John frequently attended those Indian dances with Caryl or Jack Farley, grandsons of Iron Eye. Iron Eye, known as Joseph La Flesche, was the last chieftain of the Omahas and a man of high distinction both among his people and among whites. Caryl would act as interpreter, and in this manner John heard many stories as told by old Indians.

One old fellow would begin a story and would sometimes be interrupted by another who remembered the tale in quite a different way. The tellings were dramatic and often truly hilarious or touching, and John was so impressed with the stories and the way in which they were told that he began to recreate them in short stories. His stories were very well received and were published in a number of magazines.

Joseph La Flesche had two daughters who became very well known: Susan and Susette. Dr. Susan La Flesche Picotte, the first Indian woman in the country to become a physician, lived for a time in Bancroft, and John came to know her quite well. Dr. Picotte read John's Indian tales with considerable enthusiasm and commented, "All the fiction I have read about Indians, from Cooper to Remington, has offended me until now. I cannot understand how you get in your stories the Indian way of feeling, the Indian's spirituality, and are even able to represent the Indian idiom in English."

Susette married a white man, a journalist and writer named Henry Tibbles (*Buckskin and Blanket Days*), and they became internationally known through their participation in the famous Standing Bear *habeas corpus* trial.

Known as *United States ex. rel. Standing Bear, v. George Crook, a Brigadier General of the U.S. Army*, the case was decided in the United States District Court for Nebraska in 1924. The trial is famous for Judge Bundy's decision that "an *Indian* is a PERSON within the meaning of the laws of the United States."

Bright Eyes (Ishta Theamba), as Suzette was known, during the trial in court translated Chief Standing Bear's testimony into English. She was strikingly beautiful, with an air of dignity and poise that would mark her in any crowd. She was also an eloquent and magnetic speaker who later lectured with her husband throughout the United States and in Europe.

They lived a few miles north of Bancroft, and it was there that Bright Eyes died. The night before she was buried, Tibbles asked Neihardt to sit up with him, which he did, and the two men reminisced, mostly about Bright Eyes. Tibbles talked all night, telling John the story of his life and of his experiences, in America and abroad, with his wife.

Often Tibbles would seem to forget that Bright Eyes was lying in the other room and would become quite merry over some diverting incident in his experience. Then he would remember, and he would say, "Let's look at her again!" He would stop talking and go into the room where she lay, gaze at her, and gently wipe her face with a damp towel.

Then he would return to his vigil with John, saying, "She is so beautiful!" Susette Tibbles is buried in the cemetery at Bancroft, Nebraska, a short distance from where John and his mother lived.

John worked three or four years for J. J. Elkin, and one day he was present when the members of the company were all in the office. They were talking about successful deals that had been made when one of them said, "Johnny, you don't want to do this all your life. What do you want to do? Maybe we can help you."

John replied, "No, I don't want to do this all my life." They urged him to tell what he would like to do, and he answered, "I want to run the Bancroft *Blade*." The *Blade* was a county paper, and in those days such a paper had considerable influence, because without rural free delivery, the city papers did not circulate throughout the countryside. Mr. Elkin suggested, "Well, why don't you buy it?"

When John protested that he had no money, the men present decided to organize a company and buy it themselves. John knew that the paper—building, plant, and its business—could be bought for $2,800, The men offered to put up $2,800 if John could come up with another $200. John hesitated at first, but at Elkins' suggestion he made application to borrow the $200 from the bank across the street from the newspaper. The shrewd owner of the bank agreed to take John's books in as collateral, possibly because he sensed that there might be bigger things in store for the young villager.

The Blade Publishing Company was organized, the paper changed hands, and John had the time of his life running the *Bancroft Blade*. It was the custom then for editors of country newspapers to engage in wordy battles with each other, and the readers enjoyed the fray. A good paper was expected to be a fighting paper, and John's paper was of this sort.

The president of Blade Publishing Company, Fred Nelson, was ambitious politically, and this had been one reason he wished to participate in acquiring the newspaper. Nelson was nominated for state senator on the Republican ticket, and John, born to that party, helped Nelson in the race against his opponent, a very intelligent liberal who was advanced for his time. The man knew more about economics and government in general than Nelson's group did, but he was considered a dangerous radical for views that would later come to be regarded as commonplace.

John ran a weekly department on the front page making fun of Nelson's Democratic opponent. It was written in the form of a primer for little children to read, all in questions and answers, and it was well illustrated with zinc etchings made by a young friend of John's who was good at drawing.

Fortunately or unfortunately, the Democratic opponent had a rock-hewn face that was immediately recognizable once it had been seen, and the most conspicuous feature of that face was a rather large nose. It was a simple matter for a young fellow to create caricatures for the primer page that made fun of such a face. The department became very popular, and readers looked forward to each new issue of the paper.

Fred Nelson, the Republican, was elected, and the defeated Democrat was reported to have made angry threats toward the smart-alecky editor of the *Blade*. One day the two met on the street, exchanged harsh words, and for a time it seemed there would be an actual physical confrontation between the two men who were so ill-matched physically.

In spite of his much smaller size, the villagers' bets were on John, for he had quite a reputation as a fighter and wrestler and had been dubbed "the biggest little man in Cuming County" and "the Cast-iron Duke." It was well known in Bancroft that John had a ten-inch chest expansion, could tear a pack of cards in two and could lift his own weight over his head with one arm.

The defeated political hopeful, however, did not have any such training in wrestling or boxing. As the two men stood facing each other, the bigger man said, "John Neihardt, you are so very small mentally and physically!" Replying very quickly, John said, "I am going to go through you like a dose of salts!"

Knowing that if his much larger opponent got hold of him, he would be able to shake him like a baby, John had been very careful not to get within reach, but he had a plan by which he would move very fast and deliver a punch that would knock out his untrained opponent.

When he was threatened, John leaped toward the big man, who turned quickly and walked the other way down the street, perhaps realizing that he could be made a laughing stock if he took part in a scrap with Neihardt. It was better that way, for—whether he won or lost in a fight with a man so much smaller than he—he could not win in the eyes of his townsmen.

Some ten years later, John saw the man he had treated so badly in his newspaper column as he was walking down the street in Bancroft. John caught up with him and said, "There is something I have wanted to say to you for some time."

Not looking at John, the defeated politician responded, "Well?"

"I want to say that I know you were right in the old days, and that I was a damn fool!"

The man looked down from his six-feet-two-inches to John's five-feet-two-inches with a kindly twinkle in his eyes and said, "Well, I'm glad you found out." The two men were on friendly terms after that. Although John did not take such direct part in politics again, he never lost interest in current events, and he kept up with the news through the papers, radio reports, and in later years, by way of eagerly watched television newscasts.

As a young boy John thought that he would be an inventor, but because of his rather intense physical training, another possibility presented itself. One pleasant summer week-end a group of young Bancroftians decided to go by train to Sioux City, Iowa, to attend a large carnival, and John was invited to go along. His pal John Chaffee was going, and John invited his current girlfriend to join the group. Once on the carnival grounds, the young Nebraskans had enjoyed themselves, laughing and talking as they walked about, devouring the foodstuffs offered in various booths, and trying their hands at the games and contests.

They came upon a punching machine that consisted of a leather pad that, when struck by someone's fist, caused a metal ball to rise up a tube, at the high end of which there was a bell. The player was supposed to strike the machine with enough force so that the ball struck the bell at the top, causing it to ring out loudly.

The group watched as several men struck the pad. No one had succeeded in making the bell ring, although several came close. After Chaffee and the other fellows in their party had also tried with no success, John was urged to step up to the machine. He took off his jacket, handed it to his lady friend, and approached the striking pad. Very swiftly and straight out from his chest, he delivered a punch in which his whole body was included. The ball flew up the tube, struck the bell soundly, and it rang so loudly that it was heard throughout the crowd.

John was just putting his jacket on when a stranger who had been standing near the back of the crowd approached. He was dressed, city-style, in a dark brown suit with a long jacket, topped by a black Derby hat, and tightly clenched in his teeth was a large, unlit cigar. He was definitely not a man from around John's part of the country; everything about him breathed an air of success and a kind of urban sophistication quite unfamiliar to John and his friends.

From under the Derby, the man's dark hair hung longer than the usual style, and above a wide, ingratiating smile, a black and sizeable moustache stretched almost half-way across his face. His appearance was strange—not particularly pleasant but nonetheless impressive.

The man stopped directly in front of John and gave him a rather cool but intense and appraising look from head to foot. Then he spoke, "Fellow, with that punch you have, I can make you the featherweight boxing champion of the world! I know because I train and handle fighters, and I go to places like this looking for young fight prospects. Kid, you have one hell of a punch!" The man looked at John and his friends, and he could plainly see that they were all of modest circumstances. He continued, "I promise you this: if you let me train you and manage you, I can make you rich! Now, how would you like that?"

John just stared at the man; he was so surprised by the offer that he hesitated to answer. His years of physical training had been for his own satisfaction, and living in a town where most of the men were much larger than he, it had been something of an equalizer. Never once had he thought of a career as a professional fighter.

John Chaffee, spoke up first. "John's going to be a poet, not a fighter!" At this point, John broke into the conversation, thanked the man, but confirmed what his friend had said. He did not want to be a fighter, he emphasized, even if he could be the featherweight champion of the world. He did not say it, but he may have thought it: as a boxer, he could only hope to be a featherweight, but as a poet, he could be a *heavyweight* champion. The offer did not tempt him.

With a look of disbelief and almost of disgust, the promoter asked, "What's the matter, kid? *Do you hate money?*" John did not reply, and the promoter disappeared again into the crowd. John had spoken correctly to the fight promoter; he had definitely made up his mind that he would be a poet, and his family, ever since the publication of *The Song of the Hoe* in 1900, had quite accustomed itself to having a poet in the house.

On one occasion, it is told, his Uncle George wryly commented, "I think John's going to have a poem; he acts queer!" He was busy writing the lyric poetry that later appeared in *A Bundle of Myrrh*, poems that grew out of the normal quest of a young man seeking to learn about women. The poetry came from personal experience, not mere imagination, just as his later major works grew out of his first-hand experiences with the old history-makers, both white and Indian, who were still alive. Titles of some of the early lyrics are revealing of this characteristic:

"A Vision of Woman," "Can This Be Sin?" "Let Down Your Hair," and "Titan-Woman."

Reviews of his poetry were enthusiastic. *The New York Times* described his poetry: "lyrics that have not been equaled by any modern poet." Bliss Carman ventured this assessment: "He is already with the English poets, and one can say no more."

Not all of his poems were about women; one entitled "When I am Dead" and the highly popular "Let Me Live Out My Years" reveal another notion that prevailed in his youthful mind. It is perhaps not unusual for an adolescent to think he might not live long, and Neihardt, although he was perfectly healthy, secretly had such a thought.

John had a notion that he might die young, as Byron had done. When he was writing *The Divine Enchantment*, he intended it to be a work that was to be "my justification for having lived in this world, and my payment for all the potatoes I had eaten and the roofs I had over my head."

The book was precious to him, and it was finally published by James T. White and Company in New York. Cost of the publication—about $250—was paid by Neihardt himself by way of a bank loan on which his farmer uncle, George Culler, co-signed. John repaid the loan in installments, but the banker, Mr. Ley, whose son Rollie was a schoolmate of John's, never dunned him if he was a bit late.

When about half of the lyrics included in *A Bundle of Myrrh* were completed, John and his printer at the *Blade* decided to make them into a book. They printed five copies, using eggshell, deckle-edged paper, bound in chamois-skin, and the book turned out well. The copies were given to his mother, Alice Neihardt, his two sisters, Lulu and Grace, John's good friend, Volney Streamer of the Players' Club in New York, and the fifth was for John.

It was at this time—about 1903—that John decided to burn all the copies he could find of *The Divine Enchantment*. The subject matter of that book did not come out of his own personal experience, as did the poetry and short stories he was then writing, and he wanted a "clean slate" in publishing the work he was doing and which he planned for the future. The few copies of the book that escaped being burned for heat in his mother's stove are valuable today.

After they moved to Bancroft the Neihardts had lived in rented houses, but in 1904 Alice Neihardt was able through her industry and with some help from the children to purchase a small house near the west edge of the town, at the corner of Elm Street and Pennsylvania Avenue. She lived there with her daughter Lulu, who was teaching in Bancroft, and with John. The small, two-bedroom house somehow managed to accommodate the family and a boarder, usually another teacher.

John's first serious love affair was with a lovely young school principal who roomed at his mother's home during the school year. Emma Engle was a spirited girl with a "pale, swift look" and an intensity of feeling similar to John's. Theirs was a beautiful romance, and they called each other by private names—Diana and Apollo—as they drove about the countryside.

Emma shared John's enthusiasm for reading and discussion; she also loved violin music and long walks through the countryside, but she did not share his literary ambitions. Hers was a wealthy family, and she thought he should be willing to be her husband and enjoy the comfort of wealth, relegating his writing to a leisure activity.

But John could not give up his pursuit of the great dream he had cherished for years. He feared that a marriage to Emma would inevitably destroy that dream, and he decided that he must break their engagement. Emma returned John's letters, and he left home to spend time with the Omaha Indians on their reservation. There he would absorb more material for his short stories, which were being well received. John's mother was relieved, for she had not entirely supported the engagement.

After a month or so with the Omahas, John returned to his home in Bancroft. One old-timer he came to know about this time, whose memories contributed greatly to John's growing store of first-hand information concerning the history of westward expansion in America, was Antoine Cabanné.

Cabanné was born around 1824 at Fort Atkinson, which is some fourteen miles up the Missouri River from Omaha and is now known as Calhoun. Antoine's father was Jean P. Cabanné, one of the most famous aristocratic French entrepreneurs in St. Louis. He had founded a fur-trading post at Ft. Atkinson and had married an Omaha Indian woman.

Antoine was their son, and he took great satisfaction in announcing that he was "the first white child born in Nebraska!"

"White" Antoine certainly was not, for he was Indian in appearance. He was of slightly less than medium height, powerfully built, and although he had no formal education whatsoever, he had the manners of a great gentleman, having learned them from his father and other French fur traders of the time. If he chanced to meet a lady whom he knew, he would stop and bow with a grand gesture and a sweep of his hat down nearly to the sidewalk.

Antoine had grown up in what was then a wilderness. When he was a young man, his father had obtained a position for him as an apprentice to a steamboat engineer on the Missouri River, and he had traveled the river from St. Louis to Ft. Benton in Montana, the head of navigation, more times than he could remember.

When John knew Antoine the man was about eighty years old and walked limpingly with a cane. His rough-hewn, bewhiskered face, his squat body, and his signeurial airs made him something of a comical figure for the wags of the town. They were mistaken, of course, for he was truly a fine gentleman, not only in manners but by instinct and training as well. Antoine's experiences, told to John from the remarkable memory of an illiterate, helped John to understand the life of the period in American history about which he would later write. He was already deep into the study of the history of the American West, and Antoine Cabanné came to seem like the spirit of the Missouri River to John.

Some readers may remember the days when the barber shop was the local—men only—social center of a town, and everything was discussed there. Old Antoine would sometimes come to the barber shop in Bancroft, and the village wags would get him started telling stories of the old days. Those fellows knew nothing of the history of the period in which Antoine had lived and worked, and they were convinced that he was nothing more than a colossal liar. One day when Antoine was not there, John insisted that he had found the man was accurate in what he told, and he made this proposition to the villagers: "I will get a list of old-time steamboats that were wrecked on the Missouri River, and we will get him in here and ask him about the boats. I will bet you that he knows what he is talking about."

It was done, and in a later session when the fellows asked him about a given boat, Antoine would say, "Oh, yes, I mind her." Then he would set forth on a detailed history of that boat and tell when and where and in what bend of the river she was wrecked. They continued the test, asking him about many of the boats on John's list, and the old fellow knew all of them. Antoine's memory was truly surprising, like that of many old Indians. Without the ability to record events in writing, they relied on memory, and as a result that ability became more reliable. After Antoine's performance the barbershop crowd was more respectful to Antoine.

Although his short stories were surprisingly successful, John's main interest was in his poetry, which he had collected into a manuscript that he entitled "A Bundle of Myrrh." He had not found a publisher for the book, but he had sent a copy of the manuscript to his friend Bob Davis, who had purchased many of his stories. Davis had shown the collection to friends in New York, where it brought the young poet to the attention of various persons of literary importance.

One such person was Volney Streamer, who had acted in Edwin Booth's company. A trained actor, he read poetry beautifully, and he was widely acquainted in literary circles in New York. In 1906 Streamer came to Nebraska to visit Neihardt, and they became good friends. In early 1907 Streamer invited John to spend six weeks in New York. John's friends in Bancroft were excited when he told them about the invitation, and one J. R. Kelly, the owner of a clothing store in Bancroft, felt privileged to assist John in choosing that most necessary new suit and topcoat. In New York, John stayed with Volney Streamer, president of the Players Club, and the sumptuous luncheons and dinners that followed were beyond anything John had known.

While he was visiting Volney Streamer at the club, John met many celebrities, including Edwin Arlington Robinson, Amy Lowell, and the publisher Henry Holt. Holt introduced him at the Players Club, saying, "You do not know him now, but you will!"

Mark Twain was also invited to come to the club, and John was particularly eager to meet him. Unfortunately, Mr. Twain became ill and could not attend, but he did send John a manuscript of the ribald "Conversations at the Fireside of Queen Elizabeth" with the comment "I think it will amuse him." It did!

Those he met while in New York were not all writers or actors, and perhaps the most important person he met so casually was a well-dressed, handsome woman by the name of Adah Martinsen. Her carriage and her striking presence would most likely reveal to anyone who took notice that she was a woman of some importance, and perhaps also that she had once been an aspiring actress.

Mrs. Martinsen was intensely impressed with John, and she loved his poetry. She noticed that he was not tall, but the suit that the Bancroft merchant had made for him with such pride did much to reveal his broad shoulders and narrow hips. His blonde hair, cut slightly long and full, fell into easy waves, and his eyes were of an almost shocking blue. They were at once penetrating and warmly friendly, and they seemed to belong naturally to his overall dynamic being. Adah had thought of her husband's Slavic ancestors when she looked at the young poet.

John was not rude or rough, but he carried himself with an air of masculine strength that was most pleasing to the ladies. Moreover, Adah Martinsen had been overcome quite to the point of tears by his recitation of the lyrics and by the passionate depth of the poetry itself. When they were introduced and Adah told John how she felt about his poetry, John received her compliments politely, but he was not then overly impressed. The lady, however, was deeply moved, and she had made a mental note that she must write to Paris and tell her daughter Mona about John Neihardt. She did not delay writing to Mona.

While in New York, John was given a contract with the John Lane Company to publish a collection of his Indian and other short stories to be called The Lonesome Trail. The book appeared and was a success, and editors of the American Magazine offered to buy all of Neihardt's stories. They particularly asked for another story like "The Alien," but John replied that the tale could not be repeated. He had already written "The Alien."

Back in Nebraska the excitement of his recent successes stayed with John. It was a happy and relaxed time, and to celebrate their good fortune he and his mother and sister Grace decided to spend the 1907 summer in Spearfish Canyon in the beautiful Black Hills of South Dakota. Lulu had gone to Minnesota to teach in Brainerd, and it was there that she would meet her husband-to-be, Donald McDonald.

It was a memorable summer. Their cabin was beside a waterfall whose happy sounds were heard night and day, and the sun came up each morning from behind tall peaks and sank in the late afternoon behind others. John awoke early and left before the sun had topped the peaks to go fly-fishing in the clear mountain stream. Alone or with friends or family, he spent many a happy day hiking in the mountains.

John was not the only one who enjoyed the Black Hills beauty. On one hike with his sister Grace, they found an abandoned mining town, complete with zero gauge railroad and unoccupied houses and businesses. The inhabitants had evidently abandoned the town in some haste, for they had left many of their belongings behind them.

Many cooking utensils remained in the kitchens of the houses, and behind the door of the barber shop John found an old buffalo rifle that was beautifully fitted with German silver mountings and silver triggerguard. It had obviously been abandoned when its owner hurriedly left town, and since there was no one to ask about it, John took the gun. Years later, after the gun had been broken in a moving accident, he had the silver fittings put on a Savage 32–20 rifle for a daughter.

The little, small-gauge railroad, once used for transporting ore down the steep mountainsides, was intact. John was able to figure out how the zero-gauge worked, and he and his mother and sister found it very exciting, riding down the steep slopes in the small cars. They also tried their hands at placer mining for gold in Spearfish Creek, but the effort was only relaxing, not materially enriching. Small matter, for John's interest was in material for more stories, and he found it in abundance. For all three of the Neihardts the time spent in the unspoiled mountains at Spearfish had been not only relaxing but a great deal of good wholesome fun.

After they returned to Bancroft John learned that his poetry would be published. When the manuscript for "A Bundle of Myrrh" had first been offered to the Outing Publishing Company, its readers assumed that it would be promptly refused, since poetry had no market at the time. But it did not happen so, for Neihardt's poetry was different. Much to their own surprise, the editors were so impressed by the poems that they decided to publish them. The book was well received, and reviewers praised Neihardt for his spiritual themes, and for the masculine boldness and originality of the verse. One reviewer compared him to Pindar and Heinrich Heine, another thought Neihardt should be compared to Whitman. One reviewer stated that the young Nebraskan "had talent to burn."

But there were reservations, one being the hope that he would not confuse unrestrained emotion with manliness. Harriet Monroe objected to his "boyish insolence and brag," but she also compared him to Ezra Pound as a high-hearted young poet with "delicately tempered weapons." John Neihardt's poems were considered to be "very frank," and—for those modest times—they were. John was happy with his new successes. He was becoming nationally known as an author.

From his earliest efforts at publication of his verses and short stories, and for all of the correspondence he carried on with those interested in his works, the postal service had been important to John. Mail was not only his principal mode of communication with the outside world, it was the means by which he conducted his life work; it was his sustenance.

Because of this dependence John was a regular and prompt patron of the post office. Seldom, indeed, did he fail to walk to the local office at mail-time, and he was almost unreasonably impatient with holiday interruptions. During this time in Bancroft there were no telephones or any other kind of electronic communication, but long after such means were available, he still relied principally upon the postal services. Grandchildren remember being asked to walk to the mailbox for him, and they were always cautioned, "Be careful!"

On one particular late fall day in 1907, John had gone immediately after breakfast to his room and closed the door. He could not write unless he was in an enclosed space, and today he was so intensely caught up in what he was composing that he did not come out of his room mid-morning to go for the mail in downtown Bancroft, as he was accustomed to do.

Alice noticed this, and, opening his door carefully and looking in at her son, she saw that he was hard at work, writing on the plain kitchen table that he used as a desk. She was not surprised to see the crumpled pieces of cheap yellow paper with which the floor of his room was strewn, for after John had made so many changes and corrections on a sheet that the wording was difficult to follow, he threw the paper on the floor and began anew on a fresh piece.

John wrote with penny pencils, and when a poem or story was completed to his satisfaction, he typed it quite handily on a Smith-Premier by means of the "hunt and peck" method. For this he used good quality white paper, and the neatly typed composition was ready to be sent to a publisher.

The door squeaked as it was opened, interrupting John's concentration, and he looked up at his mother with a blank, almost unknowing stare. "John, I am going to town, and I will stop by the post office for you, if you wish." John acknowledged her absent-mindedly: "Yes, Thanks." His gaze returned to the paper on which he was writing, and Alice closed the door quietly.

Putting on a light jacket, for the weather had already become quite cool, Alice walked down Elm Street to Main, and then to the small grocery that she frequented. She had come to the store for only a few items, and they filled only part of the cloth bag that she took with her when she shopped. There would be plenty of room for John's mail—and for hers, if she received anything.

Alice was smiling when she returned from town, and as she came into the house, she called to her son, who this time came out of his room, for he was eager as always to see the day's mail. It happened that among the several pieces of mail John received that day was a letter addressed carefully in feminine handwriting.

Since *A Bundle of Myrrh* with its many love poems had appeared, this was not an unusual occurrence, for a number of eager young women in various parts of the country had written to him. John always seemed to take the effusive letters in his stride. Today, however, was different.

Alice held up a letter that, like two or three others, had been forwarded from New York by the publisher. It was addressed carefully, and the rather artistic handwriting was definitely that of a woman, but what had caught Alice's attention was this: *the postmark on this letter was foreign.* Alice was plainly excited as she handed the envelope to her son: "John, you have a letter from *Paris!*"

3

The Couple

22

John and Mona

I would that my tongue could shape the sound my spirit calls you.
It would be as a rose leaf becoming vocal, as a
honeycomb talking of sweetness.

"The Sound My Spirit Calls You"

JOHN THANKED HIS MOTHER, took the proffered mail to his room, and sat down to read. He glanced quickly at all the envelopes, but he opened the one from Paris first. The lady—for it was obvious to John that this letter was from a very special woman—had written in purple ink on fine paper. The latter characteristic caught John's eye, for as a publisher he had become well acquainted with papers of various qualities, and he valued the really good ones. The handwriting was firm and clear, with carefully formed letters, and many of the nouns were capitalized, in the manner of the education of Mona's youth.

John noticed that the letter had taken nearly three weeks to reach him. Then he began to read:

Dear Mr. Neihardt:

I must apologize for taking the Liberty to write to a Man to whom I have not been properly introduced. I take this Liberty because I somehow feel that we are not Strangers. I have been reading *A Bundle of Myrrh* which was sent to me by my Mother, Mrs. Adah Martinsen of New York City. Mother met you some time ago at a gathering of Artists and Writers, and she was so impressed with you and with your Poetry that she wrote to me. Recently she sent me your beautiful volume of Lyrics.

Now that I have been reading it, I want to tell you that I am thrilled by the beauty of your verse and by the depth of meaning which I feel in it. I have shown *A Bundle of Myrrh* to a number of other students in Paris, where I am at present studying sculpture with Auguste Rodin. M. Rodin is a true spiritual light as well as a foremost Artist. I am learning much from that Great Man.

Mr. Neihardt, I do not want to take up too much of your time by trying to express the Thoughts and Feelings that come to me while reading your Poems, but let me say that I am moved by your Poetry as I have never been moved before. You express emotions that I have felt within me and experiences that I have had, and you reach up to spiritual heights which I, too, should like to gain.

She went on to mention a few poems which she particularly liked, among them "The Sound My Spirit Calls You" and "The Last Altar." About the first poem she wrote: "Such beautiful Language, Mr. Neihardt! I find the unrhymed Lyrics very appealing, although I am more familiar with Poetry that has Rhyme." She shared Neihardt's desire expressed in the closing lines of "The Last Altar:"

> I wish to grasp the joy of being humble,
> To build great Love an altar ere I die.

Mona's letter closed with the gentle suggestion, "I should be happy to hear from you, Mr. Neihardt" and ended simply, "Sincerely yours, Mona Martinsen."

John sat at his table longer than usual. He carefully read Mona's letter more than once, for in its whole he felt a spirit that cast a warm glow over the words. A number of appreciative women had written to John since *A Bundle of Myrrh* appeared, but what they said had not impressed him as did this letter from Mona.

The others had been enthusiastic and complimentary, but that was all. Mona's letter went beyond that; it had substance. As he told friends in later years, "A number of ladies wrote letters to me, but hers were the best." Reading it, he could tell that she truly understood what he was trying to say. For a young poet, striving to tell the untellable, this was success of the most encouraging kind.

"Mona," he mused to himself, "I don't know anyone else by that name. A sculptress—studying in Paris with Rodin! I wonder what she looks like . . ." Throughout the remainder of that day, John's thoughts kept returning to the letter that had come to him from so far away, and with those thoughts came a warm surge of feeling.

He waited until the next day to answer Mona's letter, writing carefully and maintaining throughout a polite and reserved manner. He did tell her that her letter "glowed" and that what she had written was mean-ingful to him. John told her about the short stories he was working on at the time and the canoe trip down the Missouri River that he had dreamed of taking.

With it all, he included a little about himself and his personal life. He also expressed the hope that she would do the same, assuring her that he was very interested in her art and in her life in Paris. In closing he said that he would be looking forward to hearing from her again, and he signed the letter "Yours truly, Jno. Neihardt."

The letter arrived in Paris some two weeks later. Mona had come home from her studio earlier than usual, and as she entered she eagerly took her mail—two letters—from the box in the entryway. She was pleased to see her mother's familiar handwriting on one of the envelopes, but her heart skipped a beat when she saw the return address on the other one. It came from Bancroft, Nebraska! Hurriedly she removed her hat and gloves but kept her outer garments on against the chill in her apartment. She would build up the fire later, but the letter came first.

Mona read John's letter eagerly, and just receiving it made her so happy that she wished to share her feelings with someone. She put her hat back on and went immediately to Olga's home. When her friend appeared at the door, Mona excitedly told her: "Olga, I have just received a letter from John Neihardt!" Olga invited her in, and Mona read aloud what John had written. "What do you think, Olga?"

"Well, Mona, you have a new friend! Didn't I tell you that Mr. Neihardt would be happy to hear from you? You will write him again, won't you?"

"Yes, yes I will! Oh, dear Olga!—my dear and understanding friend!" Caught up in emotion, Mona put her arms around Olga and hugged her.

Then, because it was nearing that time of day, she suggested that they go out for dinner together at a nearby restaurant. They did, and very little of their conversation that evening was about anything except John Neihardt.

Mona wrote again to Nebraska the very next day, and she mailed the letter at the post office on her way to the studio. As she worked on her sculpture, her usually intense concentration was interrupted a number of times as she tried to picture the young man in the far-away American Midwest. She herself had never been west of New York City, but she had known that her father had important business connections in the West.

"I wonder what Mr. Neihardt looks like? How large a city is Bancroft? His family—what kind of people are they?" Questions such as these began to break their way into Mona's thoughts. Well-disciplined through her former association with Elwell and now with Rodin, she at first was able to put the interfering thoughts aside. Gradually, however, as the days and weeks passed, this became more and more difficult to do.

The correspondence between John and Mona continued, and the beginning tone of polite reserve each had used gave way to friendly companionship and later to much more than that. "We told each other everything," John later explained, "we held nothing back." In this way they came to know each other, even though they did not meet face to face. John asked for a picture, and in the next letter from Mona a photograph was included. It showed a slender, rather serious young woman (Mona seemed never to smile for a picture) standing in front of a brick building of foreign design. She wore a beautifully cut dark suit like none John had seen, and over her darkening blond hair, done up high on her head, was a large hat worn at an angle.

It was a very nice face, John thought, a face that was more than pretty, and he was particularly drawn to her unusually large eyes. He could not tell their color from the picture, but Mona had told him they were gray and sometimes appeared to be blue. John looked into her eyes, which seemed to fasten themselves steadily and warmly upon him, and for a brief moment he imagined how Mona would look, sitting across the table from him at breakfast. The moment passed, but the feeling did not.

John had carefully chosen the picture that he would send to Mona.

It had been taken to serve as frontispiece of a book, and it revealed a well-dressed, rather handsome young man whose intense expression suggested he was capable of creating the poetry that it would introduce. It gave no hint, however, of the little frontier town that was his home or of the small house in which he lived with his mother. As she gazed—almost adoringly—at John's picture, Mona could hardly realize that the material wealth and comforts she had from babyhood enjoyed and taken for granted were entirely lacking in his life. John had been truthful with her, but could full realization of one another come from correspondence alone?

As Mona looked at the photograph, did some memory perhaps remind her of the peasant families of Gernsbach—who had so very little—laughing and singing together as they gathered wood for their fires? Because of such early experiences Mona had since childhood wondered whether one needed to be wealthy in order to be happy.

Mona saved all of John's letters, putting them into a box she prepared for the purpose. It is likely that John also kept Mona's letters. The two collections would no doubt make a most interesting book on their own. As their fondness for each other grew, these two artistic people created a soulful and—yes—a romantic relationship in their unusual courtship.

It was only partly because of her interest in John that Mona was no longer completely happy in Paris. She talked to Olga about her disapproval of the lax way of life in certain quarters of Paris, and she spoke often of John Neihardt and the feelings his poetry awakened in her. Olga, dear and understanding friend that she was, encouraged her: "Mona, you must follow your heart. If you do not, you will never be happy. I am sure of that! Listen to what your heart tells you, dear Mona, and I will help you in any way I can."

Mona listened to her friend and to her own thoughts. Early in 1908 she decided to return to New York to be with her mother and nearer to her brother Ottocar. Rudi, sensitive and brilliant Rudi, who had decided to remain in Germany when the family returned to New York, had died following an accident. It was sad but not entirely unexpected, for there had always been something about Rudi that hinted that life would not be kind to him.

Mona did return to New York, leaving behind the studies with Rodin that were so meaningful to her but also freeing herself from a way of life she could not accept. She was hopeful that she could carry on her career in the city of her birth, but a new yearning had gradually grown within her that could no longer be ignored.

Mona had never put the memory of her father or her sorrow at his death completely out of her thoughts. She had felt completely happy as a child when he was part of their family, when all was as it should have been, but after he was gone, her world was never the same again. Despite the persistence of these memories they in no way handicapped Mona. She simply never forgot. Now, as she became closer in thought and feeling with John through their many honest and heartfelt outpourings, Mona recognized in herself a growing new strength, a feeling that if a new doorway opened for her, she would be able to redirect her life.

John continued to pursue a writing career. He had often dreamed of a trip down the Missouri, the river that had been so important to him since childhood, when, holding his father's hand, he had been awed by its destructive power in the Kansas City flood. Now, in his pursuit of history, he was beginning to realize the major role this river had played in the development of the American West.

While he was still involved in planning the river trip, John met Grant Marsh, captain of the steamboat *Far West*, which had served as the "navy" during the Indian wars by bringing supplies to the army. John served as deckhand on the steamboat, carrying supplies from the dock and up the gangplank.

John learned a lot from Captain Marsh, not only about life on the river but also something about the captain's part in western history. Marsh told how one day a young Indian scout came to the *Far West* after the battle in which Custer and his men were wiped out. This is how the captain's story went:

One day when Marsh had the *Far West* tied up on the west bank of the Missouri River in Montana, a young Crow Indian came out of the brush at the side of the steamer, "crying and tearing his hair." Indicating that the scout should come aboard, Marsh asked the young fellow what the trouble was, and, realizing that he spoke no English, he gave the Indian a small stick, urging him to tell his story by means of a drawing.

The Indian told his story in this way. With the stick he drew a circle in the dust on the boat's deck, saying all the while, "Absorika! Absorika! Absorika!" (meaning "our people"). Then he used the stick to jab the dusty deck many times outside the circle, crying out, "Sioux! Sioux! Sioux!"

Finally, bringing both hands from the outside to the center of his drawing, he breathed loudly, "Poof!" The fight was all over! The Crow scout's crushing news that Custer and his soldiers had been wiped out was brought to the white world by Captain Marsh on July 4, 1876, when the young country was celebrating its independence.

John still yearned to make a canoe trip down the Missouri, and he was excited when Casper Whitney, editor of *Outing Magazine*, in which many of his short stories had appeared, approached him with a proposition. He suggested that John descend the Missouri River, beginning at the head of navigation at Fort Benton, Montana, and describe the adventure in articles for serial publication. John had dreamed of building a boat and undertaking just such an adventure, but accepting Whitney's offer would mean that he had to stop writing poetry for a while.

Even so, John agreed, and he began looking for companions to make the trip with him. He found one partner for the enterprise, a photographer from a nearby town. He was still looking about for another when a young adventurous neighbor, sixteen-year-old Chester "Chet" Marshall, learned about the proposed trip and begged John to take him along. Because of the boy's youth, John was at first doubtful about including Marshall, but two matters changed his mind. The boy was tremendously enthusiastic and insisted that he was man enough to do whatever was needed, and, secondly, no one else offered to go.

Materials for the boat were sent to the site, and in June the two men and the boy began to build their boat on a gravel bar across from Fort Benton. The plans John had chosen were for a fine, large canoe, complete with a gasoline motor in the rear. When the boat was finished and the motor installed, they tried out their masterpiece on the big water at Benton. Then they commissioned it *Atom I*, breaking a bottle of beer over its prow. A pan thoughtfully placed beneath the point of commissioning saved the beer for the thirsty and thrifty boatmen.

Bystanders on the docks, men who had been around the river for many years and who claimed to have considerable knowledge of the

Missouri, dolefully expressed doubts that the two men and a boy could make it down that stream. The Missouri, they told John, in its lower regions meandered, sometimes almost waterless, through confusing sandbars.

It was doubtful, John and his partners were told, that they could even *get down to* the lower part of the river, for there were a number of powerful rapids on the upper Missouri that could easily sink their small craft. Secure in their superior knowledge of boats and rivers, the men looked askance at the small boat, and more than one sly wink passed among them. John thanked them all for their advice, and the three adventurers set off downriver at high speed in their heavily loaded canoe. A lover of classical music, John had included among their supplies a record player and a few recordings.

Before they left, John had found time to write a short letter to his mother and a slightly longer one to Mona in New York. For a few weeks, there would not be much opportunity to keep those ladies informed.

The motor worked well at first, and they made good time with it for a day or two. All too soon, however, it began to sputter, and finally it quit altogether. John was kept busy looking for parts for the engine, and later he tried to get a new engine.

The rapids in the upper river proved to be almost as dangerous as the dockside engineers had warned, and when they were farther down the river, low water grounded them often on sandbars. This forced them to get into the water and push the boat to where the water was deeper, and the stream meandered so much that at times it was hard to tell in which direction the river actually ran. They managed the early rapids well, but they came to one so powerful that their canoe was overturned, and most of their supplies, including the record player, were lost. After that, they had only the food they had been able to salvage from the accident, and John supplemented their rations by hunting and fishing.

Once, when they were very hungry, he shot a blue heron, and on another day a deer as it ran along the bluffs above the river. The blue heron was tough and tasteless, and John decided blue herons should be forever kept for Japanese artwork and never, never used in a stew! But the deer, roasted over hot coals, was delicious, and the hungry men feasted late into the night.

When they reached the lower river, they remembered the warnings given them at Ft. Benton, for the water level was in fact seriously low, and the river's path around the sandbars was so confusing that they hardly knew in which direction it actually ran. Their boat was often grounded on the sand, and this meant they had to get out and push it until they found water deep enough to float it.

When they learned at a railway stop that the new engine John had ordered had not arrived, they decided to forget about power and row the remainder of the way. For this they found a fisherman who would trade them his sturdy rowboat for the now rather battered canoe. They gave it the name *Atom II*.

Before they had reached the half-way mark down-river, the photographer, a grown man, deciding that he was no longer willing to undergo the hardships of the venture, asked to be put off at a town where there was a railway that would take him home. The reason he gave—"I am sensitive"—would seem almost comical, spoken as it was to a poet!

On the other hand, the sixteen-year-old Chet Marshall, whom John nicknamed "the Kid," lived up to his promises, and under the grueling difficulties presented by the river, he became a man. Burned by the sun or drenched by rain during the day and fighting off mosquitoes at night, he and John rowed for some two thousand miles, landing in Sioux City, Iowa, in late August of 1908. Alice was at the dock to meet her son.

Accomplished before dams had slowed the great stream, while its many rapids still roared, the trip was immensely satisfying to John. He loved the adventure of it, and he relished the thought that he had been tried by difficulty and found worthy. His story of the experience, first serialized in *Putnam's Magazine*, is told in *The River and I*, published in 1910.

Although adventurers have since written a number of books about river trips in which they sought to relive the achievements of early explorers, John's book is generally considered an American first. Throughout the tale he remembers the feats of heroes, both ancient and new, and it seems that in it he is anticipating the historical series to which he would later devote many years of his life.

23

A New Life

AS HE ENDED HIS STORY of the river trip, John revealed to his readers the most important discovery he had made in his weeks on the great river. "What I found," he wrote, "was more of myself."

Nowhere in John's recounting of his weeks on the river is Mona mentioned, but she could not have been far from his thoughts, and everything he told her about the exploit fired her imagination. Their friendship, created through a remarkable correspondence over a few short months, had opened the doorway to something greater.

They were two separate beings who yearned to be whole, and each felt in the other the possibility that they could share a lifelong understanding of ideas and values that both held dear. While a passionate young man and an eager young woman sent and received letters, Nature had worked its new-old magic upon them. They were in love!

John sat down one day in the room that was to him both home and office, and he began to write the letter that would express to the girl in New York—the woman he had never seen with his eyes—how he had come to feel about her. His statement was simple and direct; she was *the one* for him, and he wanted them to be together always.

"I see now that I was hoping to find *you* when I wrote the lines *I want to build true love an altar ere I die.* I was dreaming of someone like *you* when the lines *I would I knew some slow, soft sound to call you* came to me. Mona," he urged, "dear, wonderful Mona, will you marry me?"

To reinforce his plea, John expressed as strongly as possible his confidence that he would be able to make a good life for them through his writing. He admitted that he did not then have much to offer in the way of money, and he did not yet have a house of his own.

"I know the kind of life you have lived, and I cannot give you such luxuries now, but, Mona, you and I understand each other, and we both care first of all about things that really matter. Mona, I am sure we can be happy, and I am sure that—together—we can build a truly good life." He sent his best regards to her mother, asked that Mona give him her answer very soon, and closed his letter: "Endless love, Jno."

When John returned from posting that most important letter, his mother was just returning from visiting the neighbors. The two sat down together, and John told her about his decision. He told his mother he had asked Mona to marry him, and he hoped for her approval and her blessing.

"Oh, John, John!" Alice was upset. "John, your marriage to her could never work. I am sure she is a fine young woman, but Mona could never fit into our lives here. John, I had no idea you had taken this long-distance friendship so far! Oh, John, it just will not work!"

"Mama, I understand how you feel, and I can tell you that I have given everything you might say a great deal of thought. In spite of all that, I know that Mona is the woman who can really understand me and help me accomplish what I want to do.

"This feeling has been growing in me for a long time. It is not just some sudden notion, and I am sure that Mona and I together can make a good life. Now, let's plan how we can arrange things here if she should agree to marry me. I hope we may live with you until I have saved enough money to buy a house of our own." Alice was the loving mother. "Of course, John, of course. You know that. Anything I have is yours. I want the best for you, only the best!"

John leaned over toward his mother, took her hands—small, strong hands that could do so much—in his and held them gently. "Thank you, Mama. Don't you remember? You are the one who brought Mona's first letter to me. Remember how surprised we were to see that the letter came from Paris? Do not worry; we are all going to be happy together. Now it all depends upon what Mona says."

Alice wondered what it would be like when all her children were gone, after all the years in which they had been her reason for trying so hard. Lulu had married Donald McDonald in February, and they lived in Minnesota. Grace had met and married Jess Ballinger, and their home was in Buffalo, New York. Grace had become a librarian and enjoyed her work at the Buffalo Public Library. Now John was having success—national success—as a writer, and she was very proud of him.

These thoughts awoke in Alice a warm and sustaining feeling of satisfaction for her accomplishments as a mother, but around the edges of her happiness she could not ignore a feeling of concern about John and Mona. Never before had the little home she loved seemed inadequate, but today it did. Always before she had met life with an unstudied sense of competence, so unlike the uncertainty she now began to feel. Mother Alice was worried.

When Mona read John's letter with its proposal of marriage, her first impulse was to accept, but that was not easy to do under the practical circumstances that she knew existed. She did understand that when she married this man she would be turning from the comfortable life of wealth that she had known to another, perhaps more difficult, life. Wishing to talk to her mother about it, Mona went into the parlor, where she found Adah sitting near a window, absorbed in reading. As Mona came into the room, however, Adah looked up at her daughter, for she could tell by her hasty entrance that something important had happened. "Yes, Mona?" Mona excitedly told her mother about John's proposal, and she read parts of his letter aloud. Then: "Mothie, I want to marry John. I really do!"

Adah was concerned. "Mona dear, are you quite sure about this? John is only beginning to be successful, and he does not even have a home of his own to offer you. I know that I introduced you to his poetry, and I was impressed with him, with his personality and his manliness, when I met him in New York.

"Even so, daughtie dear, you must think about it carefully. If you marry him and move to that little town in Nebraska, what will happen to your career as a sculptor? Are you willing to give up your own career, just when it is beginning to take shape? Are you really willing to do this?"

"Yes, Mothie, I am, if that is necessary. I have decided that his art is greater than my own. I have wished from the first time I read his lyrics that I could be a part of what he is doing. Mothie, it is simple: I feel that I must follow my heart. I can only marry a man who *believes* in the ideas and the values that are important to me. Mothie, I have always remembered what Ruth said to her mother-in-law: *my God is thy God*, and I have felt that when I marry, I must be able to say the same to the man I have chosen.

"I can—I do—say that about John. Mothie, I believe in him, and I want to help him. As for my sculpture, can I not continue that? John has said that he loves what I have done. If he can write such beautiful poetry in that little town, then I can do my sculpture there! Oh, Mothie, I could never give that up!"

Adah's eyes filled with tears. She understood only too well what her daughter was experiencing, and in a mixture of emotion and wisdom she knew how she must reply. "Mona, if you are as convinced about John as you say, then by all means you must follow your heart. I had not accomplished anything at the time, but I did give up my girlish dreams of acting when I married your father. If I had not done that, I should never have had you—or Ottocar.

"I was only seventeen and completely inexperienced, but, Mona, you know that your father was just as fine and good a man as I thought he was. I gave up my dreams of an acting career, but I have never actually regretted my marriage to your father."

Adah was silent a minute or so, seeking to control emotions that almost overpowered her. Then, with tears running down her cheeks, she shook her head in the proud, emotional way Mona knew so well. There was a catch in her throat as she spoke: "Yes, daughtie dear, I do know how you feel, and I understand so well. Follow your heart, Mona, and I will always be there for you. After all, what else is there in life? We must follow where our hearts would lead."

Adah was tempted to add but did not, "even though that may end in heartbreak." Instead, she drew her daughter close to her own fast-beating heart and repeated: "Yes, we must follow where our love would have us go. I only want you to be happy, Mona dear!"

Mona went immediately to her room and sat down at her desk near a tall window that looked out on the backyard of their home. It was only September, but a few trees were already beginning to lose their leaves. For Mona, fall had always seemed a time of ending, with perhaps a touch of sadness because it came with the passing of summer. Today her thoughts were not sad, but they were complicated, and many different feelings competed within her.

As she sat at her desk, pen in hand, looking out at the buildings beyond now bathed in the rays of the setting sun, her emotions quieted. In their place a single, calm determination took hold of Mona. John had asked her to marry him, and she knew what she must do. Mona remembered the first letter she had written to him only a few months before, and the words she had breathed as she posted that letter were still bright in her memory: "Dear God, let him not be married!" He was not married then, but he soon would be. Mona wrote quickly: "Dear John, my *herzallerliebster Mann!* Yes, Yes, I will marry you!"

Now that their course was settled, John and Mona set about planning for their wedding. After some correspondence back and forth, they decided that it would be best if Mona came to Omaha, where they could be married at the home of friends. The decision was based upon economic considerations, for if John went to New York for the wedding and the two returned to Nebraska, the cost would be considerably greater. Sensibly, Mona agreed, for since the wheel-within-a-wheel fiasco, the Martinsen resources were also considerably reduced.

Both were eager to set the date as early as possible, and they decided upon late November. That would give John time to finish what he was working on and also permit him to sell a number of short stories. John wished to treat his bride well, and that would take money.

For Mona it would mean completing her own activities in New York and planning what she would take with her—her clothing, household goods, china, and, especially, the tea set she had purchased at the Bon Marché in Paris. She would need all of those things to make a gracious home for John! Lastly, but first in importance to her, Mona packed her very large Bible—"Die Heilige Schrift" with illustrations by Gustave Doré. In it she would record the important happenings of her marriage.

John and his mother wanted Mona to feel as comfortable as possible in their modest home, which they felt had so little to offer a woman who had lived in Paris, Dresden, and New York. But Alice was an immaculate housekeeper, and rearranging was all that they needed to do.

Alice created new draperies to match the quilt she placed on the bed in the room that the newlyweds would use. John, a good amateur carpenter, made improvements in the small outside building used as a summer kitchen, which he thought might serve temporarily as a studio for Mona.

Alice's home, which stood at the corner of Pennsylvania Avenue and Elm Street, was a white frame, hip-roofed house with two bedrooms, a living room, and a dining-kitchen. A partial, unfinished basement gave space for a furnace, and open porches and the summer kitchen added extra space. Another equally small frame house occupied lots at the south end of their block, which lay at the extreme western edge of the village.

To the west beyond their street lay miles of farmlands. In 1908 Bancroft boasted a railway, a newspaper, a large frame hotel, several stores, and some thousand inhabitants. The town was set amid rolling hills whose rich soil encouraged fields of grain that stretched in all directions as far as the eye could see.

Even though they were both busy doing the many things that had to be done before their marriage, John and Mona did not slow their correspondence. It seemed that they had even more to say to each other—a greater need to communicate—and as the days of waiting passed one by one, the warmth and the passion of their love increased. John responded to each of her letters, and Mona sometimes did not wait for his response to write again. Her past disappointments became fuel for the intensity of the love she felt for this man—the poet who thought and cared as she did.

October came and went, and then November almost passed. On Saturday, November 28, John, dressed in his best suit and carrying a marriage license in his breast pocket, arrived at the Union Station in Omaha. Rumor has it that to save money so that he would be able to treat his bride well John had walked from Bancroft to Omaha.

With John at the station was Keene Abbott, a feature writer of the *Omaha World-Herald* who had remained John's good friend from his city newspaper days. John's mother had arrived in Omaha the day before, and she was waiting for them at the Abbott home. A Presbyterian minister had been alerted for the wedding, which was planned for the very next day.

The Omaha Union Station was a large masonry building, partially filled with rows of benches that stretched from side to side across its interior. The air in the high-vaulted waiting room was smoky, dimming the lights placed high near the ceiling, and the cavernous room was filled with the jumbled sounds of trains, announcers, and travelers. Mona's train, Number 112, was set to arrive on Track 13, and John was, well, frankly, John was *scared*.

Suddenly the enormity of what he was doing, joining for life with a person he had not yet met, seemed almost overpowering. What, he wondered, would he think of her? More important than that, what would she think of him? John wished that he were taller, and for one brief moment he felt the urge to turn and run. His good friend Keene, recognizing John's consternation, was encouraging. "Keep your tail up, old horse! You brought this on yourself, and it's all been done many times before. You must go and fetch her, and I will be waiting here to back you up!"

This is how—years later—John described the occasion:

> It was my moment of truth, and I plunged to meet it. A swift memory of her first glowing letter to me thrilled and strengthened me. It came from Paris. . . .
>
> The brakeman was placing the footstep on the depot platform. I remember my impatience with the first passenger to appear from the Pullman car, a corpulent lady who fussily blocked the doorway to the coach with a collection of handboxes. The second was certainly not Mona if her photographs were accurate. But the third! My god, the third!
>
> A stately young woman of more than average height stepped grace-fully through the coach door. She wore a velvet cape, and her hat of like material was almost ample enough to serve as an umbrella, I thought. I recall that I felt a momentary twinge of embarrassment.
>
> She, placing her hand upon the gallantly offered arm of the brake-man, anxiously scanned the crowd a moment. Then, with a joyous shout of recognition, she shouldered her way to me, crying "John! John!"

Excited happiness took the place of John's earlier concern, and the nervous anticipation that both had felt only emphasized the joy of their meeting. As she hurried to him through the crowd, Mona held both arms outstretched to John, and he took her hands in his as they met. For a moment, they just looked, for it was the first time they had seen each other in person. Their embrace—their first—was a shy one, fortunately soon interrupted by Keene's appearance. From one end of the waiting room, where he had stood since he urged John to go alone to meet Mona, he had seen Mona step down from the railway car and hurry to John's side.

Obviously greatly impressed with Mona Martinsen, Keene removed his hat when they were introduced and made an unaccustomed bow in her direction. After a few polite observations, Keene suggested they start for his home. "Well, now, let's get your baggage together, Miss Martinsen. I have a cab waiting outside. Mrs. Abbott and your mother, John, will be worried if we do not arrive soon at the apartment."

As they left the station with Keene, followed by a porter who wheeled Mona's considerable baggage to a waiting horse-drawn cab, John held his right arm close to his side, for tucked under it was his Mona's hand. They were married the next day at the Abbott home. Her hair pulled up high atop her head, Mona was radiant in the dress she had chosen. It was her favorite color—a soft rose—and the fine chiffon of which it was made fell in flattering fullness from a high empire waist. A pearl necklace and small matching earrings blended modestly with her gown. John wore the suit he had worn the day before, except that he added the matching vest and substituted the second pair of trousers, which retained their original crispness and sharp crease. For a tie, he had chosen his very best. A gift from an admirer, the tie was of silk, and it was a bright blue.

Pastor Mackey arrived promptly, and after greetings and introductions, he took Mona and John into an alcove off the living room, where they visited. While the three talked together, Keene went to the oak cabinet standing in one corner of the room that housed the phonograph. After lifting the lid and winding the machine carefully, he chose a record, and soon the beautiful tones of "Elégie" from Thaïs played by a noted violinist set a proper tone for the event. The music was stopped when the pastor brought his charges back into the living room, chose a spot near one end, and indicated where John and Mona should stand, with mother Alice as matron of honor beside the bride and Keene, the best man, beside the groom.

The ceremony was Pastor Mackey's standard, without the benefit of any embellishment, but it was nonetheless impressive. John and Mona repeated their vows with considerable feeling—John in somewhat elevated, steady tones, and Mona in a warm, full voice slightly shaken with emotion. Smiling warmly at the couple, the reverend T. J. Mackey pronounced them man and wife, and it was done: John and Mona were united in holy matrimony.

With mother Alice's help, Mrs. Abbott had prepared a reception for guests who came to greet the newlyweds. In an area at one end of the living room, the dining table, so carefully arranged, offered small sandwiches, cakes and cookies, and tea and coffee.

John and Mona, smiling happily in their new status, did their best to be appreciative and to accept the greetings of the guests, but it was quite apparent that they were eager to be alone. John had reserved a hotel room, and it is not surprising that he chose the European Hotel at Tenth and Howard, near the Union Station. As quickly as they could in good conscience leave the gathering, they did so.

John found a cab standing near the corner of the street, asked the driver to come to the apartment building, and soon, showered with rice and good wishes by the folks who celebrated with them, Mr. and Mrs. John Neihardt left to begin their life together. The cab they took was not like the small, two-wheeled variety to which Mona was accustomed in New York. It had four wheels, the driver sat in front, and the larger, enclosed passenger section provided adequate room for riders and their baggage. John and Mona stepped briskly into the cab, the driver cracked his whip, and they were gone.

Inside the apartment, all the occupants but one chatted happily together. Alice smiled bravely, but she was quiet, and Keene, the sympathetic host, could not help noticing that her eyes were damp with a mother's tears. It is not always out of sadness that a mother cries, and Alice's tears were partially prompted by a new happiness.

When the newlyweds arrived at the European, John paid the cabbie, who had carried Mona's considerable bags and baggage into the lobby.

Mona stood beside her husband as John registered them as Mr. and Mrs. John Neihardt, after which the porter showed them to their room on the second floor. It was small, and, in spite of the hotel's name, it was really rather plain, but for John and Mona, in their happiness, it would do very well. After months of impassioned correspondence, their wishes had come true: they were married!

The honeymoon was short, for John had been able to afford only a three-day stay at the hotel. Brief though it was, it accomplished what a honeymoon is intended to do: it gave substance to the pastor's statement that they were man and wife. Well matched in spirit, John and Mona had much to communicate to each other, and since through experience both had a certain maturity, the embarrassment or bashfulness each felt at first soon vanished.

For the first time Mona heard John recite the poems that had brought her to him, for the first time he saw the loving glow that transformed her face as she listened. We shall not presume to invade their privacy in that little hotel room, but and it may well be that sparks illumined its darkness.

Their honeymoon over, on Wednesday next they packed and took a cab to the railway station. They were bound for Bancroft and home. Meanwhile, the article that Keene Abbott had written for the *Omaha World-Herald* had reached Bancroft on Monday, the day after the wedding. Its headlines proclaimed:

MARRIAGE OF AN AUTHOR AND ARTIST

John G. Neihardt of Bancroft and Miss Mona Martinsen of New York Married. Ceremony Performed in Omaha Sunday Afternoon by Rev. T. J. Mackey.

"Here is a partnership in art as well as a nuptial partnership".

As their train sped toward Bancroft, Mona looked out the window at a world that was new to her. They passed seemingly endless fields, now bare of vegetation and covered with snow, interspersed with all too few black, leafless trees, and several times they stopped at small, uninspiring towns.

The reluctant tinge of bashfulness they had felt when they met was now almost entirely gone, and John and Mona talked easily, he doing his best to answer the many questions she had about the strange countryside. Even so, underneath their pleasant conversation, both felt a nervous concern—Mona wondering what her new life in Bancroft would be like and John worried about her reaction when she saw their small town, which he knew was not pretty, and the plain little house that would be their home.

They would both soon know the answers to their troublesome questions, for the train was slowing, and a sign on the small station building just ahead assured the travelers that they were arriving in Bancroft. It was an exciting moment—a momentous moment—which many years later John remembered in this way:

> The daily arrival of the evening train from Omaha was always an event in our little town of Bancroft, but this Wednesday the gathering at the station platform indicated something special was abroad. The *Omaha World-Herald* article announcing our marriage and return to Bancroft must have gotten around. The assemblage on the platform at the railroad station was notably larger than usual.
>
> As I stepped off the train ahead of Mona and offered my arm to her, I was aware that men who certainly were not given to the gallantry of hat tipping shyly touched the brims of their hats, evidently striving to make it seem quite accidental. Further, it was to be observed that Mr. Cabanné stood stiffly at attention against the station wall, his head bared, his hat pressed against his left shoulder. He might have been saluting the passing flag!
>
> The city bus line, consisting of a light spring wagon furnished with a canvas roof and cross seats, was obligingly on hand, and soon we were on our way home with our baggage. But anyone watching our progress (and who wasn't?) must have noted that its young driver was deliberately taking the route up Main Street where there were the most observers.
>
> It was something of a triumphal procession. Eager faces jostled each other in the barbershop door. There was a gathering in front of the drugstore. All seats were occupied on the steps of the Cary and Ransom Farm Implement establishment. Curtains fluttered and

window shades went up as we turned into the residential section of town.

And so—the bride came home.

Yes, the bride came home with her husband, and never again could one truly speak of John Neihardt without also speaking of Mona Martinsen, the artist who became his wife.

24

A Prosy Little Village

Mighty givers, meager takers—mother, sister, wife.

"The Quest"

THE SPRING WAGON THAT provided the town's transportation had
stopped in front of a very small, square white frame house set on Pennsylvania Avenue, the last street on the west side of Bancroft. On the
north side of the house, a wide side yard extended to Elm Street, up
which they had driven from the main street of Bancroft. John and Mona
had both been concerned about her reaction when she first saw her new
home, and their concerns were well grounded.

Mona was shocked, for, even though it was obviously well cared-for,
the house was of the type that in her experience was home to servants.
Indeed, for her it presented a most depressing appearance, and she tried
hard not to show her disappointment.

Fortunately, John was helping the driver carry luggage to the front
porch and did not see the expression on Mona's face, but Alice had
come to the door as the vehicle approached, and she had hurried to the
edge of the road to greet her new daughter-in-law. Alice saw the hastily
suppressed look of shock and disappointment on Mona's face.

Once inside the dwelling, though, Mona felt almost at home in the
warm and pretty living room. The floors were of polished oak, partially
covered with hand-made hooked rugs of artistic design. Although the
furniture was not expensive, it was tastefully arranged, and the windows, hung with lace curtains, allowed the late fall sunlight to cast a
pleasing glow over the room.

Directly ahead as one entered the living room was another fair-sized room that held a cooking stove and a round oak dining table, over which a crocheted white runner hung half-way to the floor. Four oak chairs encircled the table, and several more were set along the wall. It was a friendly room that could accommodate several persons for a meal.

On her right as Mona stood just inside the living room was a door that led to the room that John had used and that had been re-arranged for the two of them. It had windows that gave to the south and to the open porch on the front of the house, and it held a double bed topped by a pretty quilt. The curtains on the tall windows were of material that matched that of the bed covering, and Mona guessed that they were newly made.

"What a pretty little room!" Mona turned to her mother-in-law. "Tell me, how did you know that pink is my favorite color?" Mona was not unappreciative of the friendly welcome from her mother-in-law, which the decoration in the little room was intended to convey. The room could not provide enough closet space to store all the luggage and boxes that Mona had brought with her, so John carefully stacked them on the front porch until use could be made of their contents.

Their train had arrived late in the afternoon, and when everything had been brought in and put someplace for safekeeping, it was time for the evening meal. Mona's anxiety lessened, and, though somewhat tired, she was ready to sit down with her husband and mother-in-law.

John guided her to a chair that allowed her to look into the living room, and he sat down across from her. He remembered the picture Mona had sent to him from Paris and how, when he first looked at it, he had imagined her sitting across from him at the breakfast table. Mona returned his smile, and John felt a warm surge of resolve. He would make this lovely, high-born person happy!

Mother Alice had planned a light supper—quite delicious, for she was a good cook—and Mona noticed that everything she prepared was appetizing and attractive to look at, especially the golden-brown rolls. The table was set with simple china and silver plate flatware on a freshly ironed cloth. The atmosphere that Alice created in her home was simple and unaffected, but it carried with it a strong air of self-respect.

Her new mother-in-law was wearing no makeup and her neat but inexpensive cotton dress might have suited the cook who managed the basement kitchen in their New York home, but Mona was well aware that any such similarities ended at once. This small, pretty woman was no servant, Alice was plainly in charge of her circumstances, and the lack of a husband seemed of no noticeable importance. John had told Mona that his father left the family when he was a small boy, but no mention was normally made of him, either by way of criticism or compliment.

As for her relationship with John, it was obvious that Alice was proud of her son and that he had great respect for his mother. Providing a home for her children entirely on her own and, beyond that, encouraging them in their quest for accomplishment, Alice had earned their gratitude. Mona admired her for all this, but it would not be easy for two such different and strong-minded women to live together.

Mona's efforts to this time had been toward an artistic career, and she had neither natural inclination nor experience in the care of a household. Except for the little she had done in Paris for herself alone, cooking and cleaning and the laundering of clothes were entirely beyond her ken, and yet she would have all of those duties as John's wife. When she decided to marry John, Mona had made a choice. She knew she was making that choice, and she was determined to "stick with it," but the reality of what now faced her was more imposing than she could have expected.

Learning from her mother-in-law and her husband could hardly be a happy task for any new bride, and it was especially difficult for Mona. Mother Alice seemed to have complete confidence in the doing of all housewifely chores, and the strength of her will more than matched Mona's. Even so, the teaching and the learning began, and all three survived. Soon Mona was doing her fair share of the housework and the cooking, and her hands, made large and strong by years of working with stubborn clay, became even stronger.

Alice's home, like all those in Bancroft, boasted none of the labor-saving conveniences that today are considered necessities, and all work was done by hand—even the wringing of sheets and towels at washtime. How Mona's skinned knuckles did pain her until she had mastered the use of a washboard!

But Mona did more than just her share of the housework. When she chose what items she would bring with her to Omaha, she had not forgotten the lovely half-Amati violin her mother had found for her while they lived in Dresden. She played for John, who had always loved fine music, and he was truly impressed by hearing a violinist right in his own home. Together they remembered his earlier tribute to a violinist in "The Witless Musician," and the bond between them became stronger.

Mona's ability to play the violin was recognized as a way she could contribute to the family finances, and she decided to give lessons on the instrument. She soon had a number of students, and the income from her teaching, though not large, was helpful.

Mona was eager to continue her sculpting, and John built a pedestal for her, using the drawing she had made as a guide. It was sturdy, the upright framework being made of two-by-twos with a square top of one inch wood, to which a centerpost was fastened, and the pedestal was tall enough to allow Mona to stand while modeling. A second square board atop the centerpost formed the base to hold the clay. Chair casters fastened on the underside of the square enabled her to turn the base as she worked. Any armature needed to support the model on which Mona worked might be fastened to the base.

They found a source of clay through the art department of the Normal School in Wayne; a space was chosen near a north window in the dining area where she could place her pedestal when she was modeling, and Mona set about to make a bust of her husband. John and Mona had planned to use a portion of the summer kitchen for a studio, but that would have to wait until springtime; in early December, the outside building, aptly called "the summer kitchen," was far too cold.

Alice had agreed—not without some reluctance—to John's suggestion that they use a space in the dining room for Mona's sculpting. To avoid damaging the hardwood floor Mona put a heavy cloth under her pedestal to catch any clay or moisture that might drop down as she worked, and at other times the pedestal was set out on the covered front porch.

Meanwhile, John was putting together a new volume of lyrics, poems that he had written after the appearance of *A Bundle of Myrrh*. John's writing had changed since he married Mona. It was not his habit of writing that was different, for he had long been self-disciplined. It was the subject matter, the thrust of his lyrics that changed. When his early, impassioned lyrics appeared in *A Bundle*, one critic wrote that the verses were so impassioned, so fiery, that they could hardly be sent safely through the mails!

As he matured—and Mona was a part of that maturing—his poetry changed. Impassioned love became devoted love, and there was a noticeable spiritual growth. One interesting story involves how he happened to write one of the poems that would appear in the new volume—a lyric he called "April Theology".

One fine Sunday morning in April, when, called by the ringing bells, most of the villagers were on their way to church, poet John remained at home, inspired by the beauty of a blossoming plum orchard. To an onlooker, he might have seemed to be idle, but he was having a profound religious experience, and out of this experience came one of his finest poems.

This is what he wrote:

April Theology

Oh, to be breathing and feeling and hearing and seeing!
Oh, the ineffably glorious privilege of being!
All of the world's lovely girlhood, unfleshed and made spirit,
Broods out in the sunlight this morning; I see it! I hear it!

So read me no text, oh my brothers, and preach me no creeds;
I am busy beholding the glory of God in his deeds.
See! Everywhere buds coming out, blossoms flaming, bees humming,
Glad athletic growers upreaching, things striving, becoming!
Oh, I know in my heart, in the sun-quickened, blossoming soul of me,
This something called self is a part, but the world is the whole of me.
I am one with these growers, these singers, these earnest becomers,
Co-heirs of the summer to be and past aeons of summers.
I kneel not, nor grovel; no prayer with my lips shall I fashion.
Close-knit in the fabric of things, fused with one common passion
To go on and become something greater, we growers are one;
None more in the world than a bird, and none less than the sun,
But all woven into the glad, indivisible scheme,
God fashioning out in the finite a part of His dream!
Out here where the world-love is flowing, unfettered, unpriced,

I feel all the depth of the man-soul and girl-heart of Christ.
'Mid this riot of pink and white flame, in this miracle weather,
Soul to soul, merged in one, God and I dream the vast dream together
We are one in the doing of things that are done and to be;
I am part of my God as a raindrop is part of the sea!
What! House me my God? Take me in where no blossoms are blowing?
Roof me in from the blue, wall me in from the green and the wonder of growing?
Parcel out what is already mine, like a vender of staples?
See! Yonder my God burns revealed in the sap-drunken maples!

Nearly seventy years after he wrote it, John recited "April Theology" in an amateur motion picture being made of his life, and introducing it he remarked: "The ideas in 'April Theology' still substantially express what I believe today." In 1909 John chose this poem to be included in his new volume, together with others that became well known—"Battle Cry," "Lonesome in Town," "When I have Gone Weird Ways," "Prayer for Pain," "On First Seeing the Ocean," "Gaea. Mother Gaea."

While John wrote and chose the poems that he would include in his new volume, Mona conceived the idea of a sculptured frieze that would be used to illustrate the book, and she suggested a name for the new volume: "Man-Song." Her frieze beautifully expresses the theme expressed by the title.

Carved at the top in a slab of clay is the title in bold capital letters: MAN-SONG. At the bottom of the frieze is another slab on which the name NEIHARDT is carved, and two figures stand on this base. On the left, looking up, is a partially draped, athletic Neihardt whose one hand seems to support the book's title. On the right is the lovely nude figure of a young woman, whose face, partially hidden by her hair, is turned modestly downward, one hand reaching to the title slab and the other resting on the shoulder of her husband.

Among the most beautifully expressive of Mona's sculptured works, this frieze apparently was never cast. The photograph used on the front of the volume and also on the dust wrapper by the publisher, Michell-Kennerly of New York, is a picture of the clay model. The dedication in the book is simple: To MONA, *wife and comrade*.

Life went on for the Neihardts much as one might expect it to be for such a couple in a small town in the early years of the twentieth century.

John spent the mornings writing, and in the afternoons he gave his attention to whatever needed to be done about the house or in the yard or garden. To use a favorite expression of his, John was definitely not "a lily-fingered" poet. He was, Mona said, "the great fixer." About this characteristic, he often remarked, "I have to make with my hands when I am making with my mind."

But there was more to this need of his than would seem. John believed that before any artist—painter, sculptor, musician, writer—had the right to be an artist, he first must live up to his responsibilities as a man. In this belief, how different he was from many who use their artistic endeavors as an excuse for lack of responsibility!

It was at least partly because Mona so strongly disapproved of the lifestyle she saw among some of her acquaintances in Paris that she yearned for a different life, and it was also because of John's poetry, with which she felt such a strong spiritual identity, that she had returned to New York from Paris. Years later in a letter to a daughter she said, "I have always wanted to do what was right. I never wanted to do what was wrong." This choice of what she held to be good over what she deemed bad was not a simple choice on her part; it was an integral characteristic of herself.

The spiritual oneness that she felt with the expressions of the young American poet seemed to her a good foundation on which to base a life, but that life—as with a host of other lives—did not prove to be an easy one. They lived in little better than frontier conditions, and as the weeks and months passed, it became more apparent that the relationship between wife and mother-in-law—each being strong-willed and of an independent nature—was not a comfortable one.

John had intended to buy a home of their own as soon as he had enough money to do so, and in the meantime both women tried to make the situation as pleasant as possible. Mona continued working on her bust of John. Part of the time John sat nearby to pose, but for most of the modeling Mona relied entirely on memory, as Rodin had taught her to do. This meant that when they were together, Mona noted and memorized her model's features with a gaze so penetrating and intense that it would have been disconcerting had John not so well understood.

Busy about her own household duties and the dressmaking that provided her support, Alice occasionally was tempted to stop what she was doing and watch the sculptor at work, a friendly gesture that pleased her daughter-in-law. Mona occasionally glanced at the little woman who seemed so interested in her work. In spite of the years of struggling to provide for her family, Alice was still pretty; natural good health and the ability to be light-hearted in the face of difficulty had seen to that. Mona appreciated and respected this lively, capable woman, and she decided that her next effort would be to portray her mother-in-law. The lovely bust of Alice that she eventually modeled was, years later, placed in the Memorial Room of the John G. Neihardt Center in Bancroft.

If growing accustomed to home life was a challenge to the young wife, becoming comfortable in the community was even more of one. To the good people of Bancroft, Mona, with her slight accent and her foreign ways, was as new and different as they were to her. For example, Mona thought her tea service and china would be a necessity for her home. She soon found that to be incorrect; in Bancroft, people were drinking coffee out of mugs! Mona was learning a great deal about people in the American Midwest!

One day when she was in the grocery store, a large container of freshly churned butter caught her eye. A notion came suddenly to her mind: the butter would make a good medium for creating a portrait. It so happened that the owner was in the store, and she decided he should be her model. Seeing that he was about to go into the back of the store, Mona called to him, "Sir, will you please stand there a few minutes? Yes, right there by the counter. And please look at me. That's good! Thank you!"

Pulling the container of butter over near her on the counter, Mona set to work. Using only her skilled fingers, she quickly converted the pliant butter into the head of a man, and when she was finished, anyone could see that the butter had become a portrait of the store's owner. That gentleman was so pleased that he kept the butter model for a number of weeks in the store's ice box, and he showed it proudly to his customers.

The winter was a time of snow and ice and fierce winds, and there was little or no outdoor activity possible, and in the morning, they dressed around the stove that stood in the living room. Spring did finally come to Nebraska. John spaded and raked a large garden plot, and together he and his mother planted the vegetables that would make up a substantial part of their food supply. Mona learned about gardening and was helpful, for she was not one to sit idly by while others accomplished what was needed.

John was dedicated to his writing and to providing for his family, but never throughout his life did he fail to set aside time for simple enjoyment. He and Mona spent long hours just walking through the countryside, and she was eager to hear about the history of the area. In neighboring towns, there were events in which local wrestlers might be seen exhibiting their prowess, and Mona shared John's interest in them. For John, who had trained many years as a wrestler, the lure was in the contests themselves. For Mona, the artist, it was the sculptured beauty of the men's bodies and the classic Greek wrestling that attracted her.

One day John learned that there was to be a wrestling contest in Lyons, a town eleven miles from Bancroft. The wrestlers who would participate were some of the better known in the area, and John wanted to see them at work. When he told Mona that he would like to go, she was enthusiastic: "John, I want to go with you. I would enjoy that very much. It would be like a sculptor's lesson in anatomy!"

"Mona, we would have to walk, and it is eleven miles by the railroad tracks to Lyons. Could you do that? And then, we'd have to walk home after the match. It would be too much for you!"

"John, dear, I am used to walking distances. In New York and even in Paris, I walked wherever I needed to go. I am sure I can do it! Do let me go with you!" John was not really convinced, but he dearly loved her companionship, so they went together, hiking along the railroad tracks from Bancroft to Lyons. Some four hours or more later they arrived at their destination.

The wrestling was impressive, and John introduced Mona to a number of his friends who were attending the event. For the sculptress, watching the classic wrestling, which presented the men's muscular, trained bodies in motion, was not only enjoyable, it was a learning experience.

Mona had watched the whole process with great enthusiasm, but John could see that she was tired. The long walk home was entirely too much. To give her some relief, John wore Mona's shoes—women's shoes that were surely not meant for such rough hiking—and gave her his to wear. When they reached Bancroft, both were ready for bed, but Mona was completely exhausted.

John realized fully then that his "wife and comrade" would not be physically able even to attempt some of the things they had planned to do together. He particularly thought of the descent of the Mackenzie River in Canada that they had talked about many times, an adventure about which Mona was wholeheartedly enthusiastic. Now he realized that such an undertaking would be beyond Mona's physical ability. They did not talk again about the Mackenzie, even though the book he was working on was about his Missouri River trip.

When the weather had become warm enough, John and Mona went swimming in Logan Creek. It was a small, muddy prairie creek, but there was one spot within walking distance of Bancroft that was large enough and deep enough to be enjoyable.

Not many Bancroftians took advantage of the pool in the small, muddy creek, and so, when they were alone there, John and Mona took delight in swimming without benefit of swimsuits. The feel of the water on their skin was pleasant, and swimming without suits was such fun! One might well assume that the excitement of swimming in the nude did no harm to the passionate side of their married life.   ·

Apparently people in the town learned of their habit of swimming without suits, and one enterprising young lad decided to catch them at it. He was seated, unbeknownst to them, in a tree over the pool when they arrived. While they were swimming, John happened to look up and see the boy, and to the lad's considerable embarrassment, he called out "Fellow, come down out of that tree and swim with us!"

The boy came bashfully down from his perch, and he did swim with John and Mona. Years later, when the lad had become an old man, he told a reporter about the Logan Creek happening and complained, "They might at least have worn bathing suits!"

25

A Home of Their Own

'Mid glad green miles of tillage, and fields where cattle graze,
A prosy little village, you drowse away the days.

"The Poet's Town"

THE TIME FINALLY CAME that they had saved enough money to get a home of their own. The little house next door was for sale, and one day John and Mona went over to look at it. From a front porch that was little more than a few steps and a landing leading up to the door, they entered into a small living room. The house was empty and was only "broom clean," but both John and Mona felt the thrill that comes with the first viewing of a new home.

Many years later, when the little house had been long abandoned, their children were grown, and his Mona was no longer with him, John told his daughter about that first home: "Mama was so excited about the prospect of having our own home, that for some reason she thought she should appear very animated. She went through the whole house, almost scurrying from room to room, looking at its closets and cabinets. There weren't very many, I can tell you!"

John's very blue eyes crinkled with a grin spreading over his well-lined face as he remembered that long-ago day. Chuckling lightly, he continued: "It was a very small house, so it didn't take long for her to see it all. When she had looked around the entire house, she seemed satisfied with what she saw.

"Then, coming back to where I stood near the front door, she exclaimed, 'Oh, John! What a *darling little cubby-hole!*' "

John told the story in a whimsical manner, but there was a look in his eyes that carried a double message; first, that he wished he might have done better for his Mona, and second, that a wonderful, magical time in his life was gone forever.

The sale of several short stories made it possible for John to pay for the house in cash, and that "darling little cubby-hole" became their home. In it there were no electric lights, no running water, no plumbing, and no central heat, but it was theirs alone. Seemingly ignoring their lack of funds, Mona set to work to make the place homelike, and with her loving and artistic touch, the "little cubbyhole" assumed a warm and almost pretty appearance. She made it a home.

It was an exciting moment when Mona told John that she was pregnant, and with what eagerness those two practical romantics did look forward to their first child! Remembering, John wrote in his nineties something of how it was.

"Mona had been growing in girth for some time, and we had our unfunny little joke about a barrel going around in girl's clothing. But back of the joking it was all a dear and thrilling mystery.

"One evening she had gone to bed early, unusually weary with her burden. After sleeping soundly for some time, she called me to her. Taking my hand in hers, she held it close against her body.

"He kicked me! I tapped upon his prison wall, and, by golly! He kicked me again! 'He wants to fight,' I said, 'the little cuss!' I remember how we hugged each other and laughed and laughed! Silly!"

It was late in the fall of 1909, and winter seemed to come early that year, with the usual Nebraska wind, snow, and ice. Just to keep *almost* warm was a challenge. Only the cast-iron cook stove in the kitchen and a tall, round wood-fired heater in the living room protected them from winter's onslaught. On severe winter days or nights, the heated air did not venture far from its source, and one needed to be very close to a stove, or bundled in many blankets, to keep warm.

One day late in the winter Mona went outdoors to bring in some clothes that had frozen dry on the lines. As she returned to the house, she was holding a bundle of clothing in front of her, making it impossible for her to see the ground on which she walked. On her way out to the clothesline, there had been only a light covering of snow as she walked to the far end of the line, but on her return to the end nearer the back porch, there was a large patch of ice that she had not noticed.

When Mona reached the ice, made exceedingly slick because it had melted the day before and refrozen, she slipped, and both feet went out from under her. Rather unwieldy because of her advanced pregnancy and the clothes she clutched in her arms, Mona was unable to regain her equilibrium, but in trying to do so, her body was twisted as she fell. It was a very hard fall, and she called out in pain to John.

Fortunately, John had come out of his study and was in the back part of the house where he was able to hear her cry. He rushed out to her, carried her into the house and laid her gently on the bed. Mother Alice chanced to be looking out a window, and she had seen Mona fall. She hurried over to her son's home. "John, you go get the doctor. I will stay here with Mona until you get back. Go on! Hurry! I will take care of Mona."

Quite distraught, John did not bother to put on a jacket before he left, running full-tilt for the doctor. The good man was home and came at once to Mona's bedside, but in spite of his efforts to help her, Mona miscarried. She was in intense pain when the lifeless baby finally came, and for a moment she almost lost consciousness. Alice immediately took the little one, wiped it clean, and wrapped it in a blanket, and when Mona weakly pleaded, "Let me see my baby!" she carefully placed the little bundle in the mother's outstretched arms.

Alice was crying as she spoke: "Mona dear, your baby did not live. Oh, dear girl, I am so sorry!"

The tiny bundle that Mona held did not move, but she held it close to her breast for a few desperate minutes. John was at her side, comforting her, as she lifted the baby so she could see its face. Her face, already wracked with the pain of delivery, was somehow able to express the shock caused by her realization of her loss—of their loss.

"Oh, John, he looks just like you! How could this have happened?" Mona looked up at her mother-in-law, who stood by the bed across from John. "Oh, Mother, I have tried to be so very careful. Look at him, doesn't he look exactly like John?" With that, she gave way to uncontrollable weeping and continued to clutch the lifeless infant close to her beating heart.

The death of their first child was an overwhelming blow for both, and Mona was ill for several weeks after that. John cared tenderly for her, and Alice was always available to help. When spring finally arrived, Mona's health had improved, and she happily greeted the return of growing things—the grass on the lawn, the new leaves on the trees, and the buds on the peonies that formed a hedge in front of her mother-in-law's home. She was well again.

The articles John had written about his 1908 descent of the Missouri River had been serialized in *Putnam's Magazine*, and royalties from that publication, together with those from *A Bundle of Myrrh*, provided income but hardly enough for a new family. Wishing to be of help in regard to their finances, Mona continued to give lessons on the violin to a little Zuhlke daughter and other people from Bancroft and to Miss Teach from nearby Pender. She had become quite fond of Miss Teach.

John began forming his Missouri River articles into a book, and together they found a title for it. Remembering what he had decided was the most important product of the river trip—"I found more of myself"—John and Mona decided the book should be called *The River and I*. It was published in 1910.

As Keene Abbot's article in the *Omaha World-Herald* had indicated, the marriage of an artist and a poet had occurred, and their life together in small-town America was a test of that union's validity and durability. With each passing day the part that Mona, the sympathizer and the believer, played in the unfolding of Neihardt's talents became more evident.

As we have seen, from her teens Mona had seriously sought a career in sculpture, and her teachers, Elwell and Rodin, had been confident of her ability. Her independence of spirit and many of her ideas about the part women should play in life would seem to mark her as an early feminist. But Mona had made a conscious choice when she decided to marry, and she placed herself in the supporting role that she deemed most likely to promote the success of her marriage and of John's literary efforts. Many times she explained her self-denying decision by saying, "I did it because I think John's art is greater than my own" or "John is the gold; I am the alloy." Seldom has gold had a stronger alloy than John had in his Mona.

In the summer of 1911 they were expecting the birth of another child. The summer was a hot one, and, without modern air conditioning, the little house did not cool off much at night. This is the way John later told how they solved that problem: "We slept in hammocks out under the cherry trees. I remember how the bloom came, and the green fruit, and the ripe. Then when the woods were glorious with reds and gold, it happened."

A girl was born on October 23, 1911, and they named her Enid Volnia, the middle name being in honor of their good friend Volney Streamer, and the first name being from the classic story "Geraint and Enid." Weeks earlier John had dreamed vividly of a blond, blue-eyed girl in her teens, and when Enid was sixteen, her father recognized the girl about whom he had dreamed.

The Neihardt lyrics had all grown out of his personal experiences, and the poems in his new volume *Stranger at the Gate*, which was dedicated to his first daughter, Enid, were written as he and Mona eagerly awaited the births of their children. He expressed the couple's awareness of the great mystery in "Hymn Before Birth":

Soon you shall come as the dawn from the dumb abysm of night,
Traveler birthward, hastener earthward out of the gloom!
Soon shall you rest on a soft white breast from the measureless mid-world flight;
Waken in fear at the miracle, light, in the pain-hushed room.

. . . .

For, ancient and new, you are flame, you are dust, you are spirit and dew,
Swirled into flesh, and the winds of the world are your breath!
The song of the thrush in the hush of the dawn is not younger than you—
And yet you are older than death!

In their early morning, over-coffee talks, John and Mona often spoke of what they wished to give to their children, and foremost in the minds of both was the desire to instill a sense of what they called "the higher values." Although John's fame as a writer was broadening, there was never quite enough money for the needs of a growing family. They did not overly dwell on this financial lack, but on one particular morning they had wrestled with the matter of bills that cried out for payment. "Mona," John hesitantly admitted, "I am worried. I do not want to let you and the kids down. . . ."

· "Oh, John, dear John, you are giving them—and me—so much more than mere money. We are rich in the things that really matter to me. I know so well how poor a rich person can feel. Yes, John, we are rich!"

Mona's attitude, so like his own, pleased John. "I know that I shall probably never be able to give my family much in the way of material things, but I *can* give them a sense of what men and women have thought and felt and done over the ages. Yes, I can do that!"

"Write about it, John! That is real wealth; that is what you will give to our children!"

John did just that, and he called the poem "Child's Heritage":

> O, There are those, a sordid clan,
> With pride in gaud and faith in gold,
> Who prize the sacred soul of man
> For what his hands have sold.
>
> And these shall deem thee humbly bred;
> They shall not hear, they shall not see
> The kings among the lordly dead
> Who walk and talk with thee!
>
> A tattered cloak may be thy dole,
> And thine the roof that Jesus had;
> The broidered garment of the soul
> Shall keep thee purple-clad!

This poem expressed Mona's overall beliefs, and she absorbed what it said, just as she had been drawn to others of his lyrics. At night, as she dropped off to sleep, desperately tired and a little heartsick after a long day spent in the housewifely duties that were so foreign to her nature, she still was able to say to herself, "Yes, in spite of all our difficulties, we are rich. We are 'purple-clad.' "

In 1912 John was tiring of writing lyrics as he had tired of writing short stories, two genres in which he had achieved nationwide success. His first biographer, Julius T. House, wrote about his change of direction in *John G. Neihardt—Man and Poet*:

> One of the higher class magazines continued for years, after Neihardt quit writing stories, to ask him for more of these, saying 'When are you going to give us another story? No one writes the kind of story you can write.' He wrote no more short stories, and probably never will.
>
> Why, with financial ease and fame before him, with opportunity to write occasional lyrics, did he not continue and become known as one of America's great short-story writers? The answer is: Neihardt. He must follow the Voice.

John wanted to devote his energies entirely to poetry and to something more comprehensive than lyrics. He experimented briefly with playwriting, but he dreamed of creating a poetic series in the classic heroic mode. Searching for a topic, he toyed with the idea of the French Revolution, and for a time he devoted his thoughts and his research to its history, but when he talked to Mona about that foreign episode, she spoke out strongly against it.

"Oh, John, don't write about *all that rot*. Write about what you know— what is new. Write about *this country*." Mona's love of America came not only from her own experiences; it had been born and bred in her from her father's early faith in the New World. Rudolf Martinsen had believed in the future of the United States and had been an early financial participant in its development.

John listened to what Mona said, and when he thought more about it, he realized that he agreed with her. Years later he commented, "I turned my attention to the history of my own part of the country, and it just came up through the soles of my feet."

The poetic series he envisioned, and which he began to write in 1912, would be about his own land and his own people, and it would not re-tell the history of "a narrow strip along the eastern seaboard." It would deal with the great period of westward expansion across the North American continent. It would treat as heroic the exploration and settlement of the United States, but it would not fail to present with honest sympathy the people who already lived on the land and who were so tragically dispossessed.

John was well prepared to do the task he imagined, for he was living in what might well be called "a watershed of history." Many of the old-timers—men and women, both Indian and white—who had taken active part in the exploration and settling of the American West were still living.

He already knew many of them, and he would continue to make it his duty to become acquainted with those who would be the heroes of his stories. As a result, what he wrote would to a notable extent be based upon first-hand information. John was completely consumed with his plans for the series, and he discussed at length with his wife and comrade his plan for the series that would later bear the title *A Cycle of the West*.

Mona was intensely interested as John told her about the exploits of the early trappers, the mountain-men and the rivermen, the explorers, the conflicts with the Indian people, and the tragic ending of those conflicts.

Although John had decided on the work that would be his major interest, the need to support his family continued, and he had an idea. He wrote to the editor of the *Minneapolis Journal*, suggesting that such a fine newspaper should have a book review department and stating that he had ideas for its development. The editor wrote back, saying in effect, "Tell me about it."

A visit to Minneapolis followed, and John outlined his plan for a page of reviews of books of the time. The editor liked the idea, and John was offered a salary of fifty dollars a week for his efforts. To the young writer, who had never been paid so much, the offer seemed almost munificent. But he was cagey. "There will be opportunity for advancement?" he asked.

Assured that there would be such opportunity, John accepted the job, and he and Mona and little Enid moved to Minneapolis. Here on December 1, 1912, another child was born, a son they named Sigurd Volsung. The first-written volume of the *Cycle*, *The Song of Hugh Glass*, would be dedicated to Sigurd, and for its publication John wrote a special dedicatory poem, "To Sigurd, Scarcely Three."

In the first stanza, he told how he would play with his son, "shaping kite and boat and bow," and in the second he promised:

Meanwhile, as on a rainy day
When 'tis not possible to play,
The while you do your best to grow,
I ply the other craft I know
And try to build for you the mood
Of daring and of fortitude
With fitted word and shapen phrase,
Against those later wonder-days
When first you glimpse the world of men
Beyond the bleaker side of ten.

John played with the children. When they were tiny, he called them "Wubs." What is a Wub? To answer that question, let us go to a prose description written by John when he was ninety—some sixty years after he had first played with his Wubs:

> What is a Wub? A Wub is a recent arrival on this planet who is still as spineless as a bowl of apple jelly. When you hold it up with the palms of your hands on its bottom, it folds together like an accordion, slumping into a helpless puddle of baby and looking exactly as all babies have looked from the beginning of time, according to the best authorities.
>
> There are various well-accredited ways of playing with a Wub. Perhaps the most popular is to tickle its belly button very gently until it removes its thumb from its mouth and remarks 'a-goo-' or words of similar import.
>
> Another more boisterous but very effective way is to dodge in an out from behind any convenient opaque object, making expressive faces the while and shouting 'Boo-oo-oo' or its variant 'Ah-kee-cha, ah-kee-cha.' This latter is generally regarded by Wubs as a perfectly killing bit of comedy, often inducing an almost croup-like paroxysm of mirth. Wubs are known to have a special appreciation for this subtle type of humor.

Before he began working on The Song of Hugh Glass, John's interest was aroused by a note that he had read in an historical work. Only a few lines, the note told of an adventurer, a hunter for the Ashley-Henry men, who was mauled by a bear and left to die by his fellows. Fearfully wounded, the man crawled a hundred miles over empty country to do vengeance, particularly to one of his party—the youthful Jamie—whom he had considered almost like the son he never had. Mona was captivated by the story. "You must write that story, John! You must!" John agreed, and he immediately set to work, planning and researching.

In Neihardt's treatment the wounded man's heroic struggle to live and to achieve vengeance is portrayed in all its geographic reality, but when Glass finally arrives at a trading post and has the opportunity to vent his anger on his unfaithful friend, it is no longer vengeance he desires. Somehow, out of his desperate efforts, crawling a hundred miles to find faithless comrades who had abandoned him—somehow out of all that hardship he had learned what in life is really important, and he had grown spiritually. The reader is given these lines, which explain it all: *The miracle of being loved at all, the privilege of loving to the end.*

Writing for the *Minneapolis Journal* was a financial godsend for the Neihardt family, but it could not last. Tiring of life in the city, John and Mona wished to return to their small-town home in Nebraska. A misunderstanding with his editor, J. T. Jones, over whether he might continue his position while living in Bancroft caused John to leave the *Minneapolis Journal*.

Fortunately, a new outlet for his abilities opened: John was invited to give readings of his works at schools and colleges. At that time, evening lecturers wore formal attire, and John had a black swallow-tail suit made for him. He looked the part in that outfit, and he was quite successful as a performer, for his writings were timely and unusual, and his delivery was surprisingly good.

An actor friend cautioned him, "John, you want to be sure the people in your audience understand every word you say to them. Remember this: you must *bite the consonants and sing the vowels.* And you must learn to project your voice so that you are heard in the back portion of whatever room you are in."

The ability to enunciate clearly and to project one's voice was in those days most important, for microphones were not used. John followed his friend's advice faithfully, his voice stood him in good stead, and he soon found that he had a new part-time career. Mona later told about a homecoming in the spring of 1916 when John had been on a lecture tour, his last "stunt" having been at his alma-mater, the Normal School at Wayne.

"Daddy was so happy! He had a pocket full of money, and I was so glad to see him! I shall never forget that time, for it was one of the most beautiful moments in our whole marriage!"

John's and Mona's family was only half complete, and in early December of 1916 another girl was born. She was named "Hilda," the sword maiden—just Hilda, with no middle name.

Mona was busy devoting herself to her children's needs. She remembered well her childhood promise: "When I have babies, I will take care of them myself!" Her children prospered in the encompassing warmth of her love. John was occupied with the need to make money, but he always kept on with his writing. He was working on the story of the Missouri River trappers and voyageurs that would take its place as the first volume of the series.

It was a time of war—the First World War—and its tensions were strongly felt even in small-town Bancroft. It was not easy for John and Mona, for each had emotional ties with the German people, and, although they were truly patriotic Americans, they could not fully be a part of the wartime hysteria. Fortunately for the family, John was not taken into the military.

There were town meetings in Bancroft, and at one such gathering John was astonished to hear a pastor excitedly tell the villagers that he would like nothing better than to "shoot a lot of Germans." John rose and faced the cleric: "And just which father, son, husband or brother do you want to murder?" A hush spread over the meeting, for it was not entirely safe, during those almost hysterical wartimes, to speak against the passions arousing the townspeople.

On November 11, 1918, the armistice was signed, and peace came to the world and to Bancroft. In 1919 The Song of Three Friends was published, and it was greeted with as much enthusiasm as its forerunner. It told the story of the young men who flocked to Ashley-Henry's call for exploration by keelboat up the Missouri—young, beardless fellows who survived the dangers and hardships of the trip and returned as men. It also told the boisterous, tangled, tragic tale of the three friends—

Mike Fink, Carpenter, and Talbeau—three men who differed in almost everything except their love for one another.

The Song of Three Friends was dedicated to Hilda, and instead of writing a poem for the purpose, John chose a selection from Sappho in the original Greek. Translated, it bore this message: "Like a red, red apple on the topmost bough, that the apple pickers overlooked. No, they did not overlook it; they could not reach it!"

This book, the second volume of the series to appear, was well received. In *Review of Reviews*, a critic shouted, "Mr. Neihardt succeeds admirably with his characterizations of the men and in the recreating of the atmosphere. No true American can read the two sections 'Ashley's Hundred' and 'The Up-Stream Men' without a thrill of patriotic devotion for the land of his birth."

William Marion Reedy in the *St. Louis Mirror* declared, "It has indisputably the great quality of making the reader live the poem with all the men in it and the vast nature in which it moves. It isn't free verse, but it frees the spirit. Salutations to Mr. John G. Neihardt!"

Also in 1919 Mona was interviewed at length by a reporter from the *Kansas City Star*. After telling the romantic story of their "long-distance courtship—Bancroft, Nebraska, to Paris, France," the enthusiastic reporter continued:

Now that was nearly a dozen years ago, long enough to prove that marriages "sight unseen" of intellectual people are—are what? Happy, that's what. Their home is a white cottage set among green trees. Their three pretty children play about the place, and she declares: "Food and babies are the most important things in the world—everything else depends upon them. Learning to cook was my greatest task. My husband helped me. He has camped out a great deal," she adds, as if that gave him the sesame in cookery, "but I was proudest when my fruits and vegetables decided to stay in the can."

And proudly the sculptress-mother showed three hundred quarts of fruits and vegetables that the poet-husband had raised in their garden.

And Mrs. Neihardt hasn't given up her career exactly, either.

"See Hilda when she's shy," gently coaxed six-year-old Sigurd, as he led the way to an alcove off the kitchen, where a model of a three-year-old baby's head was almost finished.

"That's the way she holds her head when she's sleepy," is the way Enid charmingly explained the pose of her cherubic baby sister. Enid stands a head taller than Sigurd and looks as if she had stepped from a Russian fairy tale.

Mrs. Neihardt came up with Hilda in her arms. "Yes, my children are my models now; they are more delight than all that studio work. Any woman artist can well afford to pause in her career to bring up her children. Now that they are growing up"—the children were flattered by that—"I shall begin my work again. The bust of a college president is under way, and a group for the statehouse is under consideration. I must make my reputation match my husband's."

"It does," was the chummy remark of her husband, the poet.

Adah Martinsen came often to visit. Now that there were children in the family, she was known as "Amama," a Russian word for grandmother. It was not surprising that Amama had been shocked when she first saw the tiny house in which John and Mona lived. It seemed to her the type of dwelling that would be suitable for servants, but certainly not for her daughter, nor for an accomplished poet. She was not particularly skilled in keeping her thoughts to herself, and what she said caused trouble in the family. John's pride was injured, and Mona, so loyal to her husband, was upset with her mother. Amama's offer to contribute money to help had been hotly refused by both, but her later offer to give clothing for the children was accepted.

Amama was not the only person who found their home unsuitable. John's fame had spread rather widely, and a number of people came to see him in Bancroft. On one occasion, Samuel Gompers, a well-known Socialist and a president of the American Federation of Labor, came to meet Neihardt, who in his early formative years had been interested in socialism as a form of government.

Gompers was well received by John and entertained by Mona, but he did not conceal what he thought about their home. Gompers made no effort to restrain himself, saying in no uncertain terms that he thought it most unsuitable that a fine poet and his family should live in such a small town as Bancroft, and in a house without running water, inside plumbing, or electricity. "I find it all," he said, "quite shocking."

Mona, always loyal to her husband, spoke up: "But Mr. Gompers, Jesus came out of Jerusalem!"

"That's just what I mean," Gompers replied, "He came *out* of Jerusalem!"

But John and Mona did not leave Bancroft, and there were other visitors with other ideas. One such man, a Brahmin from India, expressed his thoughts so:

"I am a very practical man. When I am near the home of a poet, I never fail to visit him. Yes, I am a very practical man!"

After completing the tale of the three explorer-adventurers in *Three Friends*, John set to work on his next volume, which would tell the story of the migration of white people across America and their ensuing conflicts with the Indian people who lived there. It would be called *The Song of the Indian Wars*, and it would take its place as the third volume of *A Cycle of the West*. While he was working on *The Indian Wars*, he experienced a remarkable interruption.

A letter came from the editor of the *Minneapolis Journal*, asking for a poem on Easter, for which he would pay fifty dollars. John was not at all interested, but when he told Mona about the offer, she urged him: "John, please don't answer right away. Wait a day or two to see what might happen!"

John agreed, and that night he had a dream. In it, a number of men—"they were good poets," he told Mona—recited lines of great beauty about the subject of Easter. But the dream-poets were rude; no one would permit the others to complete what they wanted to say. When John told Mona about his dream the next morning at coffee, she quite practically urged him to put those lines together and get that money. "John, fifty dollars would be such a help to us now!"

"It is all just like rags in a rag-bag, Mona," John protested. "There is no connection between the lines, and I can't do anything with them. Besides, I must keep writing on the *Cycle*." And so John went into his study, sat down, turned to the manuscript on his table, and read back a few hundred lines to get into the flow of the story.

But he could not concentrate; those beautiful lines that the dream-poets had recited kept running through his mind John was definitely annoyed by the interruption, but he pushed back the manuscript and was quickly able to put the recurring lines together. He called the poem "Easter," and in it he tells of the return of springtime with its awakening of winter-bound rivers, and he treats the returning migratory birds as apostles. The poem ends with these lines:

Oh who can be a stranger
To what has come to pass?
The pity of the manger
Is mighty in the grass!

Undaunted by Decembers,
The sap is faithful yet.
The giving Earth remembers,
And only men forget!

John sent his poem to the editor, and soon the Neihardts were fifty dollars richer! In those simple days, fifty dollars had considerable buying power.

Some time later the editor told John he liked the poem, but part of it was a bit "highbrow" for him. John responded, "Which are the offending lines?" The editor referred to the two in which the poet had said "the pity of the manger is mighty in the grass."

"I never explain my poetry," John said, "but if you will go to the high plains of Wyoming in the very early spring, when grass is just beginning to grow among patches of melted snow, you will see two starving cattle for every bunch of that grass. Just take one of the cows aside and ask her. She will explain the lines."

In 1919 when the reporter from the *Kansas City Star* had found John and Mona "happy," there is little doubt that she was not mistaken. They were happy together, and happy in the work they were doing. However, the severe climate of Nebraska, where it was very cold in the winter and hot and humid in the summer, was wearying. For Mona, housework in the winter was desperately unpleasant. John had frequent severe colds, and their little house could not provide a comfortable home for them and their children. Mother Alice, too, was ready to make a change, so John and Mona began to think about where they would like to move.

They decided upon the Ozark Mountains of southern Missouri. John thought the beautiful land and the warmer climate would provide an enjoyable place to live, and he eagerly anticipated being in an area suited to the camping, fishing, and hunting he loved. Mona agreed with him, but for another reason. No doubt she was hoping the Ozarks would be something like the Black Forest of Germany, where she had been so happy as a girl.

26

In the Ozark Mountains of Missouri

The sun was teaching gladness to the hills . . .

"The End of the Dream"

IN 1920 THE TWO NEIHARDT homes in Bancroft were sold, and the family, including Grandma Alice, prepared to move to Missouri. John and Sigurd went on ahead to find a place where they might live, and Mona, her mother-in-law, and the two girls were to follow as soon as possible. Their furniture was shipped by train, but not everything could be sent. Many of Mona's pieces of sculpture remained in a small building on their property, and what became of them, no one knows.

Mona, Grandma Alice, and the two girls took the train to Branson after they had completed matters in Bancroft. John had found a home just west of the town, a two-story white frame farmhouse on eight acres, and the family stayed in a Branson hotel until they could move into their new home. Grandma would live with them for a time, but she had purchased four of the eight acres and intended to build her own home on that land.

It was starting over for them all, without central heat, running water, or other niceties, but Mona had already mastered such challenges. The house needed a great deal of help to make it habitable for the Neihardts. Mona and Alice set about the task of making the house look good—cleaning and painting and making curtains and draperies—until it became quite homey.

Grandma found a capable carpenter, a Mr. Drumiller who lived up the street toward the town, and he agreed to build the stone bungalow she wanted. When it was finished it was much finer than John's simple farmhouse; it even had hardwood floors, space for a bathroom, and a fireplace! Grandma moved into her home, and it was a happy thing for the children, having her living next door. Alice just naturally knew how to be a grandmother. Like everything else she did, Alice put her heart into "grandmothering."

When the Neihardts arrived Branson and Lake Taneycomo (Taney County Missouri) were already known as pleasant spots for tourists or retirees, but the area was still largely undeveloped, and the Ozark hills were hauntingly beautiful with the blue haze covering them much of the time. With no town lights to interfere, there were stars at night— millions of them. As Mona had hoped, the Ozarks did remind her of her childhood home in the Black Forest of Germany. Like the *Schwarzwald*, the mountainous land was covered with trees, which gave it an appearance similar to that of the pine-covered hills in Germany.

They lived on the main road from Branson, and regularly the country-folk came past their homes on the way to town. The Neihardt children often watched with admiration as a "hillbilly" man stood casually in his wagon, reins held loosely in his hands, his knees slightly bent to absorb the shock, while the iron-bound wheels of the wagon rattled on the rocky road as it sped toward town.

Evenings, the younger hill folk came to town on horseback for whatever entertainment Branson could offer. Young men placed their hands loosely on their hips as they sat behind their saddles so that their girls could sit more comfortably in front. Later, as the young people rode home on moonlit nights, John and Mona often heard them singing, and they recognized the songs. They were old English ballads handed down to them through several generations of hill people.

Those were the days when small, spunky, stocky Pearl Spurlock, who provided local transportation for the town, drove her big black Dodge taxicab over rocky roads to the Shepherd of the Hills country made famous by Harold Bell Wright. She escorted countless awe-struck tourists through the beautiful and unspoiled hill country, over near-impassable roads—the one up and over Dewey Bald mountain being little more than a path over a series of rock ledges—to Marvel Cave, formerly owned by the Lynch sisters but which is now the site of the much-frequented Silver Dollar City. Pearl was a little dynamo, an "original" in every way, and she entertained her passengers with many humorous tales about the Ozark area and the "hillbillies" who lived there. Pearl was intriguing, and she was a friend to the Neihardts.

Unlike Mona's beloved Schwarzwald, the Ozark hills had few pines, and most of the forests covering the hills were of hickory, oak, cedar, and walnut, with beautiful dogwood, redbud, and a profusion of wild-flowers in the springtime. If Mona's memory served her well, there were other differences between the Missouri woodlands and the land of her childhood. There were flies in Missouri—Mona remembered there had been none in Gernsbach—and there were mosquitoes and wood ticks in the summertime.

The whole family learned a hard lesson from the pests that abounded in the forests, for if a tick were not properly removed when its head was buried in its victim's skin, a bad infection followed. John and the children soon learned that in the Ozarks one goes into the woods only in winter, after the first freeze. Camping, hiking, and hunting were pursued only in winter, and in the summer, swimming in crystal-clear Roark Creek or boating and fishing on Lake Taneycomo, as the dammed White River was known, would have to suffice.

John found almost boundless opportunity for fun with the children, of which there were now four. In August of 1921, another girl was born and was named after her grandmother: Alice May. The morning of her birth, John brought Mona a bouquet of the lovely blue flowers of the wild hemp plant, and after that those blooms were known as "Alice flowers."

Mona seldom accompanied the others when they went camping, horseback riding, or swimming but preferred to remain at home. Perhaps it was her never-forgotten sorrow over the death of her father when she was only eight years old that made her so eager for her children to "do things with Daddy." Left at home alone, there was always house-work for her to do, but Mona also saw the happy times the children spent with their father as opportunities for her to turn her thoughts, uninhibited, to her sculpture. Or, when she was very tired, those times gave her an opportunity for much-needed rest.

It was not until Hilda was a grown woman with children of her own that it occurred to her that it was to give Mother some relief from the duties of child-care that her father had taken the children on so many outings. She remembered that when they returned on a summer's afternoon from a swim or a boat ride, Mother was either sleeping or she was in her studio, busily working on her latest model. Although Mona seldom went swimming, Grandma Alice upon occasion did, and the children watched as she paddled around in the shallow water of the creek. It was, she said, good for her rheumatism!

There was a happy custom: often when they returned from a swim, the remainder of the hot afternoon was devoted to the making of ice cream. Rich Jersey milk and cream and home-hatched eggs went into a custard to be frozen in an ice cream maker that required much turning of a crank. The children took turns with their father in this occupation, each cranking until he or she was tired. And when the ice cream was frozen, how good it did taste!

They often anticipated the ice cream as they walked up the steep, rocky road after a swim in Roark Creek. Still cool from their long swim in the fresh waters but hungry and a bit tired, they were almost "slap-happy." On one occasion the children became almost hysterical, laughing at a suggestion made by John.

"We could invite Mrs. Ballentine and Mrs. Corlis to have ice cream with us," he said, referring to two refined and gracious ladies who lived in the town. "We could put sauerkraut juice in the mix for the ice cream and then watch to see how they would look when they tasted the sour, salty stuff! They are both so polite that they would never say anything bad about it!"

The almost scandalously ridiculous idea caused John to chuckle as he recounted it, and how Enid, Sigurd, Hilda, and Alice did laugh as they imagined the scene! It is not necessary—is it?—to report that the sauerkraut ice cream was never made.

John loved to ride a horse, and beautiful, black Pet, a Kentucky sad-dlehorse, was later added to the family for Hilda and Alice to ride. She was not only a riding horse, she was a companion, an understanding friend to whom a child could go when she felt unhappy or perhaps misunderstood. At such times, just hugging her long horse-neck soothed hurt feelings and restored a happy mood.

During the winter, the Neihardts kept a horse or two from the local riding stable, so the three horse lovers—John, Hilda, and Alice—might go together on long rides through the countryside. The stable owner, Rosie Rozell, was more than willing to have any of his horses fed and cared for through the winter, when they would be of no use to him. One particular big, rawboned mare, Red Ribbon, had once been a racing pacer. Ribbon was a favorite of John's, and he rode her like the wind. So fast was she when she paced that another horse had to gallop or nearly run to keep up with her. If a child were riding behind John's saddle, she was hard put to keep from sliding off the rear of the speeding animal. John did like to go fast.

Mona devoted herself to her family, and she wanted her children to have uninhibited freedom to play out-of-doors. "I just want you to be happy!" she often told them, and that statement at times carried with it something of a bittersweet touch. Was there too much intensity in the way she said the words, and did her smile try to hide her own lack? But Hilda and Alice were young, and they felt secure in their mother's love. They took full advantage of Mona's lenient attitude, and for them there was never a dull or boring moment. In spite of the fact that girls and women did not wear trousers at that time even though the Ozarks were already a tourist playground, Mona said, "If they are going to hang upside down from trees, they should be properly dressed." And so, two little girls wore boys' clothing when they played outdoors! Mona, with her independent spirit, was surely ahead of her time.

The unusual Mrs. Neihardt brought more than a touch of refinement to their life in Branson, and—even though money was scarce—the warmth and simple beauty of the home reflected her artistic nature. Perhaps not often, but occasionally, the Neihardts entertained with dinner, and the table was always beautifully set with fine cloths which Mona still had from the Gernsbach days—linens woven with the large Martinsen M and matching napkins large enough to cover a card table. Dishes were Mona's favorite Gold Key pattern, and the food was her own creation. Son Sigurd teased his mother because for salad she often—well, nearly always—served a tomato aspic on fresh lettuce leaves, with home-made mayonnaise. When she was planning her menu for a company dinner, Sigurd would add, "and *tomato aspic!*" Mona joined him in his silly giggle.

On one such occasion, the guest of honor was a writer who also was accomplished as a wine connoisseur. He could, John had learned, identify any wine just by its taste. The dinner had been served, and the time for the wine-tasting arrived. John left the room and returned with a bottle of imported wine that he had wrapped completely in a towel. He handed it to the guest, who opened the bottle and poured a small amount into the waiting glass. He swished the wine around in the glass, tested its fragrance, took a taste, contemplated it, and took another small taste. Then he told the amazed diners not only the year of the wine but the exact valley in France from which it came!

Of all the good times the family had, the Christmas celebration was the one most filled with wonder. Even though his childhood experience with the season of giving had been marred by disappointment, John joined with Mona in re-creating the happy and mysterious times she remembered from her childhood. Weeks before the big day, the children wrote letters to Santa, telling that jolly elf what they would like to receive, and some, at least, of what they asked for would be under the tree on Christmas morning.

It was not until the morning of Christmas Day that they saw the decorated tree. John had gone out the day before to find the prettiest cedar available, and after the children had been sent upstairs to bed on Christmas Eve (after they had hung their stockings, of course!), Santa Mona, with the help of Santa John, made the tree beautiful with tinsel and candles. Later, when electricity was available, the much safer bulbs were used for the tree.

Early Christmas morning Mona called up the staircase in her melodious voice, telling the four eager youngsters that the long-awaited time had finally come. As they gathered around the tree, Mona said, as she always did, "This is the *best* Christmas we have ever had!" Then they all joined with her in singing "Merry Christmas, Merry Christmas, see the lights how they shine! Merry Christmas, Merry Christmas, it is holiday time." Everyone's eyes were on the brightly wrapped gifts, but, before the presents might be opened, a special Christmas breakfast, with oranges, cinnamon rolls Mona had made the day before, and hot chocolate, had to be eaten. Then, and only then, the gifts were opened.

Christmas of 1922 was special in a particular way. Six-year-old Hilda came home from school and told her mother that teacher had said she must have a "piece" to recite for the school Christmas program. For mother it was simple: "Go ask Daddy, dear. He will find just the right poem for you to memorize."

She did go to her father, who was in his study, reading. "Daddy, I have to have a 'piece' for school. Can you find me one about Christmas? I am going to be in the program next week at school!"

John was blunt: "There *is not one* poem written for children which has anything whatever to do with the real meaning of Christmas."

By this time Mona had come into the study, and she saw the disappointed look on the little girl's face. "Oh, John, if that is true, why don't you just write one for her?"

Well, he did, and this is how it looked after John had carefully typed it:

THE MEANING OF CHRISTMAS
(Hilda's "Piece")

This holiest of all the nights,
I wonder what it means?
It's surely more than candlelights
On tinselled evergreens.
It's more than toys that make it dear
And eating pleasant things,
For if you listen right, you'll hear
A murmuring of wings!
My Grandma says it's more than fun
And hanging up your stocking;
It's knowing any needy one
Might be the Savior knocking.
It's helping those who feel the rod
Of grief and heavy labors;
I guess it's being nice to God
By loving all your neighbors!

A happy little girl recited her "piece" for the school program, and teachers and parents said they liked it very much!

Now and then, on a cold winter evening, John would come into the living room where the other members of the family were gathered, perhaps listening to a favorite radio program. "Who wants to go for a walk?" he would ask. Two always did: Hilda and Alice were eager to take part in any adventure with their father, for somehow no matter what they did, an *adventure* it always was. So, out the door they would go, the two girls hastily pulling on their jackets as they followed their dad into the wooded area across the road from their home. John plunged ahead swiftly, seemingly unbothered that he carried no flashlight, and the girls followed, all the while catching the limbs of the trees that he parted as he walked.

And those moonlit or starlit nights were embroidered by the poetry he declaimed as he strode along. When he chose Tennyson's powerful description of the time when the dying King Arthur asked his loyal knight to throw the sword Excalibur back into the lake, whence it had come, John's stride took on the rhythm of the poetry:

> Dry clash'd his harness in the icy caves
> And barren chasms, and all to left and right
> The bare, black cliff clanged round him, as he based
> His feet on juts of slippery crag that rang
> Sharp-smitten with the dint of armed heels—
> And on a sudden, lo, the level lake,
> And the long glories of the winter moon!

Truly, the chills that Hilda remembers going down their backs were not entirely caused by the cold of the night air, and the Ozark moon had its own "long glories."

Sometimes he quoted, in the original ancient Greek, from the Agamemnon of Aeschylus, or perhaps from a play by Sophocles. Not knowing Greek, Hilda and Alice could not understand what he said, but the language was melodious, and the impassioned, warm baritone of his voice was good to hear.

Oftentimes, when it was raining outside and there seemed nothing much to do, John would suggest to his adventurous daughters, "Would you like to go down in the pasture and start a fire in the rain?" Of course, they wanted to do that, for all of Daddy's suggestions were full of fun. They did get a fire started under a large sycamore tree whose giant leaves kept the ground under it almost dry. "Daddy" showed how the very small, dry, dead limbs that clung to the center of a cedar tree could quickly be made to burn, allowing larger, even damp sticks to join in the flames.

At such a time, after they were gathered around the crackling fire, John—always the poet—might change his thoughts to Swinburne and a gentler, warmer scene:

> In a coign of the cliff between lowland and highland,
> At the sea-down's edge between windward and lee,
> Walled round with rocks as an inland island,
> The ghost of a garden fronts the sea!

Or, for a change, he might recite one of the many humorous or naughty-boy limericks or verses he had written in idle moments, perhaps this tender bit of nonsense:

> If I had a lumpty-tum-tumpty-tum-too
> In the land of the olive and fig,
> I would sing of the lumpty-tum-tumpty to you
> And play on the thing-a-ma-jig!
> And if in some far-distant land I should fall,
> A lumpty-tum's all I would crave!
> Oh, bury me deep in the what-you-may-call,
> And plant thing-a-bobs on my grave!

Usually, as they sat there in the warmth of the fire, the family horse, cow, goat, dog, and cat would gather in a circle around them, their faces toward the fire and their tails to the outside. John likened the animals to "the Holy Family," and their friendly presence made the occasion warmly memorable.

Those were never-to-be-forgotten times, and for the family the memory of them would always be tinged with the hopeful trust that happiness and beauty are real and that it is indeed a good thing to be a member of the human race.

As soon as he could, John had a room added to the north side of the house. It had windows on three sides, and it served beautifully as a studio for Mona. The room had a flat roof with a wooden railing around the edges, and that space served as a sleeping area in the hot summertime. One could see the stars there, and mosquitoes did not come up as high as the second floor.

There were many happy and busy times in the afternoons, for John continued his habit of writing only in the mornings. After breakfast—an early breakfast with Mona—he went directly to his study to write, just as he would, if otherwise employed, have gone to work. He had begun *The Song of the Indian Wars* while they were still in Nebraska, but he finished it in Branson.

The final chapter telling about the death of Crazy Horse was so hard to write but so successful that John wrote "Thank you" in the margin at the end of the manuscript. John had learned the details surrounding the death of that great Sioux hero from his friend Major Henry Lemly, who was in charge of the cordon of troops at Fort Robinson at the time Crazy Horse was killed there. Because that chapter so grippingly told a story that somehow capsulized the white-Indian conquest, John would use it often later in his lecture-readings.

One night after the book was finished, Mona awoke while dreaming. Still half asleep, she murmured, "John, your sister Lulu is not tall. I guess I am dreaming, but this woman who calls herself 'Lulu' is tall and very pretty, and she has blond hair piled high on her head. She is smiling as she points to a small boy sitting at a desk. John, she is so *warm* and I can see how proud she is as she points at . . . that . . . little . . . boy."

Mona had fallen back into her dream, but the next morning she remembered and talked about it again. "That was Miss Lulu Lobb!" John told her. "I was in school in Kansas City when she was my teacher, and I thought she was so beautiful that she must be a goddess!"

"Now I understand why she was so proud, John. She knows about your writing; I am sure of that!" Mona's face glowed as she spoke. She too was proud of the man sitting across from her at breakfast.

The Song of the Indian Wars was beautifully brought out with Allan True's illustrations by Macmillan Publishing Company in 1925, and it was dedicated "To Alice, Three Years Old." Although the publisher had contracted in advance for this work, as it had also done for previous volumes, there was little if any advertising, not even an announcement of its publication in the *New York Times*.

In 1926 John bought his first big car. Before that, the family had driven a Ford Model T up and down the hill to the town, taking a "run" at its base in an effort to "make the hill on high." The new car was a 1924 cobalt blue Buick touring car, complete with side curtains to keep out the dust of the road, and when Mr. Binkley drove it up to their home, the children and Mona were overwhelmed by its long, sleek beauty. The vehicle more than lived up to its manufacturer's bragging advertisement: "When better cars are built, Buick will build them." John learned to drive on that car, and while learning on the dirt and gravel roads, he declared, "Yes, eighteen miles an hour is *my speed*." How he did change, for he became quite a fast driver for the times! Touring in that open car, which offered neither heat nor air conditioning to its occupants, brought new excitement and fun for the family, but riding in it was a dusty, chilly, or hot business!

Once more John turned to writing for a newspaper, and in 1926 he accepted the position of literary editor of the *St. Louis Post-Dispatch*. He was to have a page for his reviews, and Mona designed its heading: "Of Making Many Book," a phrase taken from Acts. John continued to write for that newspaper for ten years. At first the family remained in Branson, and John took Enid to St. Louis with him to act as his secretary.

Later, the family joined him, and they lived for a time in suburban Kirkwood, where the children enjoyed the good schools and happy playtimes with the neighbors.

It was during the time of prohibition, and Mona had a problem for which she sought the answer. She telephoned the local police station. "This is Mrs. John Neihardt," she said, "and I have a question. My husband likes to drink beer, and I want to make it for him. But, if I do make some home brew for him, am I disobeying the law?"

Through a barely concealed chuckle, the officer replied, "If you are disobeying the law by making home brew, then so are half the people in this town—including myself!" After that, John had his favorite drink, perhaps no more than one bottle on most days, and Mona was no longer worried.

While the family lived near St. Louis, Hilda and Alice spent the summers in Branson with Grandma Alice. Who could forget the raspberry sandwiches on homemade bread she sent with them when they went swimming in the creek? And one of the girls thought Grandma must have psychic powers when she said, "Dear, you have been eating onions in the garden, haven't you?" Surely she made life happy for the girls, but more than that, she was an inspiration to them, much as she had been to her son. Through the years, one granddaughter never forgot her admonition: "Hilda, *do something!*"

It was during the summer of 1928 that Nick Neihart came back. Or did he? This is how it happened: The two sisters were asleep in a back bedroom at Grandma's, and sometime during the night Hilda awoke to witness a strange sight. She told no one about it the next day, not even Grandma; instead she decided to wait until her father came from St. Louis. That next weekend, John did come down to Branson, and, while she was standing with her father near the gate which led to the pasture from Grandma's backyard, she told him what she had seen.

"Daddy, a few nights ago I woke up in the middle of the night and looked out the window into Grandma's back yard. Right there under the clothesline was a man. He had on a cap that looked like a soldier's, and he was wearing a uniform. He was standing at a big desk like the one in the post office down town, and he was writing something on it. I pinched myself the way people do in stories, just to make sure I was awake, and looked back into the bedroom.

"Then I looked out into the yard again. The man was still standing there. He was still writing on that post office desk. Then, all at once he disappeared."

John was excited "Kid, that was my father you saw!" Then he told Hilda something about his father, including that he had been in the army and had fought in the Philippines, all of which came as total news to her. John's father had never been mentioned in the family, for after he left when John was a little boy in Kansas City, he did not return.

After learning of Hilda's experience, John wrote to a lawyer friend in Omaha, who was able to learn that Nickolas Neihart had died in an old soldiers' home in California near the time when his granddaughter had looked out her bedroom window and seen the soldier standing there. With Judge Vinsonhaler's help, and after relatives had signed affidavits saying that there had never been a divorce, Grandma Alice received a widow's pension for the remainder of her life.

Did Nick Neihart finally come home to his family?

While she was working at the newspaper with her father, Enid met Oliver Fink, a feature writer a number of years older than she, fell in love, and married. They lived for a time in Overland, a suburb of St. Louis, then moved to Columbia, Missouri. Sigurd found his life partner in Branson—pretty, vivacious Maxine Melton. Hilda remembers how smitten he was when he met her, and when he was told, "I know her; she is one of the nicest girls in high school," he added, "Yes, but you don't know how *cute* she is!" Maxine became a much-loved member of the family.

John's work at the St. Louis Post-Dispatch was grueling. In addition to planning and arranging for his page "Of Making Many Books" John read and reviewed a book a day. Busy as he was, John could not be entirely happy when he was not devoting full time to the poetic series that he considered his main life work. Normally a happy, joking person, he at times gave way to the strain and expressed himself at home in a pessimistic manner that was unsettling to the children.

Mona understood, and she explained, "When Daddy is not working on his stuff ["stuff" was the word by which he referred to his writings], his wheels turn backward."

During this period Lindbergh had made his historic solo flight to France, and John was again asked to write a poem, this time one that would commemorate that achievement. Again he rose to the occasion, and the editor of the paper was pleased. The poem ends with the thought: " . . . and Lindbergh rides with God!"

In spite of unwelcome interruptions and the time devoted to his work on the Post-Dispatch, John did make headway on his "stuff," for he never completely stopped working on the Cycle, even though he was occupied with another job. When he had written some five hundred lines on what would be the final volume of the Cycle, The Song of the Messiah, John hit a snag.

This third *Song* would tell the tragic story of the final struggle between the Plains Indians and the whites who were streaming across the land. The Indians of the Great Plains were never actually conquered militarily, but they were near starvation because the seemingly endless herds of buffalo and deer, upon which they relied for food, clothing, and even shelter, had been decimated by the invading white men. Hungry and suffering from diseases alien to them, the Indian people had turned, in their helplessness, to spiritual belief for their salvation.

A Paiute Indian by the name of Wovoka had a vision in which he was told that if the Indian people would dance, wear certain shirts while they danced, and pray all the while, a new world would appear. The various "improvements" made by the invading whites that the Native peoples found so desecrating to Mother Earth—the railroads, the fences, the plowed land—would all disappear; the Indian people who had been killed would come back, and all would live happily together on a green, green earth, under a blue, blue sky. Many tribes joined in this hope, and their participation was popularly referred to as "the Ghost Dance movement." It all came to a tragic end with the massacre of Sitanka's (Big Foot's) band at Wounded Knee on December 29, 1890.

For all of his works, in addition to historical research, John relied upon personal—or near-personal—acquaintance with actual partici-pants. This was possible for him because he was writing at a time that he called "a watershed in history," when old men and women who had taken part in the historical events he would chronicle—both whites and Indians—were still alive. John decided he needed to find a Sioux holy man who had participated in the Ghost Dance movement. He had completed all the background historical research for the book, but he needed to feel close to a spiritual leader who had actually been involved in the "dance of the ghost."

Throughout much of his life, John supported his family by lecturing widely at schools and colleges throughout the United States. During one period, his pianist son, Sigurd, added music to his father's readings and, with his wife, Maxine, acted also as agent for the tours. On one such trip in August 1930, they diverted from their lecture tour and drove to the agency office at the Pine Ridge Reservation in South Dakota and asked the agent if he knew of a holy man who had actually contributed to the Messiah, or Ghost Dance, movement. The agent knew of no such person, but from a group of old "long hair" Indians who were sitting around outside the agency office, John learned of an old holy man who might be the one he sought.

He was warned, however, that the man—Black Elk—was a bit strange and most probably would not talk to him. "Just about two weeks ago," he was told, "a writer came up from Lincoln and asked Black Elk to talk with her. He refused. He always refuses. I don't think he will talk to you either."

"I have never known an Indian who would not talk to me," John said, and he asked young Flying Hawk, who acted as an interpreter at the agency, to go with him and Sigurd some twenty miles or so to the home of the holy man, which was near Manderson.

As they drove along the narrow dirt road west of the town, they approached a small log cabin near the top of a low, barren hill. In front of the pine shade that had been built near the cabin, a slender old man was standing, shading his eyes with one hand as he peered down the road toward the approaching car. It was Black Elk, and after Flying Hawk had introduced the two visitors, they all sat down together on the ground under the pine shade, smoking the cigarettes that John had brought. Cigarettes were then much in demand and made welcome gifts.

Black Elk did talk to John. The four men had sat together for a time, visiting and smoking, when he made a most surprising statement. "I feel in this man sitting beside me," he announced to the hillside in front of him, "a strong desire to know the things of the Other World, and he has been sent to learn what I know. He must come back so that I may teach him."

Then he spoke in Lakota to a young boy who was sitting properly apart from the older folk. The boy got up and went into the cabin, soon returning with an ornament that he gave to his grandfather. As Black Elk took the piece, he stated that it was sacred and that he had used it many years before in sun dances. Holding the ornament in front of him and speaking to John, he explained its sacred meaning.

Black Elk pointed to a circular piece of leather suspended on a narrow thong. It was painted a light blue with a yellow center, and there were indentations around its circumference. "This star represents light and the wisdom and understanding which come from the light. The piece of buffalo hide hanging here is for the good things of this life which come from the buffalo—something to eat, something to wear, and a place to live. And this eagle feather hanging down from the star means that our thoughts should rise high as the eagle does."

Then, offering the ornament to John, Black Elk said, "I wish you all these things, my friend!" The gift was so unexpected, and Black Elk's description so meaningful that John was quite overcome. He could only breathe the words "Thank you! Thank you!" as he took the sacred ornament into his hands.

In response to the holy man's words "he must come back so that I may teach him," which had both surprised and intrigued him, John asked, "When do you want me to come back, Black Elk?"

"In the spring, when the grass is so high," the old holy man said, indicating by the breadth of his hand how tall the grass should be.

"I will come back, Black Elk, and I will learn what you have to teach me."

The men talked a while longer, and before they left, John thanked Black Elk for his courtesy, promising to return the following spring. As they drove down the narrow dirt road toward the village of Manderson, Flying Hawk remarked, "Funny thing! When we came up the hill to his house, it looked like the old man was expecting us. . . ."

"I noticed that too," Sigurd said. "He certainly did not seem at all surprised to see us. He seemed to be waiting for someone to come."

They had sensed for the first time the mysterious power of Black Elk.

By the time he had returned to his home in Branson, John's interest in Black Elk had increased so much that he immediately wrote to a publisher he knew—William Morrow of the New York company that bore his name. John told him about the meeting with Black Elk and his conviction that the holy man's story would make a book that would reveal as never before the true nature of American Indians.

The book he envisioned would be, he told Morrow, "entirely out of the Indian consciousness." The publisher was interested and offered to give John an advance that would make it possible for him to go to Pine Ridge Reservation to gather material for the book. With two of his daughters—Enid, who had graduated from a St. Louis business school, to do the shorthand reporting and Hilda as "official observer"—John returned to Manderson the first of May 1931.

Mona did not go with them. As always when she remained at home, she did so not only because it was necessary for her to care for the home. Remaining at home also gave her an extended period of time when she could work on her sculpture. Mona was creating a series of small figures that she called "Ozark Babies" and that she hoped to be able to market. Although she occupied herself primarily as wife and mother, Mona never gave up her desire for some success as a sculptor.

It was not easy for John to get official permission to spend time on the reservation for the interviews, but he did finally get that authorization from the current secretary of the interior, Lyman Wilbur. Although there had apparently been considerable concern on the part of certain authorities that his interviews might cause problems on the reservation, it was decided that John was not likely to stir up trouble among the Indian people. He was not, someone urged, a rabble rouser!

In the brief three-week time they were allowed, John and Enid, with Black Elk's son Ben as the chosen translator for the interviews, spent long hours—often well into the night—eliciting and recording the stories of Black Elk and several of his old friends. Although he had known Indian people rather intimately for some thirty years, what he learned during those sessions was excitingly new to John. Black Elk's friends too recounted much of historical interest, for they had lived the old way of life and had taken part in many battles against the army.

But most of all, John was overwhelmed by the beauty and spiritual meaning of what Black Elk revealed. Never before to anyone, and particularly not to a white man, had Black Elk told in its entirety the Great Vision that had come to him when he was nine years old. Many times during the conversations, John was so impressed and surprised by the depth of meaning and the beauty of what the old man said that he interrupted, asking Ben, "Did he really say that?

"Yes," Ben would reply, "Old Man, he really say that!"

Ben too was impressed, for most of what his father related was new to him. Black Elk had given a partial account of his dream to a holy man when, as a young fellow, he was worried about what his vision meant for him to do, but other than that Black Elk had told no one, not even his family, about the vision or his early life.

One day when he and John were visiting during a break in the interviews, Ben remarked, "Ain't it great; ain't it wonderful!"

"What is wonderful?" John inquired.

"What the old man is sayin'. I always knew he had something, but I didn't know what in hell it was!"

The contributions from Standing Bear, the old man's lifelong friend, and from Fire Thunder and Iron Hawk added authentic historical and human touches, and Neihardt was more than ever convinced that the resulting book would be "entirely out of the Indian consciousness."

When John and the girls returned from their weeks on the Pine Ridge Reservation, they were tremendously excited about the experience. It had been a happy adventure for all three, but it was much more than that. The spiritual concepts learned during the interviews were as intensely meaningful to Mona and the family as they had been to John. Black Elk's telling about the Sacred Hoop had been a high point in the interviews.

"Imagine," Black Elk said as he made a circle with his arms, "a hoop so large that everything is in it—all the two-leggeds, the four-leggeds, the fishes of the stream, the wings of the air, and all green things that grow. Across this Hoop, beginning in the east where the days of men begin, and ending in the west, where the days of men end, runs the black road of worldly difficulties. Everyone must walk along this road." Then, seemingly by way of explanation, he added a comment that seems a gross understatement: "It is not easy to live in this world."

"But if the black road of worldly difficulties were the only one, then this life would not mean much. There is another road—the Good Red Road of Spiritual Understanding—which begins in the south, whence comes the power to grow, and goes up to the north, where the Great White Giant lives, the region of white hairs and death. Where the good red road of understanding crosses the black road of worldly difficulties, that place is holy, and there stands the sacred Tree, which shall fill with blooms and singing birds. Under this Tree, the people will be safe, as her babies are protected under the mother sheo's wings."

John's general knowledge of the history of the American West made it possible for him to make choices and to form the interviews with

Black Elk into a valid sequence. In the diary that she kept, Enid had commented, "Black Elk is very good at telling his vision, but he is not much good at history." The book was quickly written and the manuscript submitted to the publisher early the next year. The matter of a title had been no little problem, and John considered many. As he usually did, he discussed the various possibilities he had in mind with Mona. She had a suggestion.

"John, why don't you just call it 'Black Elk Speaks?' "

" 'Black Elk Speaks,' " John agreed, "yes, that would be a good title. It will show that the book is all Indian. Truly Indian. And I do want to give full credit to Black Elk. I will suggest that title to the publisher."

William Morrow, John's friend, had died in the meantime, and the editor who took over the manuscript suggested that Black Elk's Great Vision be put in an appendix. John was horrified, and he stamped around the house, bitterly expressing his feelings:

"Mona, I will not stand for that. The vision is the heart of the book! If that's the way they think about it, they can just return the manuscript! They can just send it right back!"

"John, dear, don't be upset." Mona's voice was soothing. "They will publish it just as you have written. You must tell them that the vision belongs in the main part of the book. It belongs there! Just insist upon that! You will see; they will publish it as you have written."

The book was published as Mona had said it would be. It received enthusiastic reviews and critics called it "a beautiful book," but it did not sell. "After a year or two, copies were remaindered for forty-five cents each, and the book was out of print for over twenty years.

Through a student, Carl Jung learned of the book, and because he was so impressed with it, he arranged to get it published in the German language by Walter Verlag of Zürich in 1955. Because she had grown up speaking German, Mona would have liked to assist with the translation, for she believed she could make sure that the story and the meanings were faithfully carried over into the new language. She was not given that opportunity. The small advance given to Neihardt in 1931 was not completely earned by the book's sales in both the original English and the German editions, and Neihardt was asked by William Morrow Company to "please send your check for the unearned balance." He did.

The concept of the Sacred Hoop—being inclusive, not exclusive, and so *true*—seemed a paradigm upon which a good understanding of life might be based. Mona was moved by it, and—having lived for years in Europe where formal gardens were everywhere—it was not surprising that she came up with a remarkable idea.

"John, why don't we make a Sacred Hoop Garden? We could have the two roads, and the four quarters could be represented in their appropriate colors with flowers. What do you think? Instead of the Tree in the center, why couldn't we have a fountain figure—a small child? I could sculpt one, and you and I could cast it in cement, and the little child could be holding a hose, out of which water would rise, just as the Tree would rise from the ground. What do you think?"

John was captivated by the idea, and they immediately set to work on the plans. A local hillbilly who often worked for them was asked to help in making the garden. When they told him what they wanted to make, Art said, "You want a vegetable garden."

No, that was not it, and they explained further. "A flower garden?" Art suggested. Not quite, they said, and they repeated their description of what they wanted to build. Art interrupted his thoughts with some neglected chewing of tobacco, turned and spat, then, in a flash of understanding, said, "Oh, you mean a *beauty garden!*" Yes, that was it, and the work to make a garden was begun.

A privet hedge enclosed the circle, with blue, white, red, and yellow flowers at the four quarters—the colors that Black Elk used for the west, the north, the east, and the south—and with the black road of worldly difficulties and the good red road of spiritual understanding crossing in the center.

There, at the crossing of the roads, was a pool, and in its middle stood a small child holding a hose from which life-giving water spurted. John cast four benches of cement, which made the enclosed area a delightful place to sit and think as one watched the fountain. John's and Mona's plan for a Sioux Prayer Garden was repeated later at the John G. Neihardt State Historic Site in Bancroft, Nebraska, and after that the meaningful plan was borrowed for a number of other public places.

Although it would be many years before the Branson area achieved the fame that later came to it, many unusual persons had already felt the allure of the Ozark hill country. Mona had become acquainted with one of these—Rose O'Neill, the creator of the Kewpie doll. Their mutual interests led to a brief friendship, and a photograph of the time shows Mona and Rose O'Neill together—two ladies of approximately the same height standing by the pool and fountain-baby in the prayer garden.

While the family was living in Branson, John learned that a group was promoting the idea of a monument to the great Sioux hero Crazy Horse. Mona yearned to be chosen to do the work, and she believed that her long association with Neihardt, who had so honored the hero and his people, together with her training with the greatest living sculptor of the time, Rodin, fitted her for the job. John wrote a letter describing her ability and recommending her, and he asked others to do the same.

A letter written by Mona to Hilda tells how she felt and why:

> It looks as though the nation is trying to erect a monument to Crazy Horse, and Daddy is going to do everything he can to turn it in my direction. They are now considering a man called ——, or something to that effect. It would be exactly my luck if a stranger did get the chance I have ached for all my married life, and misrepresented all Daddy's heroes in bronze—now wouldn't it?
>
> I would do the work for nothing in the way of profit—so that may carry some weight, and I would do it according to John's ideas of how Crazy Horse *really* looked.
>
> In *The Song of the Indian Wars*, when Daddy first got the lines "*Don't touch me; I am Crazy Horse!*" I got a mental picture of just how he stood when he said that—and I have never forgotten it. I so wanted at the time to model him that way—now do you suppose some "foreigner" without the true *feel* of the Cycle will be given the chance? If he does— then I am *through*.

Sadly, Mona was not chosen. Instead, a man was chosen to do the sculpture—a man from Europe! Hilda remembered the day Mona learned of the appointment. She and her mother were in the front yard of the Branson home when the disappointed sculptor, overcome with the bad news, expressed her feelings: "*It's just because I'm a woman!*" Hard words, but possibly they were correct.

As he forged ahead with the writing of his epic *Cycle*, Mona was John's sounding board. Each day when he left his study after a morning's work, he read to her the lines that during that morning he had been able "to get." Mona listened, and each day it was the same. Her mobile face was illumined by the wonderful glow he had first seen when their marriage was new, and unfailingly she cried out, "Oh, John, that's great stuff!"

The Song of the Messiah, begun before John had gone to South Dakota to find Black Elk in 1930, was completed in 1935, and it was dedicated to John's life partner:

> FOR MONA
> His woman was a mother to the Word.

The quoted words in the dedication are taken from the first part of the Paiute Wovoka's telling of a powerful dream he had, in which the Indian people were promised that the beautiful, unspoiled world that had been taken from them would be returned, and with it the people who had died. He told of the vision that would lead to the Messiah Movement:

> And before she heard,
> His woman was a mother to the word,
> The first of all believers to believe.

The lines had grown out of Mona's dedication to his work and his love for her, and she expressed her joy in a letter to Enid in this way: "Just think of it, the greatest and noblest of all his poems—to me!"

Before he sent the manuscript to the publisher, Mona begged, "John, you're not sending this one to Macmillan's too?"

"They're the largest publisher in the world," John responded.

"Oh, but John, they're *killing* you!"

Again, the book was beautifully put together, but there was no advertising for it in the *New York Times*. Even so, it was given a prize by the Poetry Society of America, and a telephone call informed John that he was to receive the Pulitzer Prize. Just how that happened John did not know, but the prize was finally awarded, not to him as he had been told but to a little-known woman whose book of verse had just been published. John was invited to go to New York and speak at the award dinner!

Mona was devastated. "John, surely you are not going!"

John Neihardt did go, and he spoke at the dinner for the Pulitzer Prize winner. John was like that.

About this time Mona wrote in a letter to a daughter:

> Dr. —— thinks a "Bust" on a pedestal is a monument! Just think how absurd to remember America's greatest Poet that way! I wrote him how it *should* be and I don't care whether they take it or leave it. But they can mess around with their men sculptors and they'll have to take something as fine as the wonderful portrait they have in Omaha! What scrambled eggs this world is! The authorities give a society lady the Pulitzer Prize the year that John Neihardt comes out with his Collected Poems—and they won't let me make Neihardt's Monument because I am a woman and an unknown quantity. But they'll pay a painter a big sum to paint a poor portrait.

Hilda had completed her first year of college, and John wanted her to attend his alma mater, Nebraska Normal College in Wayne. She transferred, and when she came home in her second year for Christmas of 1935, it was a happy time being home for the holidays with her family. As always, she did not neglect Grandma. One day that dear lady cautioned, "Now Hilda, Grandma will not be here when you come home in the spring."

"Oh, Grandma, *yes you will!*" Hilda could not think of her grandmother's dying; she loved her so.

Grandmother's response was spoken calmly. "No, dear, Grandma will not be here. But when you hear about it, do not leave your studies and come home. Do not interrupt your studies. Do not do that! You must not neglect your studies. Promise me!" Hilda sadly agreed, and when she was back at school after the holidays, it happened—in February 1936—just as Grandma had said it would.

To Mona, who—living next door—had been the one to give Alice the loving care she needed during the last years of her life, the dying mother-in-law confided, "Mona, you are my daughter, my real daughter!" Mona was deeply touched by the heartening admission. It was the truth, she thought, but she could not help remembering, somewhat wryly, how many times she and Mother Alice had argued. She recalled that at one such time out in the yard they had been so upset that they threw buckets of water on each other! "Fact and truth are not always the same," Mona thought.

Many years before, when John had first held in his hand the picture Mona sent him from Paris, he had for a fleeting moment tried to imagine how it would seem if that cosmopolitan young lady were sitting across from him at breakfast. That thought had become real, for during more than two dozen years they had sat together at early breakfast, before other members of the family were up, and had talked, mostly about what they called "the higher values"—poetry, art, music, and spiritual concepts.

Sometimes their young second daughter had awakened and slipped quietly down the stairs, to sit with them and listen. Although she could not fully know just what was meant by "the higher values," that very young girl thought they must be something wonderful! Their early morning visits became almost a ritual for John and Mona. Not only was the conversation good, so was the coffee. Mona had seen to that; she blended two of the available brands—one mild, and one strong—to make their brew just right.

The Branson home was a white frame farmhouse that they had done over in stucco. There was an extension on each side, the east side being given to a kitchen, which housed the deep well, some cabinets and a wood cook stove. The other extension housed a furnace and the bathroom, which had been made possible when Branson got electricity and city water.

Each year Mona planted red salvia beside the gray stucco home. It did look pretty, the red against the gray, but it seemed to Hilda that there was something more than color that prompted Mama's choice of flowers. They seemed especially important to her. Years later, when she was in Paris, Hilda saw that the same red salvia flowers were planted around the Louvre! She asked a Parisian acquaintance if the same flowers were planted, year after year. "Oh, yes!" was the answer. Mona did not complain about the change in her life, for it had been both truly satisfying and disheartening, but she never forgot the time she had spent in Paris.

On the first floor of the Branson home, the main part of the house between the two extensions held the dining room. Here upon occasion Mona hosted a company dinner, complete with linens she still had from the Vrohmberg home and beautifully set with china dishes, individual glass salt cellars, and napkin rings. It was from these happy occasions that her daughters learned about table settings and warm and friendly dining.

From the dining room, toward the south, one entered the living room, simply furnished in wicker but displaying a grand piano for Sigurd, who was becoming an accomplished pianist. It seemed to his siblings that Sigurd practiced all the time, with the family friend, "Boycat," sitting beside him. Mornings, when Daddy was writing, were quiet.

In this room Mona's "Cottage Orchestra" performed. Its members were people from Branson—with the owner and editor of the *White River Leader*, Rollo Fletcher, on the cello, Mona on the violin, and Mrs. Hays, a sizeable lady and one of Mona's best friends, holding it all together with the piano. It was near the children's bedtime when they practiced, and Hilda remembers sitting on one of the bottom steps leading to the upstairs, secretly watching and listening. Mr. Fletcher was very thin, with an unusually large Adam's Apple, and his large eyes seemed to stare with an intensely serious expression. Mrs. Fletcher was quite the opposite; her pretty face was happy, atop a soft and rather cuddly body.

A door off the living room led to an almost sacrosanct space devoted entirely to John's study and his extensive personal library, which, because of his broad interests, contained books on widely differing subjects. When, mornings, he went into his room to write, the children knew that they must be quiet, and that he was not to be disturbed until one of them was asked to tell him dinner (country expression for lunch) was ready. If, when a knock on the door was not answered, or its opening revealed a man who, seemingly unseeing, looked right through the one at the door, it was quietly closed, and dinner waited.

Although John was dedicated to his life work—writing—about which he was intensely serious, during the afternoons he played either with his children or with a series of young men who came to confer or to "play" with him. He was a jovial companion, and he joked frequently. He especially joked when times were difficult or when there was not much money. At such times, joking concealed his worry.

A favorite hobby of John's was to go sharpshooting with a rifle or a pistol, and he developed the idea of a rifle sight that would quickly change for elevation—distance shooting—and for windage. It consisted of a number of interchangeable discs with peep holes at different locations, which would provide the correct position of the rifle for whatever circumstance existed.

A member of the National Rifle Association, he wrote to its then president, Colonel Whelan, who stated that such a sight was needed. John had painstakingly made a model of the sight, and he wanted to get his idea patented, but the attorney he had chosen to do the legal work kept asking for more money, until John's finances could no longer keep up. The sight was never fully developed.

The difficult economic conditions of the time made it seem helpful for Mona and John to care for their two grandchildren. Sigurd and Maxine were having difficulty establishing themselves, and until they had a satisfactory home for themselves and their two little girls, John and Mona suggested that Joan and Elaine stay for awhile with them in Branson. It was a happy time for the grandparents, even though taking care of a second batch of children would seem not to be part of the usual plan. Mona made busts of the two, and she made a full-figure statuette of Elaine in her "birthday suit." It stood at the turn of their driveway, in the midst of cannas and other flowers.

Because the little girls were sometimes afraid of the dark, John wrote a special prayer for them to say before they went to bed:

> Great Spirit, you are everywhere;
> You made the lovely earth and air.
> You made the creek that runs and sings,
> And everything with legs or wings.
> You made each blade of grass and tree,
> And all the little girls like me.
> So good is everything you made,
> That I should never be afraid.
> Great Spirit, teach me what to do,
> So I can be as good as you!

Every evening they said the prayer, with the fond grandparents listening. After the prayer, Joanie would enumerate all the creatures that should be blessed, beginning with members of the family and continuing through all the animals she knew, ending with bugs and spiders. "Bugs and spiders need our help," Gaki would agree, "because nobody likes them." She and Elaine did their best to draw out the happy experience as long as possible so that bedtime would not come too soon. It was wonderful being with their grandparents, but mother and father returned before too long, and they were glad to go to their new home.

One thing resulted from the time the two little Neihardts spent in Branson: Elaine could not properly pronounce the word "grandfather." In her baby way she said "Ga-ki," and that name stuck with John until he died. Those who might not for the sake of proper politeness call him "John" but who wished to use a more affectionate term than "Mr. Neihardt" or "Dr. Neihardt" were allowed to call him "Gaki."

When Elaine had grown to lovely womanhood, she recalled how it was when she and her sister Joan lived with their grandparents, John and Mona. "I remember how it was when I was sick. Nanny would come into my room, and I shall never forget the radiant look on her face. She was so warm and so loving, and she always did something that made us feel better. No, I can never forget how good she was to us."

While John was away from their Branson home writing on the St. Louis paper, Mona had an accident. She stepped on a rusty nail and, possibly because of inadequate medical care, her entire system was poisoned. Becoming very seriously ill with what was termed "erysipelas," she was taken to the hospital in Springfield, Missouri. John came to visit her as often as he could, and when she was able to do so, she returned to the Branson home.

Still unable to take care of herself, a special nurse was hired to help her regain her health, and Hilda and Alice were there to do their part. Because she was not strong enough to stand or walk, they concocted an idea by which she could see the flowers in her garden. They put comforters in a wheelbarrow, carried their mother outside, placed her atop the comforters, and wheeled her about. In a letter, Mona reported that Hilda "laughed and laughed," and indeed she did find it comical to see a queenly lady riding in such a modest conveyance.

Grateful for the professional care her husband provided, Mona wrote to him, first by way of dictating her letter to Hilda, and when she improved, doing her own writing. Those letters reveal much about their relationship:

Dearest Husband:

When I think how much you've been doing for me the last month or so, I wonder how I can ever be worth it—either to you or the children. . . . And all this money that was supposed to be used to write *Jed Smith* is being used to keep the same old girl going. And you, dear, need a summer suit badly.

The children have been so good. Everything is convenient and so well kept. Hilda's meals are so delicious that I eat big farmer meals for dinner.

It's so wonderful to be at home. It makes me so grateful to you that I have such a lovely hone. I marvel how you keep hitting the ball with your beautiful page. Don't forget that your letters are just eaten up. . . . It's been a month since I've been able to write to you, but you know I've thought of you every day. All I want now is to live, to be worth all your goodness.

Mona.

(In her own handwriting)

My own Darling

My thoughts are once more with you—and I am so grateful St. Louis is having a cool spell. . . . I wonder if Amama is with you and when she will come here, exactly. . . .

At 6 a.m. this morning I washed myself and started the little coffee percolator going on a table right beside my bed, where the folks had placed everything I needed. It seemed so wonderful to be able to do things myself. Now in a few hours I'll bathe and put on a clean nightgown for the day. Then Alice and Hilda will carry me into the front room which Hilda will have cleaned up so nicely.

I must get that mattress remade before anyone can sleep comfortably. . . . Amama will doubtless stay for a week or so at least, am so eager to see her, and so glad she will not have to rush.

Many thanks to you, dearest! Oceans of love. Always your old girl, Mona.

Dearest:

Your huge cheque once more received, with many, many thanks. Please do not send any more extra money now. You cannot pile up savings toward the writing of *Jed Smith* if you don't draw in a little now. You are so good to so many of us, and all of us are a part of me.

. . . Please excuse this. I am no good now. . . . Must quit, with endless loads and loads of love. Mona.

My own Darling:

When I have such faith in you, and in the great work you have yet to do—why cannot you just let go and know, without thinking, that you will be used to the utmost? It seems to me that this job is just what you say, and I am so grateful and glad for all you are doing with it. But it should not last long.

Enid should attain what she needs before long, and by that time you should have enough in savings so you can come back here and write *Jed Smith*. I feel you really must, because if you don't, something else will come in to take you elsewhere . . .

John dear, I do feel so much better today—worked a little and am progressing nicely. Darling, please don't think I am thinking of myself in a professional way, for I know too well how limited are my powers. But if I could help you, Oh, God! How happy I would be!

Loads of love to my own Darling, from Mona.

In one of her letters, after all of the years they had been together, Mona expressed this touching thought: "Oh, John, I wish I could be pretty for you!" She ended another in this way: "I love you more than any fat lady could!" Mona always thought she was too thin, but when she consulted a physician about that fault, he told her she was indeed fortunate.

Then: "Yes, dear, some day we will be together once more, and it will be more wonderful than any honeymoon!" In another letter she was ecstatic about John's return home: "Then, dear, perhaps we can sleep outside under the stars, the way we slept under the cherry trees so long ago!"

While they were apart, John expressed his feelings: "That was another dear letter yesterday, and you make me feel that I ought to be a lot gooder than I am. . . . I get lost when you are away."

While she was so ill with erysipelas, Mona was not able to be active, and as a result she thought and thought—and thought—about many things. All her thoughts were not about honeymoons: "John, do you know I have thought so much of that first baby we lost who looked so much like you, and I've had the distinct feeling that we should have been thinking of him more constructively and loving him—oh, so much— because of the accident that stopped his growth in this world. Oh, God, what a terrible thing that was—and how can I ever make it right? Of course, I cannot. But I feel I should not try to forget but rather feel and think of him as an entity that has developed in spite of the handicap I placed upon him—so unintentionally. Please tell me what you think about this." Mona's thought of another world in which the little stillborn could grow and develop would not be surprising to one who knew her as John did.

Although she had great faith and was most often in good spirits, there were times when Mona was distressed. To portray her as never having such interludes would be to depict her as something more than human. In one letter, late in her illness, she confessed: "Before, I did feel that if I could just drop out now in some decent way, it would be just as well or better for you and the children."

It was no doubt during one such discouraged time that she decided to do a desperate thing; she decided to burn all the letters that they had written to each other before they married. She did so, and one can only shudder to think of the loss that resulted from that act of destruction. Communications between the poet John Neihardt and the sculptor Mona Martinsen as they came to know each other's hearts and finally to fall in love, would have made a most gripping book!

It is not surprising that many of the early letters she had saved spoke of passionately romantic feelings, and Hilda remembers how Sigurd would go up to the attic where the box holding them was kept, would take one of the letters from it and read parts of it to her, giggling naughty-boyishly all the while. Of course, Hilda would not have dared doing such a naughty thing, but she could listen! It was not an easy time they had in their marriage, and one cannot fully know why Mona burned those letters, but she must indeed have felt desperate when she destroyed the collection she had so fondly kept.

Mona recovered nicely, and she was soon once more the strong, guiding spirit she had been. In a letter to Hilda from Branson, she made her beliefs clear, and what she said seems to answer any questions one might have had about how a young woman from her Fifth Avenue background could accept a life so different.

"I have always felt that doing the best we can is right. One can always look back and say 'What if I had done some other way.' One must not think that way; it is *wrong* and good for nothing at all. Think, act, and then go ahead with the assurance that God is with you. This I believe in. . . . She (Amama) says it is wonderful and so unusual for husband and wife to be so happy together, and for parents and children to be close to each other as we are to you children, and vice versa! So I think my attitude cannot be so wrong! I have never truly wanted anything that was not *right*. I simply do not want what is *wrong*."

As Mona had wished, John did leave his work in St. Louis and arranged to come home to Branson. They had survived the Great Depression, and because John kept so well informed about the country's conditions, the family savings were not lost by the banking failures. John had taken his money out of the bank and invested it in United States Postal Savings. Once more in their Branson home, he began immediately to write The Song of Jed Smith. Though written last, that volume would later take its place as the third in A Cycle of the West. It would tell the story of Jedediah Smith, whom John considered the greatest of American western explorers after Lewis and Clark.

It was Jed who, with his adventurous followers, discovered the South Pass, which opened up an overland route to California—a journey that up until that time had to be negotiated via vessel around Cape Horn. Smith, a powerful man physically and, most unusual, spiritually, would prove a worthy and tremendously interesting hero for the Song. John finished The Song of Jed Smith and it was published in 1941.

On a particular morning in 1941, when the Cycle had at last been completed, John and Mona were sitting at early breakfast in the dining room of their Branson home. Because of the completion of *A Cycle of the West*, a task they had begun twenty-nine years before, John and Mona were unusually happy.

They had been visiting together over their early morning coffee for some time when Mona, quite overcome with her emotion, suddenly announced: "Well, John, *we did it, didn't we?*"

John's response was immediate: "*Yes, by God, we did!*"

Together they had completed the poetic work begun so many years before. The five volumes included in *A Cycle of the West* "sing" about the early history of the United States, beginning with the rivermen and trappers who first ventured into the unsettled regions, continuing with the exploration across mountains and deserts to California, the migration of white settlers and the wars with the Indian people, and rising spiritually to the tragic ending of Indian resistance with the Massacre at Wounded Knee in 1890. The *Cycle* was later included in a choosing of the "Three Thousand Best Works from Homer to Hemingway."

It had been a long road for John and Mona—not an easy one nor an unfailingly happy one. Always there was the problem of a lack of money, and they skimped most of the time in order to make John's writing possible. In a letter to Hilda, Mona explained, "Daddy could never have completed the Cycle if I had asked for (money to buy) even the most normal things for the home." She also spoke upon occasion of the almost royal treatment he was given on his lecture tours, while at home she had to continue to make do on little. Always, however, she softened the effect of her complaint by adding, " . . . but Daddy never fails to provide for us. He is always so good to us. . . ."

In spite of the fact that the *Cycle* was completed, the need for cash continued, and John's joking, always increased by difficulties, became at times almost too much for his family. There could be no way to earn money in Branson, so John and Mona went to Chicago, where they had been invited to visit with long-time friends, George Steele Seymour of the Pullman Company, and his writer-wife, Flora Warren Seymour. John sought gainful employment in the city; the author who had been justly famed for his lyrics and short stories and who had completed *A Cycle of the West* was job-hunting in Chicago!

For a time they remained with their friends, who had a large home on Blackstone Avenue. Amama came to be with them, and Hilda also, who was discharged from the WAVES and expecting the arrival of her first child. Though a white-haired lady in her eighty-fifth year, Amama was still the *grande dame* she had always been, and with her dramatic ways she graced the dinner table. One funny little habit was strangely charming: she shook the saltshaker both ways—back and forth!

More than once, over the years, John had urged Amama to record her worldwide travels and tell about the many famous people she had met. During much of her later life, thanks to the generous support of financially successful Ottocar—her "hero of daily life"—she had done little except travel, and places from the Riviera in France to mysterious Sumatra and Bali were commonplace to her.

John now continued to ask her to tell or dictate the story of at least some of her experiences. In reponse to his repeated urgings, a small, deprecating smile would cross Amama's still pretty face, and, shaking her head, she would dismiss the idea. Her voice was almost a whimper: "Oh, John," she said, "it's nothing. I can't . . ." That was all she said, and the others at table could only think of the loss caused by her reluctance.

Amama died while she was in Chicago with her family and friends. To preserve her dignity even in death, John tied a soft scarf around her head to hold her mouth shut until it would stay that way by itself. Ottocar came from New York, and as they stood beside the bed where she still lay, he remarked, "But, John, you understood her." A very distinctive character and a dear, loving lady was gone. She had ended one of her last letters to John and Mona with these words: "And so thanks again to my idealistic, spiritually precious children, & please don't stop loving your somehow heartsick old Mommie, Mothie, Amama."

John had found work in Chicago—two unsuitable, low-paying jobs— but before long he was asked to work with a man he knew and admired, John Collier, director of the Bureau of Indian Affairs. While working for the Bureau, he edited and wrote for its magazine, *Indians at Work*.

It was because of Collier's interest in a Siouxan cultural history that he asked John to go again in 1944, with Hilda as his reporter, to interview Black Elk and another ninety-year-old Sioux named Eagle Elk.

The interviews from this time are incorporated in *When the Tree Flowered*. Successful in England under the title *Eagle Voice*, and though its contents are quite as authentic as *Black Elk Speaks*, it has not been as widely received as the earlier work. Because of this, John often remarked, "I am jealous for *When the Tree Flowered*."

While they were in Chicago, Mona also took a job as a proof reader for Donnelly and Co., a publishing firm, and it was the first time she had worked outside the home during their marriage. The two left the Seymour home and found rooms at Hotel Metropol, a residence hotel in downtown Chicago. Together there, they were almost like newlyweds. Mona wore pretty dresses and big hats again, and Hilda commented that never before had she seen her mother so happy.

It was war again—the Second World War. Hilda's husband, Albert Petri, was in the navy, and Alice and Hilda had both joined the women's branch—the WAVES. While serving, Alice met a handsome young sailor—Charles Thompson. After the war ended, they married, and the two came to live with Alice's parents.

27

Skyrim

Forward is the only way.

John G. Neihardt

DISENCHANTED WITH CITY LIFE in Chicago, John and Mona returned to their home in Branson, but nothing seemed the same there, and they felt it was time to make a change. To sell the home they had loved in the Ozarks was not a sudden decision, for they had for some time considered doing so. Both had wanted to find a farm home near Columbia, and in 1948 they found just the right spot and moved to central Missouri.

The home they chose on eighty acres just three miles north of Columbia was a white farmhouse on a hill, and Mona immediately recognized it. She had, she said, dreamed of just such a house on just such a hill, where she felt that all the family would gather and be safe. Because of the way it lay on the top of a hill, with a view in all directions, Mona named the home "Skyrim."

The house needed improvement, and Mona wanted her kitchen to be in the basement, for she remembered fondly the kitchen in the basement of their New York home. John built an electricity-powered dumb waiter for her, which would carry food up to the first-floor dining room. This too was like the home she remembered.

Urged by Mona, who longed for her family to be together, Enid and Ollie, with their children, Nei and Mona, found a home nearby, and Hilda and Albert brought their three children, Gail, Robin, and Coralie, from

California to Columbia, where they purchased a home near the town. Sigurd and Maxine, with their three daughters, remained in Phoenix, where they had sought a climate that would be more healthful. Sigurd had cancer.

Together, John and Mona gradually did many things to make Skyrim the home they wanted it to be. A garage was built in the basement of the house; the driveway from the road was made circular, somewhat like the one they had in the Ozarks; and a Sacred Hoop prayer garden was created in front of the house. In the pasture near the house, a pond was dug. On its banks, below the flagpole that Mona had wanted, the family celebrated Fourth of July, and at Mona's request, Hilda sang Irving Berlin's "God Bless America." Alice's beautiful horses and John's Angus cattle grazed happily on Skyrim's pastures, and John was proud of the hay and crops grown on the land.

Deer and other wild creatures lived unafraid at Skyrim, for John no longer cared to hunt. He remained fond of his firearms for themselves and for the marksmanship they provided, but he did not want to kill anything. One day a man from the town came to Skyrim and asked if he might hunt on Skyrim land, for he had heard that quail were plentiful there. John's unexpected response came quickly: "Fellow, I'll make you a deal: you don't shoot my quail, and I won't shoot yours. How is that?" The disappointed and quail-less townsman could only agree to John's "deal."

A professor of history at the University of Missouri learned that the Neihardts were living near Columbia, and John was invited to join the English faculty. John accepted, although he was sixty-seven years old at the time and had considered himself retired. The association was a happy one. John created courses, and for a number of years he taught classes on his epic *A Cycle of the West* and the creative writing of poetry. His teaching was so popular that an auditorium was needed for his classroom.

John was impressed with his students. More than once he declared, "They are far superior to the young people of my own generation!" He was, as many a teacher would be, particularly pleased by the maturity and genuine interest in learning shown by those who had returned from the war and were studying under the G.I. Bill. As for his students, many of them have over the years since expressed their appreciation of him as a teacher. The famed actor George C. Scott was one of his students, and he later told a *Columbia Missourian* reporter that he recalled how Neihardt sat on his desk and dangled his legs—"and I do mean *dangled*," he said—then added, "we really learned from that man!"

During the Columbia years John was often asked to read his poetry at university or other social gatherings, "stunts" for which he had formerly been well paid. Mona was usually with him, and it was often remarked by those attending that the most striking part of the whole affair was the special glow that spread across her face as she listened to her husband's recitation of the poetry she loved so well.

On one such evening he was talking to a large group of fraternity students. A young man with a strained look on his face raised his hand to interrupt. "Dr. Neihardt," he complained, "you keep saying that life is good, but I wonder how you can say that when all around us we see so much that is bad. I just cannot understand how you can keep saying that life is good!"

John's response was immediate. "Young man, it is true that people of good will could talk together for twenty-four hours, listing all the things that are wrong with this world, and they would be right. The same people could spend another twenty-four hours listing what is good about this life. They too would be right." Then, looking intently at the young man he pointedly asked, "Young man, do you like to eat?"

Perhaps thinking that the question was not relevant, the confused fellow replied, "Why, yes, sir, I do like to eat. Why do you ask?"

Neihardt's tone was rather severe when he asked, "Well, *do you eat swill?*" The young man—quite obviously shocked—responded that of course he did not, whereupon Neihardt asked, "Why not? The world is full of it!" Then, in a softer tone he explained, "You see, fellow, you have to be selective in this life. You must choose."

His face still bore a puzzled look when the troubled young man settled back in his seat, but his voice had lost its antagonistic tone. "Yes, sir, I see what you mean. Thank you."

It had long been the custom for the family to gather for dinner on Thanksgiving Day, and while the family was in Columbia, they were usually invited to Hilda's home for that event. Before they ate, the family's gratitude was expressed by someone, and on one particular day one of the children recited: *Thank you for the world so sweet, Thank you for the food we eat, Thank you for the birds that sing, Thank you, God, for everything!*

Grandmother Mona was seated at one end of the table, and as the children finished the little prayer, she broke in. Almost tearfully, and shaking her head with the strength of her emotion, she added, "Yes, and I *do* mean *everything—the bad as well as the good!*"

Mona never stopped working on her sculpture. She made busts of Alice's two children, Lynn and Erica, as she had done for Sigurd's children, Joan and Elaine, when they stayed with their grandparents in Branson. Sigurd's and Maxine's third daughter, affectionately known as "Maxie Pie" had not joined the family at that time, so she was never the subject of her grandmother's modeling.

While Mona devoted herself to her sculpting, John turned to making jewelry. In St. Louis he had frequented pawnshops and jewelry stores, finding many precious gems that during wartime had been removed from gold settings. Knowing of his interest, some friends gave him a large block of American jade, and from this, with tools of only the most primitive sort, he created for his Mona a choker necklace, earrings, and a hololithic ring, all made of the jade and some gold. She often wore these beautiful pieces when they were entertained in Columbia, and on occasion she chose instead the large topaz pendant with matching earrings that he had given her.

Mona made a point of being with her daughters when a child was to be born, and in January 1946 when her granddaughter Gail Evelyn Petri was born in Chicago, she recorded her first days by sculpting a baby head— just the forepart of the head, with a soft, cloudlike background that reminded one of Rodin. Later in Columbia Mona made a three-quarter sized bust of her only grandson, Hilda's boy, Robin, when he was eight years old. How pleased she would have been, had she known that he would later become a fine classical guitarist! Her other granddaughter, Coralie Joyce, she unfortunately did not model, although she was fond of that little girl. Perhaps she had just "run out of steam."

Children and grandchildren remember how she would at times look at them with an intensity that was almost disturbing, memorizing the shapes, sizes, and arrangement of their features. Then too she often took hold of an arm, moving it up and down and sideways. When she was satisfied that she saw just how it worked, she returned the arm to its owner and said, "Thank you, dear!"

Although they loved their white house on a hill north of Columbia, the life there, with its seemingly endless housekeeping and care of children, was too hard for Mona, whose health was failing. On April 17, 1958, just a few months before their fiftieth wedding anniversary, Mona died from complications following a minor automobile accident. For all her family, her passing was a monumental trauma.

The day of the accident, Mona had asked John to drive to Columbia to get the daily newspaper. Their Studebaker was in good running order, and a week or so before, John had taken it to a local garage for repair of the brakes, but on that fateful day they failed. John had just stopped at Ninth Street and Broadway with no problem, but when he crossed Broadway and attempted to stop for a truck that was double-parked on Ninth Street, the brake pedal went to the floor. John swerved to the left to avoid striking the truck, but unfortunately he met and collided with an automobile coming toward him.

It was a minor accident at very slow speeds, and behind the steering wheel John was unhurt, but without the protection of a seat belt, Mona was thrown forward, her head striking the metal band above the windshield. Quickly getting out of the vehicle, she insisted that she too was unhurt, but because of the blow to her forehead, she was taken to the hospital. A bump had arisen on her head, but the examining physician, after making what may have been perfunctory tests, thought it of little consequence, and she was released to go home.

It became obvious that the examining doctor was mistaken, for Mona's condition worsened. She was taken more than once to the hospital, but the doctors who saw her, failing to realize the seriousness of her condition, did nothing for her except send her to a nursing facility for care. Hilda consulted a highly respected local physician, Dr. James Baker, who chanced to come into the law office where she worked, and when she told him what had happened to her mother, he was so concerned that he ran to her bedside. He immediately referred Mona to Dr. Charles Black, a noted brain surgeon who was in practice at the University Hospital.

On April 16, 1958, Dr. Black successfully drained the hematoma that had formed in her brain, and Mona seemed on the road to recovery. John and the family members with him, after visiting with Mona as she came out from under the anesthetic, were told late that evening to go home: "You can't do anything for her here, Dr. Neihardt, and you need the rest. Come back in the morning!"

Relying on what they were told, and also much relieved to see that Mona was semi-alert and able to speak to them, John and his daughters embraced her tenderly and left for home. Rejoicing as they drove, they talked together about how happy they would be when she could be back in their care. "No matter what her condition—even if she has to be in a wheelchair—we will take such good care of her! Oh, how happy we will be to do that!"

But when on the morning of April 17 John, Hilda, and Alice returned to the hospital, eagerly expectant that they would find Mona much improved, they were abruptly stopped as they neared her room. Mona had awakened early, John was told, had seemed to be feeling much better, and had asked for a cup of tea. The tea was brought to her, and as she drank it she visited with a family friend, young Dr. David Scherr. Her condition seemed quite hopeful, but in the middle of a sentence she stopped talking and just simply fell over in her bed. A blood clot had snuffed out her life.

Dr. Black was warmly sympathetic as he told John about Mona's sudden and unexpected passing. Looking down, the surgeon drew a circle on the floor with the toe of one shoe as he spoke. "Oh, Dr. Neihardt," he said softly, "Dr. Neihardt, I am sorry! I am so sorry!"

Had Mona been ill for a long time, her death would not have brought such desperate sorrow to her family, but the manner in which it had happened was so *wrong* that her passing would not be forgotten—ever. The loss caused by her death was not alone the loss of a loving wife, mother, and grandmother. A great spirit, a rich and vibrant soul, had left, and one could only wonder whither it had gone.

She was irrevocably gone from them in one way, but not in another, for Mona found a means to comfort her family. Twice they heard it, her family gathered there. Two times, on two different days, a large glass bowl on a table in the living room at Skyrim rang out loud and clear, as though struck sharply several times by an invisible hand. The same bowl continued to stand where it had been, but never again was it so musical.

On April 23, six days after her death, John answered a letter of sympathy from a long-time friend, a professor at Cornell University in New York:

> Dear Slade: Your dear letter means everything to me. Bless you! All you say is true, and I am so glad you wrote about the glow of spirit on her face. It was so strikingly characteristic that even strangers have remarked about it. It was the spirit shining through.
>
> She had been preparing to go for a long while, getting things straightened out—boxes and barrels of papers and trinkets—all our rings made strong for the children. A ring had lost a diamond. That had to be reset, because the ring would go to Sigurd after I was through wearing it.
>
> She gave me orders about the funeral long before her illness. All this was done with no hint of morbidity. We believed together, and we knew, and I know.
>
> At her funeral, I recited poetry she had chosen; Sigurd played a Bach piece she loved, and Hilda sang a beautiful song Mona knew well.

His life partner gone, for many months John gave the appearance of one who had been hit over the head with a sledgehammer. He did not complain, for that was not his way, and in his loss he found some comfort in knowing that Mona was not the one who would have to live on alone. It was a bleak prospect that he faced, but courage never failed him, nor did the memory of his Mona.

Never had she forgotten her vow, made when she was just a child: "When I have babies, I will take care of them myself!" She had enveloped her own children with the warmth of her love and inspired them with her spirit, and she had done the same for two sets of grandchildren. Always her strong presence had been an unswerving power for good in the family, and her faithful partnership with John throughout the rocky ups-and-downs of a life dedicated to spiritual ideals surely validated the premise upon which her marriage had been based: She had always said: "I must be able to tell my husband: *my God is thy God!*" She could certainly tell that to John, for the things in life that they most honored were the same.

Life sometimes plays tragic tricks on mortals. It was so with Mona, who had been so loyal a supporter during their life together, for many of Neihardt's honors and rewards came to him after she was gone. Published again by the University of Nebraska Press, *Black Elk Speaks* became an international success, and numerous awards were given to John for his poetic accomplishments.

John continued to live at Skyrim until, after twenty years of teaching, he retired in 1968 from the University of Missouri. His career at the University over, life at Skyrim was no longer satisfying to him. Alice and her daughters, Lynn and Erica, were still there, but without Mona, the place could not be home for him. She had been the warming, beautifying soul of it, and she was gone. Long-time friends Julius and Myrtle Young drove from Lincoln, Nebraska, in 1969 to see John, and when they asked him to return with them for a visit, he did so.

It was more than a visit, and John continued to live with the Youngs for several years. His presence in Nebraska renewed that state's interest in Neihardt, and it awakened in him a desire to write again. While in Lincoln he composed two wise and charmingly nostalgic volumes of reminiscences—*All Is But a Beginning* and *Patterns and Coincidences*. The latter volume was published posthumously, and it contained John's only written tribute to Mona in the chapter (quoted earlier) entitled "Homecoming of the Bride."

Considering John's advanced age, it is not surprising that he was often asked by a friend or an interviewer if he despaired of modern attitudes and conditions and whether he perhaps looked longingly back at former times. "Oh, no," he quickly responded, "the 'Good Old Days' were not always so good!" Then, with an understanding smile and with noticeable intensity, he added, "The only way is *forward*. No, we cannot even think about going back. Forward is the *only* way!"

While he was living in Lincoln, John returned often to Columbia to visit, but he never again stayed at his Skyrim home. In 1972, when he was ninety-one, he was visiting at Hilda's farm home hear Columbia. It was a rainy evening, and the renovations being accomplished on the home made it necessary to enter through the back door. Those were the conditions when a former student of John's at the university brought famed Swami Satchidananda to see the poet. The eager young man, then studying with the Swami, thought the seer and the poet should meet, because he knew that from his youth John had been a student and admirer of the Hindu religion and that his first book-length poem—*The Divine Enchantment*—was inspired by that interest.

When Hilda opened the door to greet the guests, she saw a tall, elegant gray-haired, bearded man in a saffron robe and a smaller, blond young man robed in white, and she quickly invited them to come in out of the rain. Once inside, they were greeted enthusiastically and respectfully by John—and by someone else as well. The family cat, a large, usually bashful gray tabby, came directly up to Swami, not quietly or slowly as one would expect a cat to do but with something of a rush. That impressive gentleman did not interrupt what he was saying as he leaned down, picked up the cat, and held him in his arms. It was a meaningful moment.

The young student beamed with delight as he sat appropriately on the carpet, while John and the holy man sat in chairs and talked. At his request Hilda brought her father the sacred ornament that Black Elk had given him when they first met, and he told Swami Satchidananda how the old Lakota holy man had explained its meanings. After they had visited together for a time, the two men pulled their chairs closer together. Holding hands as they looked into each other's eyes, they sat for some time in silence. No one in the room disturbed that reverent quiet. Then, after minutes had passed wordlessly, John looked up, smiled under raised eyebrows at the holy man, and said simply, "Yes!"

For both of them, and for the others in the room, "Yes" seemed to be all that needed to be said. It was the answer.

It is the answer.

After John died, Swami Satchidananda wrote the family a beautiful letter in which he commemorated John's life and the contributions his works had made.

John never ceased writing, nor did he discontinue his lectures and recitations. In the spring of 1973 United Artists of Hollywood sent Bill McIntire to Columbia to record his recitations. Bill stayed for three weeks, living in a trailer on Hilda's farm, and helped John record excerpts from almost all of his works, after which he chose enough of the conversations and recitations to fill a three-disc album. Much of 'his wisdom and humor, his knowledge of our western history, and recitations of poetry and prose remain unused in the number of eight-track tapes recorded at that time.

The people of Bancroft and of Nebraska did not forget John Neihardt, even though he and his family had moved away in 1920. A monument was placed in the park at Wayne, Nebraska, and his mother, Alice Neihardt, attended its dedication. In 1921, by act of the state legislature, John Neihardt had been made Poet Laureate of Nebraska, a designation that after his death was officially changed to "Poet Laureate in Perpetuity." Neihardt had been Nebraska's poet laureate for fifty-two years—longer, it has been suggested, than any other poet laureate in history.

In 1965 a most significant honor was given to the poet. The John G. Neihardt Foundation was established by a group in Bancroft, working with fans in other parts of Nebraska. Its stated purpose was to promote works of John Neihardt. In 1976, after statewide efforts by the Foundation board, spearheaded by its executive director Marie Vogt, a beautiful brick building of unique design was dedicated. The State of Nebraska had appropriated the needed funds, and today the building, its grounds, and the little one-room house that had served as John's study are referred to as the John G. Neihardt State Historic Site.

Visitors from all over the United States and all over the world come to that site. Presently operated by the Neihardt Foundation Board under a contract with the State Historical Society, the work of the Neihardt Center is carried on by an executive director and staff. A sacred hoop prayer garden, fashioned after the original plan John and Mona designed for their home in the Ozarks, graces the grounds of the historic site.

Years after they had left Branson, at the urging of long-time friends, among them members of the family of the journalist-cellist Rollo Fletcher, Branson also managed to remember the Neihardts, who had lived there for nearly three decades. A stone monument on Highway 76 leading west from Branson reminds any passerby who chances to see it that the Neihardt home formerly stood on that spot. Branson has become a major tourist center, and the house was torn down to make way for a much-desired store and parking lot.

All of Neihardt's works are presently in print at the University of Nebraska Press. Dr. Lori Utecht, formerly director of the Neihardt Center, selected and edited a collection of essays under the title *Knowledge and Opinion*; Neihardt wrote the pieces in his book-reviewing days. They represent what he considered "some of my best work." Nebraska Press is publishing a fourth biography, written by Nebraskan Tim Anderson of the *New York Times*, and a critical work on *Black Elk Speaks* by Brian Holloway, in which the author seeks to portray fairly the relationship between Neihardt and the holy man, will appear under the aegis of Colorado University Press.

Although career wise she had given up so much, Mona's art did not go unrecognized. Bronze examples of her portrait busts of John are displayed at the University of Missouri in a special room holding his personal library; at Wayne State College in Wayne, Nebraska; and in the Hall of Fame in the tower of the Nebraska Capitol in Lincoln. The beautiful plaster casting of her first bust of John, completed in 1909, is in the John G. Neihardt State Historic Site in Bancroft, as well as the plaster cast of the bust she made of her mother-in-law, Alice Neihardt.

It would have been only fair for Mona to share in the successes that came to John, all of which would have made her rejoice. It seems greatly unfair that she was not fated to share those successes, for they came after she was no longer with him. But is not fairness perhaps a concept that we humans have created and which may or may not exist in the cosmos?

Sorrow does not live alone; it often neighbors with regret. Once, when he was overcome with sorrow after Mona's untimely death, John blurted out, "Oh, Hiddy, there were so many times when I could have made her heart sing! I could have made her dear heart sing, but I did not do it." As he spoke, the expression in his eyes and on his lined face was one of admission, as though he were telling a secret about which he was not pleased.

Before his daughter could think what she might say in reply, John brightened. "But," he said with particular emphasis, "when Mama and I were alone together, we had perfect understanding." On another day, he repeated what he had said, with considerable emphasis. The matter seemed of real importance to him. Hilda listened, but she did not feel the need to reply. "What more," she thought, "could anyone hope for beyond perfect understanding?"

In 1971, thirteen years after Mona's death, in an interview with Dick Cavett on ABC, a ninety-year-old, white-haired John Neihardt tapped his slender, jewel-topped cane lightly on the floor as he answered Dick's question about his marriage to Mona Martinsen:

> We were more in love at the end—oh, much more—than we were when we first met! Oh, yes, we were much more in love at the end!

Afterword

. . . the Spirit keeps the Secret yet awhile. . . .

"Song of the Messiah"

JOHN NEIHARDT RETURNED OFTEN to visit in Columbia, but he never again lived in his own home at Skyrim. In August 1973, lonely for his family and perhaps feeling that the end was near, he asked to leave Lincoln, and his friends drove him to a daughter's farm home near Columbia, Missouri. Grateful for his return, his children and grandchildren gathered around him, fearful that their time with Gaki was short.

One of Columbia's most respected physicians, Dr. Lohmar, was asked to care for John, and he came to the home to examine him. Taking Hilda and Alice into another room, he told them in confidence, "Your father is dying." They had known in their hearts that what he said was true; even so, those words were sharply painful to the daughters. The doctor continued, "I want you to know this—the man who wrote *The Song of Hugh Glass*, I would not connect the man who wrote that book to tubes and wires in a hospital. I would not subject him to that."

"Doctor, we would not let you. We have promised our father that he would be cared for at home, not in a hospital," was the quick response.

John's wonderful memory and his great mind were never taken from him, and he was confined to bed only a short while. One day when many members of the family were present, at Alice's suggestion his grandson, Robin, back from three years in the Vietnam War and once more applying himself to the study of the classical guitar, sat at Grandfather John's bedside and played for him. When the piece ended, the others sitting in the next room heard John's comment: "Beautiful! Beautiful!" It was the last music John would hear this side of eternity.

John Neihardt died at his daughter's farm home north of Columbia on November 3, 1973, lovingly attended by children, grandchildren, and special friends. It was late afternoon when he passed, and one could almost hear—or *feel*—his spirit as it flashed away, leaving behind only the body of a barely recognizable little old man.

A service was conducted for John in the same place where Mona's service had been held. He was not a member of the Methodist Church ("I am a member of all churches," he had claimed), but Bishop Monk Bryan, who was then in Columbia, was asked to conduct his service. Bishop Bryan conducted a meaningful and beautiful service, and members of the family were permitted to participate. Many good friends from Columbia and from Nebraska attended. It was a heartwarming service, but it was not the end.

A couple of mornings after the service, something remarkable happened. Hilda, alone in the house, had taken his faithful poodle Jacquot outdoors and returned. She had just closed the door behind her when the little antique upright piano in the living room gave out a loud sound—almost a roar. Hurrying to the instrument, she saw that there was nothing that could have fallen on the piano, and no strings were broken. It seemed as though the sounding board on the back of the instrument would have to be struck with great vigor to cause such an explosive sound, but such a blow was not possible, even if someone had been there to do it. The little piano was backed up tightly against a wall.

On the next morning, it happened again—the same very loud roar of the strings from the sounding board, while the piano was still backed up against the living room wall. When she told her sister Alice about the happenings, the reply was: "That was so like Daddy. He *would* make the sound when you were up. He would not make it in the night, when it might frighten you." For Hilda, that repeated sound was a loving greeting. It did not come again.

In accordance with the family's long custom, they gathered again in 1973 for Thanksgiving dinner at the home where John had died.

Something wonderful happened on that day. Robin was with others in the yard outside his mother's hilltop house when he called out, "Look! There's an eagle!"

Indeed there *was* a bald eagle, and it flew low over the house in a counterclockwise circle, went a short distance to the south, then returned and flew—again in a counterclockwise circle—over the house and very close to the rooftop. Alice and her daughters arrived just in time to see the eagle fly away to the south. Excited, granddaughter Lynn exclaimed, "*I have never seen an eagle before in my whole life!*"

The family did not know how, nor did they try, to explain it, but the unexpected and entirely unusual appearance of the eagle gave them a warm and uplifting feeling. They could only think of Neihardt's good friend, the Sioux holy man Black Elk. Eagles were Black Elk's thing.

The family had known—always, it seemed—that John and Mona Neihardt did not want any place to exist where their children and grandchildren might go and be unhappy. There was no hint of the morbid in what they knew was to be done: their parents' remains were to be strewn from an airplane over the Missouri River.

Arrangements were made with the local Cotton Mather airport for an airplane to fly them on November 29, 1973—the sixty-fifth anniversary of John's and Mona's marriage—out over the Missouri River, which had been of such importance in Neihardt's life and in his writings. From the family, only Hilda and Alice would go in the plane. Sigurd had died a few months before, after fighting cancer for some fourteen years. His final words to wife Maxine and youngest daughter Maxie had been: "I love you!" and his comment as he passed: "Oh, it is so beautiful!" Enid was not well enough to make the trip. A young Missouri University professor, Bob Dyer, who had been a good friend to John, was invited to go along.

When the three arrived at the airport a few minutes before the appointed time, their somewhat somber mood did not match the bright November day, which seemed unaware that anything much was happening at all. On the runway, a fine, twin-engined plane awaited them. It boasted two pilots—a young man and the daughter of the airport's owner. Against Hilda's protests, she smilingly insisted that no charge would be made for the trip.

Alice brought a volume from Skyrim that contained the two poems chosen to set the tone for the flight. "When I Have Gone Weird Ways" and "L'Envoi" were written by John after his marriage to Mona, and the poems gave expression to her beliefs as well as to his. Readers may remember that on her first exposure to John's poetry she realized that her thoughts, her feelings, and her unswerving beliefs were in sympathy with those expressed in his lyrics, and that is why Mona left her studies and her home and came to him. On more than one occasion John gratefully gave credit to *A Bundle of Myrrh*, saying, "that little book went all the way to Paris, where it found my Mona for me!" Together they had lived out the beliefs they shared, all the while meeting headlong the joys, difficulties and sorrows of a normal life.

All that was over now. Hilda had brought two urns with her, one of which she handed to Alice. Boarding the plane, the sisters carefully carried those urns, one holding the newly cremated remains of John Neihardt; the other containing Mona's remains, which had been waiting for some fifteen years.

As the plane took off and made its way the few miles to the river, lines from "When I Have Gone Weird Ways" expressed the intensity of the moment:

> When I have finished with this episode,
> Left the hard, uphill road,
> And gone weird ways to seek another load,
> Oh, Friend, regret me not nor weep for me—
> Child of Infinity!
>
> Nor dig a grave, nor rear for me a tomb
> To say with lying writ: Here in the gloom
> He who loved bigness takes a narrow room,
> For he is dead.

As the airplane flew over the river the two fond daughters could see below them the tracks of the Missouri, Kansas, and Texas Railway, of which their grandfather had been president. No doubt Rudolf Martinsen had traveled more than once along those very rails as they made their way below the bluffs at the edge of the great river.

Now another poem—"L'Envoi"—accompanied what was happening:

> Seek not for me within a tomb;
> You shall not find me in the clay.
> I pierce a little wall of gloom
> To mingle with the day.

Silently, and unaware of whose remains were in the urn she held, each daughter opened a window on her side of the plane, held her urn outside, and removed the lid from her container. The crumbled remains of John Neihardt and Mona Martinsen, so colorless and white, reflected the bright rays of the sun as they mingled and fell into the swirling, muddy waters below.

Its purpose completed, the plane rose and straightened to return to Columbia.

More lines of poetry expressed the feelings of those who had gone:

> Not Death can sheathe me in a shroud,
> A joy-sword whetted keen with pain,
> I join the armies of the Cloud,
> The Lightning and the Rain.

> My God and I shall interknit
> As rain and Ocean, breath and Air,
> And O, the luring thought of it
> Is prayer!

As it glided toward home the airplane's silver body was bathed in gold by the rays of the lowering sun. Its occupants were silent. Its three passengers were filled with a sense of loss that clung to them like an ache, and with a special sort of happiness tinged with sorrow. Over it all hovered a soothing feeling of relief, for they had done as John and Mona wished. Now it was all over. The story of John and Mona was ended.

. . . Or was it perhaps only a new beginning?

Bibliography

Crowder, Richard. Notes and reminiscences of John G. Neihardt. Courtesy Andy Crowder, Chicago IL.

Davis, Richard Harding. *About Paris.* New York: Harper & Bros, 1903.

"Disposing of the Wreck." *New York Times,* Sept. 25, 1898.

Elwell, F. Edwin, "Mart." *The Arena* 24, no. 191 (October 1905).

Faragher, John Mack, et al. *Out of Many.* Upper Saddle River NJ: Prentice Hall, 1999.

James, Henry. *Italian Hours.* Boston: Houghton Mifflin Company, 1909.

Kansas City Star, April 27, 1919, article on Mona.

"Mrs. Neihardt." *Missourian,* April 4, 1951.

Neihardt, John G., and Mona Martinsen. Letters. In possession of the author's family.

"Marriage of an Artist and a Writer." *Omaha World Herald,* November 30, 1908.

Palladium, June 21, 1866.

Rodin, Auguste. *Art.* Translated from the French of Paul Gsell by Mrs. Romilly Fedden. Boston: Small Maynard & Company, 1912.

"Rudolph V. Martinsen." *New Amsterdam Gazette,* July 24, 1891.

Whiting, Lillian. *Italy, the Magic Land.* Boston: Little, Brown, 1907.